DAILY AFFIRMATIONS

STRENGTHENING
My RECOVERY

Meditations for
Adult Children of Alcoholics/
Dysfunctional Families

STRENGTHENING *My* RECOVERY

Approved by the 2013 ACA
Annual Business Conference
ACA WSO, Inc.
Signal Hill, California
www.adultchildren.org

Mailing Address:
Post Office Box 811
Lakewood, California USA 90714
www.adultchildren.org

Printed in the United States of America

ISBN: 978-0-978-0-9789797-6-8 (softcover)
ISBN: 978-0-9965049-0-4 (hardcover)

9 10 11   21 20

"Our solution appeals to cultures across the globe." BRB p. 94

Introduction

History of the ACA Meditation Book

Strengthening My Recovery is a Daily Meditation Book written by and for the Adult Children of Alcoholics (ACA/ACoA) Fellowship. The seeds of this book were planted during the final development of the Fellowship Text, also known as the Big Red Book (BRB). The idea slowly moved forward, eventually gaining a sense of definition.

In August of 2012, when "the time was right," volunteers made a commitment that led to this book becoming a reality. Meditations were gathered from ACAs worldwide for the next eight months, at which time the book's draft received final approval by Delegates from 13 countries at the 2013 World Service Organization (WSO) Annual Business Conference (ABC) in Birkerod, Denmark. This was the first ever ABC held outside of the U.S., a truly historic and unifying event. The draft was subsequently made available on the ACA WSO website for 90 days for Fellowship review and feedback.

The Writers

Those who contributed to this meditation book shared their experience, strength and hope as part of their recovery journey. We are deeply grateful for their willingness to do so. Because individuals wrote about where they were on their journey, all stages and views of ACA recovery may not be covered. Such is the nature of a volunteer effort. However, we believe that you will find immense value in what you read, just as we have in putting this book together.

The Topics

The topics were chosen by the volunteers. Thus, this book offers a snapshot of how some of our members, from many different backgrounds, understand and experience their recovery at this particular point in time.

The Format

Each meditation starts with a quote from the BRB. The writer's recovery experience is then shared. The affirmation at the end is intended as a message of hope to carry us through our day.

The volunteers were asked to write in the nominative, plural case (the "we" format). Although their observations may be personal in nature, they are also thought to be universal to most of us. Using the nominative case makes them our stories, reminding us that we are a recovery family.

Artwork

We are also grateful to the artists and photographers who shared their talent with the Fellowship so this book could be even richer.

Suggested Uses

It should be noted that "Strengthening Our Recovery" is not meant to facilitate study of the BRB. It is meant as a companion to the BRB and our Twelve Steps of Adult Children Workbook. Taken together, they are powerful tools for recovery that complement each other.

In addition to making this book a part of your personal daily recovery reading, we hope that each group will read the meditation of the day as part of their meeting format.

The ACA Meditation Book Trusted Servants
November 2013

---

*What you are about to read was created from a space
of love and gratitude for a Program that has saved
countless lives, physically, emotionally and spiritually.*

January

"Each ACA member is equal to the next and has an equal voice regardless of job status or career track. We are all adult children who relate to one another at the level of empathy instead of the level of employment or lack of employment." BRB p. 528

Fellow Travelers

"Each ACA member is equal to the next and has an equal voice regardless of job status or career track. We are all adult children who relate to one another at the level of empathy instead of the level of employment or lack of employment." BRB p. 528

In the rooms of recovery, we may sit next to a doctor, a priest, a janitor, a housewife, or just about any profession we can think of. But who are we really sitting next to? We are sitting next to another adult child, with all of the fears, insecurities and trauma that can entail. In a society where our worth appears to be measured in material things or the position we hold, there are few other places besides a 12 Step meeting where we are all on equal footing, where no one of us makes decisions for the others.

In ACA we are spiritual beings going through a human experience. We are reaching out to each other for the love and understanding that was not given to us in our family of origin. We celebrate each other's victories and support each other in our times of sorrow.

Success in ACA is not measured with money or social status, but with inner peace and serenity. We share our experience, strength and hope with each other as we laugh together, cry together and know that we are home.

On this day I know that in this world I am not alone as long as I have my fellow travelers.

Commonality

"The first time I read the common behaviors of an adult child, I felt like a bell that had been fetched up and rang hard. I was calm on the outside, but I was vibrating on the inside." BRB p. 118

When we first heard "our" story told, it seemed like we floated around the room for the rest of the meeting. What just happened? Did we really hear that? How does this person know about us? We felt frightened, but we weren't sure why.

We may have even gone home and taken a nap, or walked through the rest of our day in a daze. When we woke up the next day, we may have felt hung over.

What we find is that we identify with the ACA Problem and the Laundry List Traits and with other adult children. We have learned many tools to deal with those defenses as we grow in the program with our sponsors and with our Step work. We lean on the people who came before us to show us the way to serenity and wholeness until we possess those qualities with stability in ourselves. We know we are not alone.

On this day I will call my sponsor. If I don't have a fellow traveler yet, I will call someone with more experience in the program than me and ask them if they're willing to walk with me through the Steps.

Step One

"We admitted we were powerless over the effects of alcoholism or other family dysfunction, that our lives had become unmanageable." BRB p. 118

Of course we are powerless. Haven't we been powerless most of our lives?

In ACA we learn to think of this word in a new light. When we hang around meetings long enough to listen, we find that our very power comes from surrender. The First Step tells us that we had actually been giving away our power at the exact time we sought to keep it. As we learn to healthfully surrender by walking away and letting go, we begin experiencing a new freedom.

We stop trying to fix others so that we can feel more comfortable, and in the process teach them how to take care of us. We take care of ourselves and allow others to fall down and *not* get up if that is what they must do. We walk away from the emotional car crashes that have caused us to feel like victims most of our lives. We realize we never really had the power to change anyone, especially those we grew up with.

As we make healthier choices, we start to see results in our lives. It is no longer the right thing to complain when we can just simply step away from the dialog. Because we now value our serenity, we release the idea that it is our job to change the world around us.

On this day I see wonderful things happening in my life as I loosen my grip…and let go.

False Self

"The mind developed the Laundry List Traits or the false self to survive." BRB p. xxvi

Many of us were born into a hostile world. Instinctively, we learned to sense danger. We were caught in the family story and played our part, doing what we had to do to survive. We couldn't be our genuine selves – who we were meant to be. We molded a personality that could change at the drop of a hat, adapting to any situation. It took a lot of skill to survive, and our false self kept us safe in childhood.

Before ACA, most of us didn't know we had carried this false self into adulthood. As we gained new awareness, it helped us notice the constant barrage of negative thoughts our false self gave off. It seemed the 14 Traits were part of our DNA.

As we move forward with courage, we use meetings and recovery friends as support. Our literature informs us and remodels our thinking. The Steps help us find who we truly are. We know the Traits were an important part of our early survival, but now they are holding us back. Standing at the crossroads, we choose to allow our Inner Child to come out of hiding. We become our True Self. As we recover, the Traits begin to soften to a point where they lose their hold on us.

On this day I will remember how far I have come. I treasure the self-knowledge I've gained in ACA that no longer gives my false self power.

Acting Purposefully

"We have seen adult children use the principles of the Twelve Steps to handle illness, despair, and death with amazing serenity and faith." BRB p. 291

The beauty of the Steps is that they guide us in our recovery from having grown up in a dysfunctional home, providing us with a healthy spiritual base from which to live our lives. When we remain engaged with our recovery by attending meetings regularly and reaching out to other adult children, we maintain a level of spiritual fitness that will assist us in coping with the inevitable challenges we will face.

With strengthened spirits, we live from a solid foundation that will not collapse, even during times of crisis. Situations and events will come at us unexpectedly, and we will be presented with difficulties and painful circumstances – this is certain. Rather than reacting unconsciously and repeating unhealthy behavior patterns, we act purposefully while maintaining our peace. The Steps are the tools that help us navigate the uncharted territory that is our life. By continuing to apply what we have learned on a regular basis, we can face the trials of life with grace.

On this day I will apply the universal wisdom contained within the Twelve Steps to whatever problem I am facing.

Abusive Relationships

"We stay in abusive relationships because they resemble how we were raised." BRB p. 197

We're going along and things seem to be working smoothly, and suddenly, "Bam!" The rug gets pulled out. We feel betrayed by the ones who supposedly love us the most. And we feel stupid for trusting again that things will be better.

This can describe what happened in our childhood and also what happens in our adult relationships. We can experience abuse as an adult, whether it's with our family of origin or another relationship.

We may get knocked down emotionally or physically, but with the help of the program, we can now learn to separate ourselves from the abuser. We are not trapped like we were as children.

In ACA, we learn to trust and to feel at a level we never experienced before. We have choices – to continue to hope the others will change as we continue to be abused, or remove ourselves and find a safe haven. There are many levels of safe haven, from a shelter to simply being in a meeting with our ACA friends. They are available if we are ready to stand free.

On this day I will choose the best path for my emotional health. I prepare myself to make life-changing decisions to remove myself from my abusive relationships.

Emotional Sobriety

"Through meditation, we begin to visualize emotional sobriety.
BRB p. 265

Many of us had trouble learning the rules of punctuation when we were in grade school. We wrote sentences without commas, such as: "We ate the dog did not," which sounded like we "ate the dog." The rules were foreign to us and seemed difficult to master. But as we trudged forward, we picked up little tips along the way, like using commas that told us to "breathe/pause here."

Emotional sobriety can be very much like punctuation because it allows us to set limits and be more clear about our wants and needs. When we pause and breathe, life becomes more manageable. As we learn to express our unexpressed grief to others in the program, we find that they understand what we're saying because we're saying it in a way they can hear us.

As we listen intently to the Problem and the Solution when they're read in our meetings, we learn to not only hear but absorb them. We begin to visualize what our life can be like if we practice the Steps and use the tools of ACA, including meditation. We learn to pause, breathe deeply, focus and start to make emotional sobriety a reality in our lives.

On this day I will pause and remember that just as it took time to learn the rules of punctuation in school, so too can I achieve emotional sobriety with practice and focus. But the effort is definitely worth it!

Triggers

"We often cannot avoid triggers, but we can change the way we deal with them." BRB p. 253

"They really know how to push my buttons!" How often have we said this to ourselves or heard others say it? The buttons are the repressed memories or resentments we have stored in that place in our mind and body that we never want to visit.

So when someone says or does something that awakens those memories, the battle begins. It's as if these old memories and resentments are poised at the gate, waiting to get out, waiting for us to finally deal with them, and reminding us that until we do, they will always be there.

Unlike most other recovery programs, ACA encourages us to resurrect those memories and resentments and put them on the table in a safe and loving environment. In doing so, the miracle happens. They begin to lose their power, and little by little we find that we can, in fact, deal with them without feeling as helpless as we did when the events actually occurred.

ACA is the safe place that allows this to happen. Our fellow travelers have also been that scared five-year-old, and they know how we feel.

On this day I know that taking away the power of old memories will also take away the power of the triggers.

Mistakes

"We also have great difficulty accepting mistakes as adults."
BRB p. 38

Many adult children find themselves being overachievers and perfectionists. Many of us live in a white-knuckled *what if?* environment created by our own need to manage everything and everyone around us. We worry things won't be done on time or be done perfectly.

As children, most of us felt we weren't loved enough because we weren't good enough. Our parents or caretakers reinforced this by letting us know we didn't measure up. So we attempted to be perfect, which of course, fell short.

As we entered adulthood we continued to equate perfection with love or the lack thereof if things didn't work out. No one needed to berate us for imperfections; we were very capable of doing that to ourselves.

Perfectionism, control, negative projection, berating ourselves: how did we ever have time to breathe, let alone have any degree of serenity in our lives?

As we work the ACA program and start to feel better about ourselves, we become okay with imperfection. We accept our human limitations, forgive ourselves for making mistakes and release ourselves from the need to control everything in our environment.

We can take time to breathe... really breathe... as in *inhale*, *exhale* and *relax*.

On this day I will give myself the freedom to make an error and know that it does not affect my worth as a human being.

Recovery Language

"We may be speaking program lingo, but we are not talking about what truly bothers us." BRB p. 432

In the beginning, many of us found great comfort in the new language of recovery. It shielded us against the old way of thinking. But some of us found that "talking the talk" without "walking the walk" did not change our actual behavior. We damaged ourselves and those around us by treading lightly. As we learned when we were children, we did not make waves, and the consequences still hurt us deeply. What we needed to see was that we were in a fight for our very lives.

As we recognize our complacence, we begin to free ourselves. We embrace our choices as adults with a firm backbone. We grow up. We do for ourselves what no one else can do: we rescue ourselves. We do this by surrendering our controlling grip and letting other people into our lives who can help us – a sponsor, a fellow traveler, a therapist – whomever we need.

We are not looking for perfection, but progress. We put aside our doubts and walk into the light of a new truth. It may feel painful to be honest and try something new, but not as painful as staying where we are.

On this day I will take action to get a sponsor if I don't already have one. I will commit to working the Steps and not just sound like I know what I'm talking about when I really don't.

False Self

"The dysfunction is encoded into our souls as the false self."
BRB p. 105

Many of us couldn't be ourselves as children. In order to survive, we bought our parent's negative messages, and then as adults, we repeated their dishonest justifications for crazy behavior. We remember our destructive false pride that wouldn't allow us to admit mistakes or feel vulnerable. On some level, we always knew what we were doing, but our false self was in charge and we didn't have the words or thought processes to do things differently or to express true feelings.

What hurts the most is that for those of us who have children, we modeled this dishonest behavior for them. As much as we tried to stop ourselves, we just couldn't see our way through to show them a better side.

In recovery, we now see that our wounds were so deep that it's hard to imagine that we had a hole that big in our soul. Today we can see that our lack of honesty for so long is constant proof of the trauma we suffered as children, and the reason we need ACA to break the cycle. This is where we strip away all the layers of shame that created our false self. We now more readily admit our shortcomings because as adults we can handle any fallout. In doing so, we help keep the family craziness from growing.

On this day I release my false self and have the courage to admit when I am wrong. I do this so that the hurts stop piling up, both for both myself and others.

Trait One

***"We became isolated and afraid of people and authority figures."
BRB p. 10***

So many of us shut down and hide because of our fear of people and authority figures. Most of this fear stems from the way we were treated when we were young. Understandably, what we learned as children carries over into most everything we do today: fear of our partner or boss, fear of success or failure, fear of conflict – the list can seem endless.

Our childhood authority figures, our parents, were often physically, verbally, or emotionally abusive. One thing many of us thought we learned for sure: if anything went wrong, it was our fault.

While working the ACA Steps with a sponsor, we gradually and bravely uncover the traumatic moments from our childhood that made such lasting impressions. No wonder we were scared. No wonder we held our breath and squeezed our muscles tight. Knowing what happened is what leads to change – one follows the other for a reason.

All of our work bears fruit. At some point, the clouds open up and the sun shines through. We get it! We don't have to live in fear anymore. Freedom feels terrific! Thank you, Higher Power!

On this day I acknowledge the fears I've carried for most of my life, and I remind myself that I am now safe. I take deep breaths and feel gratitude for the people in my life who are kind and loving.

Taking a Risk

"Talking about our feelings is a risk; however, this is a risk worth taking because the rewards are great." BRB p. 186

Where is it safe to talk about our secret fears, our perceived shortcomings, and our doubts about our own sanity? Our Higher Power gave us a group of ACAs who listen to our feelings and do not judge us.

Our ACA fellow travelers feel what we feel and share many of our same doubts and our often misguided perceptions. They do so without trying to fix us and without telling us to "get over it." Their hands are outstretched to newcomers who take the risk of walking through the meeting doors to tell their secrets.

It is very difficult *not* to believe in a Higher Power when we walk into the rooms of ACA and see the unconditional love we display to one another. The ability to share our feelings in this safe environment moves us toward the rewards of the program. We experience the miracle of learning to love ourselves, and we project a new image to the world.

On this day I know that in ACA I can risk sharing my innermost feelings. They will be met with acceptance and love.

Unvoiced Pain

"In acting out, I was screaming when I could not voice my pain."
BRB p. 503

Many of us spent years drinking to numb our pain, eating for comfort, using drugs for escape, using sex while hoping for love, or whatever worked for us. While some of us found other Twelve Step programs that helped us with our self-harming, addictive behaviors, others of us may have lived life rotating from one behavior to another. We felt we needed something to help us separate ourselves from the pain, so we "acted out" as a way to avoid "feeling in."

As children, we went through so many tough experiences alone. We couldn't tell anyone what was happening or how we felt. We couldn't even admit that the craziness we observed was really occurring. No one would listen, or if they did, they would smooth it over with excuses or tell us there was something wrong with us for even saying it out loud. As a result, these thoughts or words festered inside.

We now are able to put a voice to our pain that can be heard by others in ACA. No one judges us for feeling the way that we do. Our True Self is able to shine through without turning to our former addictions, our silent partners. We are freeing ourselves from the guilt, shame and loneliness of our past.

On this day, if I feel the pull to act out, I will stay in the moment and try to find out what is triggering my reaction. I will use whatever ACA tools I need to in order to help myself.

Promise One

"We will discover our real identities by loving and accepting ourselves." *BRB p. 591*

Real identity? The idea that we aren't "real" can be very confusing at first. The concept is difficult, even maddening. As we go to meetings, we may begin to hear about a critical inner parent, an inner loving parent, and the hidden Inner Child. It seems complicated.

Somewhere in the first few months of attending meetings, it clicks. Slowly we learn, understand, and apply the information we have been gathering, and one day the realization of our dilemma becomes clear. The picture finally comes into view. Without knowing it, we have been perpetrating a fraud: impersonating our True Self with our false self.

As we dive into Step work, we begin to reparent ourselves. In the same instant, we become accepting of ourselves. No longer untethered and wandering aimlessly, our course is made clear with each day of practicing this simple, Higher Power-given program.

A miracle occurs as a result of the work we do in ACA: we unshackle our True Self from our false self, embrace our hidden Inner Child with the caring arms of our inner loving parent, and are carried to higher and higher levels of freedom.

On this day I will listen, learn, and apply the concepts and principles of ACA recovery. They are the means of discovering my real identity, allowing me to love and accept myself.

Hitting Bottom

"All bottoms have meaning, and all bottoms can be a starting point for a new way of life. There is hope. Healing is possible."
BRB p. 124

We come to ACA because we've hit some type of a bottom. Maybe we feel hopeless because life hasn't gone as we hoped. Or we've lost too much because of our dysfunctional behaviors, and we realize that we don't know how to change on our own. We tried, but it didn't work. Maybe we find our way to a meeting because deep down we know there has to be something more.

Working the ACA program doesn't mean we might not hit more bottoms. Some of us are often blindsided by something we thought we'd dealt with. Maybe we've spent eons working on our over-responsibility character defect and have made great strides. Then in the face of overwhelming stress and grief, it feels as if we find ourselves right back where we were before we began recovery. We're in there trying to take care of everyone, being the buffer, trying to control the situation.

The difference this time is that we're not really in the same place. We now have tools: the telephone, the BRB, and the meetings. This new bottom tells us that we're a complex individual who doesn't have all the answers.

On this day, when I slip so far that I think I can't see daylight, I will not abandon myself. I will look at my situation as another opportunity for growth in the program.

Service

"Fortunately, our Second Tradition reminds us that our real authority in ACA meetings and service work is 'a loving God as expressed in our group conscience.'" BRB p. 499

There may often be few, if any, experienced members in our ACA meetings. Who then makes the group's decisions? Who chairs? Who buys the literature? Who sponsors the newcomer when we are all newcomers?

Others of us who started ACA meetings have dealt with this situation by just opening the meetings and asking if anyone wished to chair. We had faith that someone would find the courage to step up. When we asked for someone to buy literature or make copies, a Higher Power brought someone to the meeting who was willing to do this bit of service. When we looked around for someone to work the Steps with us, a comfortable person seemed to appear.

So it is for our group's purpose. When confronted by a situation that seems greater than us, we can feel reassured that by turning it over to the group's Higher Power in the form of a group conscience, a decision can be made. We trust that we can work out the details when we have the best interest of the meeting in mind. If our egos get in the way, we talk to someone and sort it out. We help the day-to-day affairs of the meeting to run smoothly.

On this day I will trust that a Higher Power will express itself through our group's conscience, giving us an opportunity for unity and spiritual growth.

New Way of Life

"We ask the adult child considering ACA to look at the program as a way of life that will unfold over time, bringing rich rewards of emotional relief and self-acceptance." BRB p. 95

We took all of the abuse we could and still thought it was our fault. What was it we were doing wrong, anyway? What was it that made us feel so different and defective? Why couldn't we just be like the rest of the people in our family and just take endless amounts of abuse without seeming to care? Why were we so wimpy? And where did negative feelings like anger get us, anyway?

Before ACA, we may have been in other programs that helped us, but where certain feelings may have been minimized. This made us feel like we were back in a place where we had to shut parts of ourselves off. We might have been told that "taking it to God" was the only important thing. That may work for many people, but we realized it wasn't enough for us.

Now, with the help of ACA and the people we have learned to trust, we can accept the value of all of our feelings. We especially accept our anger and no longer run from it, knowing it can help teach us where our boundaries should be. We talk to others who are in touch with their feelings in a healthy way and can really hear us when we express our emotions. We know we are in the right place where healing takes place.

On this day I will realize my emotions are part of a gift from my Higher Power, a gift called "Me."

Re-Creation

"Yet, our children and relationships were still mired in our dysfunction. We recreated the abandonment and loss of our own childhood." BRB p. 21

Many of us tried to raise our families differently. But without ACA or another type of intervention, we were like our parents – we could only give what we had. This meant we made a lot of wrong choices. We may even have become alienated from our children, finding that they resented us, just as we resented our parents.

ACA presents us with a choice: stay and get better in a way that might someday repair our relationships, or feel hopeless and continue to fill ourselves with self-blame and shame.

If we choose ACA, we must let go of the fact that we didn't find help earlier, when it could have prevented so much pain. We accept that change takes time, so we "get our heads on straight" and concentrate on taking care of ourselves. As we're ready, we learn to be present in a healthy way for our children. If we're separated from them, we hope they come back to us, but if they don't, we continue to love them and pray they find their way.

On this day I will take care of myself first. Only then will I be available to my family if they ask for emotional support.

Grief Work

"We can pinpoint and measure our loss by comparing the treatment we received as children in dysfunctional families with the care we could have received if raised by loving, consistent parents." BRB p. 204

The grief exercises in Step Five ask us to journal about childhood incidents to help access emotions about events. If they don't surface, we try to see how a present-day child would feel in our situation. We can also look at childhood pictures to help connect with our innocence and what was lost.

Then we're asked to re-read our Step Four "Shame and Abandonment" worksheets and reframe each incident. We describe what would have been different if there were a loving parent in each scenario.

Experiencing loss in this way can help us release it. But if we're blocked, it may be that we switch from grief to anger when it hurts too much. It's like a button is pushed that sends us into shutdown, blame, or rage mode. But the deep sadness of our grief can also help us see the true level of destruction of our emotions, minds, and bodies.

In choosing the recovery process over dysfunction, we realize that grief work helps us find our strong, capable Inner Child. We are learning what a loving parent would do and how we can reparent ourselves. The ACA program is not easy work, but the reward is freedom!

On this day I will hold on to the ACA process when the grief and emotions are screaming. I will stop at nothing to recover my original self.

Relationships

"We remember we can talk, trust, and feel instead of control, isolate, and fume. Relationships can be different in recovery."
BRB p. 291

As children we relied on our survival traits to protect us from harm. Gradually, they grew stronger and more ingrained as we encountered greater levels of family dysfunction and the resulting fear. We carried our traits into adulthood. Initially, we were unaware of their effects, but our relationships suffered.

Through ACA, we realize our survival traits no longer serve us. When we consider emotional intimacy, we may feel scared and at risk for hurt. However, if we risk sharing ourselves with another, we become capable of having a true relationship.

Trusting another person with our most vulnerable selves is a new and maybe scary practice. We can let the other person earn our trust gradually as the relationship develops. We can ask for what we need rather than manipulate to get what we want. We can identify and share our feelings without shutting down or ruminating endlessly. We no longer need to keep our True Selves locked inside. When we risk honesty and openness with another, we discover a world of new possibilities, including love.

On this day I have the courage to break old patterns that keep me from deeper connections with the people in my life.

Step Four

"Without knowing the meaning of the abandonment encoded within the past, the adult child is doomed to repeat it. The unexamined past becomes the future of the next generation." BRB p. 154

Many of us came from other Twelve Step programs, and our experiences with the Fourth Step may not have been positive. Like medicine, it was something we took because we were supposed to. It didn't feel like an action of love, but rather like a listing of how we were defective people. We were confused by this, but we did as we were told.

When we arrived at ACA, we may have carried that Fourth Step baggage and cringed at the thought of doing another one. What in the world could we be blamed for about our childhood? How could we be at fault?

But we began the work anyway. We may have been confused when we started, but we soon saw that this would be a completely different experience. We answered the questions in the Fourth Step exercises, which gave us a well-rounded view of what actually happened to us. We began to see the reasons why we act the way we do today, and why we could not have turned out differently.

This was an amazing discovery. We now believe with great hope that we can recover from the effects of our dysfunctional childhood so that we can leave a new legacy for future generations.

On this day I affirm my commitment to examining my past so that I can help change the path of my future and the future of those close to me.

Exact Nature

"When we look at the exact nature of our wrongs, we see that we have harmed ourselves based on our sense of being unacceptable, inferior, or lost." BRB p. 198

For years we blamed ourselves for everything – what we did and what others did. To keep the peace, we made amends, both verbal and non-verbal, to unsafe, often violent people in our lives. We were the doormats we were raised to be. We hid our feelings and confided to no one.

Some of us, even after we started recovery in ACA, continued to keep things bottled up and wondered why we weren't changing. Somehow, we had interpreted "taking it to God" to mean just praying the uncomfortable things in our life away. We thought that expressing our feelings, especially anger, to others wasn't acceptable.

We now view anger as a normal, healthy emotion that can help us know when we need to set a boundary, get out of a specific situation, or let go of an unhealthy relationship. We no longer ignore how we feel.

We may create a list of triggers to help us get in touch with our feelings. We might keep lists of emotions to more accurately identify our own. We realize that even the seemingly negative ones are a part of the gift of being completely human.

On this day I will sit with my feelings instead of pushing them away. Then I will make a phone call to share them with a fellow traveler.

Actor vs. Reactor

"This book will...truly move you from a place of reactor to actor in life. As said in many Twelve Step programs, 'It works if you work it.'" BRB p. xix

As children, most of us learned to be reactive as a survival mechanism. If we didn't "jump to it" without questioning, we were usually punished. We learned to be defensive, often having to explain even the smallest of our actions. We reacted out of fear and did what was necessary to avoid getting into trouble.

As adults, this conditioning may have an upside – maybe we're the ones who react quickly to a crisis and save the day. But we also might be the ones who react quickly to answer someone's intrusive question, later realizing it wasn't their business. Then we berate ourselves for being so "stupid." Or maybe we're the ones who blurt out something inappropriate because something triggered us.

ACA's Big Red Book was written to help us uncover and understand the roots of our dysfunctions. We learn that we carry around a critical inner parent that causes us to react in ways we are no longer comfortable with. As we work the program to silence that critical voice, we feel calmer. We learn to stop, question and decide what our role is and should be, rather than jump to conclusions. Gradually, we become the actors who think for ourselves...and the critical voice fades.

On this day I will take time to read from the Big Red Book to help me further silence the critical voice that may still cause me to be reactive.

PTSD and Survival

"The memory contains PTSD elements of fear, threat to survival, and feeling alone, perhaps destitute." BRB p. 180

Many of us experienced the trauma of being left alone for hours, having to feed ourselves and to do whatever else was necessary to survive. We ate what we could find, even if it was half-rotten; we wore what was there, even if it wasn't clean, had holes, and didn't fit. We were desperately afraid, we were neglected, and we didn't know if we would survive.

We suffer from PTSD, just as sure as if we were raised in a war zone. As a result, we often developed addictions directly related to what we experienced. If we didn't have enough food, we may have developed an eating disorder; if we didn't have enough to wear, we may have become a compulsive shopper or a shoplifter; if we were terrified of being alone, we may have learned to manipulate others to keep them around.

In ACA, we discover the Laundry List traits, the survival behaviors we developed as a way of coping with our childhood trauma. As we continue to learn more, we use this knowledge to begin to take care of ourselves in a healthy way. We make a commitment that even if we feel overwhelmed, we will not abandon ourselves and our program. We know recovery is possible in ACA because we see it in others.

On this day, if I reach outside of myself for an unhealthy solution, I will remember to reach inside for the experience, strength, and hope the program gives me.

Sponsorship

"Sponsorship is the vehicle by which we take the road less traveled to a true connection with others and a God of our understanding."
BRB p. 368

Coming from a family of dysfunction, we developed a fear of authority. We learned early that our opinions, feelings, and attitudes were insignificant. The power belonged to the raging alcoholic, the enabling spouse, and any older children in the family who were given authority over us because they had been put in charge of most of our care. In alcoholic homes, the parents were too involved in fighting or manipulating each other over alcoholic rages and abusive behavior to care for us.

When we escaped, we vowed never to let another person control us; yet, we found ourselves either being the abuser or the dependent one in most relationships we developed, including working relationships, religious relationships, and friendships.

When we finally found ACA, for some of us, choosing a sponsor to help us work the Steps often lead to the same type of relationship we were familiar with. Then we discovered the "fellow traveler" model of sponsorship. We found this peer-to-peer concept helped keep us out of our people-pleasing or running-someone-else's-life behaviors. It put us on equal footing and allowed us to travel the road to recovery together.

On this day I will walk hand-in-hand with my fellow traveler so we can help each other recover on the less-traveled road.

Overly Responsible

"Before finding recovery, we suppressed our feelings and were overly responsible. We tried to anticipate the needs of others and meet those needs so we would not be abandoned." BRB p. 94

Many of us have focused all our efforts on spouses, significant others, or children, trying to do everything possible to make them comfortable and happy. We may have spent so much time with our children and their friends that we were uncomfortably intrusive. Because we feared abandonment, we may have sacrificed ourselves in an attempt to keep our spouses from becoming bored with us.

These actions kept us from admitting, "I'm tired. I'm not interested. I don't have time." Eventually, we began to resent them. We deserved to do things we wanted to do, and our family members needed space to breathe, to make their own decisions, to make mistakes and learn from them.

With ACA recovery, we finally get the message that it's okay to let loved ones do their own thing. It's okay to let them find happiness through their own actions. Not being constantly involved in their lives does not mean they will abandon us. In fact, it can strengthen our relationships when we all feel the relief of being responsible for ourselves.

On this day I will remember that I do not need to micromanage the lives of those close to me. They will not abandon me simply because I let them live their own lives.

Buried Feelings

"We learned to keep our feelings down as children and kept them buried as adults." BRB p. 589

How can we honor our feelings when many of us were brought up by parents who implied or directly told us that we shouldn't talk about, think about, our even *have* our feelings? They told us we were "imagining things," or said "Stop making a big deal out of nothing." They said showing feelings and emotion would turn us into weaklings. It was more important to look good and not be concerned with feelings, especially those related to fear, anger, and sadness. How would we be able to stand on our own two feet if we were shadow-boxing with unnecessary emotions? We got the message loud and clear and kept our feelings buried for decades.

But how long can we go on stuffing things before it affects us emotionally, mentally, and physically; before people shun us because these denied feelings start manifesting themselves as inappropriate behavior?

In ACA, we begin to recognize and honor our feelings in real time. When fear, anger, envy, greed, and jealousy appear, we identify and filter them as honestly as possible. Sometimes simple acknowledgement and perspective-gathering is enough. But we also should be prepared to talk about our feelings for the purpose of gaining true understanding and acceptance. As we do so, resilience and serenity begin to permeate our minds and our souls.

On this day I will honor my feelings by unlocking them and accepting them as an essential part of my whole being that deserves love and respect.

Blame

"We cannot reach the level of spiritual growth that we are seeking by blaming sick people." BRB p. 158

The hard truth about alcoholism and family dysfunction is that there is no one to blame. It may feel as if our parents caused our suffering, but we forget that dysfunction is inherited. They were simply working with what they were given. They may not have willingly set out to harm us; they were reacting to their own sickness and in turn passed down the disease of dysfunction.

As children, we experienced unfair treatment and wished our parents would get help. However, we had no control over their actions.

But today we have control over whether we hang on to blaming people who could not help themselves at the time. When we let go of accusing sick people, we can focus on ourselves and what can be done in the here and now to help ourselves heal. We loosen the ties that keep us bound to circumstances that couldn't have turned out differently, thereby creating the possibility of limitless growth within us.

On this day I will do all that I am capable of to help stop the generational dysfunction in my family. In doing so, I will let go of any blame that is keeping me from experiencing greater levels of recovery.

Tradition One

"Can we even have personal recovery without ACA unity?" Our First Tradition frankly says 'No.' ACA members working the Twelve Steps recognize the need to place the group's survival ahead of their own selfish needs or their fear-based urge to control others." BRB p. 492

Our feelings of self-doubt are often revealed by the exchanges we have at a business meeting. They tend to surface in clandestine forms of control and its close cousin, manipulation.

When the group is considering taking an action, we may voice a concern or point out that it may violate a Tradition. If a course of action is taken that we disagree with, our personal program helps us to admit we are powerless and accept the things we cannot change.

We are mindful that unity does not mean complete agreement. Still, we strive for substantial unanimity in making the group's decisions. We actively seek out the voices of dissent, giving them an opportunity to be heard. This ensures that all sides of a discussion are heard, and perhaps compromises may be reached.

Actively listening to each other is an exercise in inclusivity. Decisions that raise rancor may have to be tabled or revisited when feelings are not running as high. Nonetheless, if the group's decision is firmly grounded in the ACA Traditions, even if we don't agree, we are called on to turn over our personal agenda.

On this day I will be mindful that everyone's voice should be heard on group issues. If I can contribute my experience, strength, and hope, I will do so without expectations. Being open-minded and tolerant is humility in action.

Other Laundry List

"Before we write in greater detail about the original Laundry List, we must note that most of the 14 Traits have an opposite. Our experience shows that the opposites are just as damaging as the counterpart." BRB p. 8

Overcoming our denial of family dysfunction was easier when we took an honest and balanced view of our life experiences. The Laundry List provided clues about some of the effects, but the compulsions and the addictiveness could not be accepted as normal. Somewhere, deep inside, we knew there was more to the issues we faced than we were currently in touch with.

The Opposites Laundry List gave some of us the rest of the puzzle. Here was a description of how we might have acted out the Traits. We could see how we set up an endless roller coaster ride between the effects of our childhood and how it affected ourselves and others today.

The Solution for both lists is the same: the Steps and reparenting. Admitting powerlessness, coming to believe, and turning our will and our lives over to the care of a Higher Power all start us on the road to our spiritual awakening. Acknowledging our critical inner parent and creating space for our inner loving parent to guide our Inner Child releases us from our affects, and gives us power to achieve integration and wholeness.

On this day I will look to both the Laundry List and the Opposite Laundry List to get a sense of the effects and my affects. I will be mindful of the Solution, using the Steps and reparenting myself in order to create integrity and wholeness.

February

"The ACA program has brought me the miracle of life. I am able to experience compassion, forgiveness, love, and gratitude, the emotions that make my life worth living." BRB p. 140

Gratitude

"The ACA program has brought me the miracle of life. I am able to experience compassion, forgiveness, love, and gratitude, the emotions that make my life worth living." BRB p. 140

Before ACA, many of us were so mired in our dysfunctions that if someone asked us how we felt, we usually just said, "Fine." We probably didn't even know how to describe our feelings, since many of us couldn't think of more than a few anyway. This was the result of consistently stuffing them in our childhood and adult lives.

In ACA, we learn to change our thoughts, to gradually free ourselves from the things that are weighing us down. We see that the sky is often a beautiful blue; it's not always cloudy. We start to see so many more possibilities for ourselves about the way we truly want to live our lives.

We find that it's possible to have compassion for others in a way that doesn't mean we want or need to fix them. We understand that we all have struggles; we offer help where we can, with no strings attached. Instead of carrying resentments, we learn forgiveness. We begin to release any bitterness and anger. Instead of being a victim and feeling as if we don't have enough, we learn to have gratitude for what we have and for our potential. We find the miracles.

On this day I will remember the emotional gifts this program has given me, and with gratitude I promise to continue to open myself up to life's possibilities through ACA.

Identity

"In childhood our identity is formed by the reflection we see in the eyes of the people around us." BRB p. 84

Who were our mirrors? It was the people who told us in words and actions how unwanted, bothersome, or stupid we were. We tried to do what they wanted, but it was usually never enough. Any approval we got was conditional. And it evaporated if we let down our guard by not getting perfect grades, not taking care of our siblings the right way, or not doing the housework well enough.

We didn't know who we really were because our identity was whatever they told us it was.

What brings most of us to ACA is that we eventually get tired of trying, isolating, and stuffing our feelings. This is where we learn to accept that our parents and families are never going to be like the ones on television or down the street. Instead of continuing to recreate the rejection and abandonment we received as children, we learn to love and affirm ourselves. Our sponsors and fellow travelers tell us to accept only what is good, and if it doesn't feel right, don't do it. We keep following these suggestions repeatedly until we notice we are no longer who we were once told we had to be. We are strong and independent.

On this day I define who I am. I am good, and I accept only what is good and healthy in my life.

Step Two

"Came to believe that a Power greater than ourselves could restore us to sanity." BRB p. 130

When we heard "restore us to sanity," some of us tried to remember when we had ever even felt sane. We had lived obsessed with control and were addicted to our families of origin. Step Two was a revelation when we realized how the dysfunction and insanity of our childhoods had affected us.

Our inventories and Step work guided us on the journey inward that would lead to our True Selves. We saw that we needed to allow the long-suppressed emotions and voices to surface.

The voices came from our Inner Child; we learned that our insanity had kept us from paying attention. But we needed to hear our full story, so we began to listen. This helped us step out of our shaming shadows and into the light. We began to realize that our personal Higher Power had been there inside of us to guide us all along. We were finally learning to embrace our feelings and not cover them up with addictions.

As we continued to recover, we realized that feeling sane meant taking care of ourselves not just emotionally, but physically, too. For some of us, this was a first.

On this day I will have faith in a power greater than myself. I will give myself permission to explore what that is for me, no matter what it looks like for others.

Spiritual Bypass

"A spiritual bypass means that the person is attempting to avoid the pain that can come with working through the trauma and neglect from childhood. In some cases, the person attempts to jump ahead in the recovery process without going through the entire process. This path invariably fails or leads to dissatisfying results." BRB p. 287

While looking for answers, many of us have read countless self-help books, put on a false face, and purchased products to boost our self-esteem. We wanted a quick fix for our empty lives, but we found temporary relief at best. We inevitably spiraled downward into a familiar despair, wondering yet again, "Will it ever be my turn to be happy?"

When we find ACA, we hear the Solution and see progress and spiritual recovery in others. This gives us hope. We learn that the tools of recovery are meant to work together, not in isolation. Many people leave ACA believing they worked the program, but it just didn't work for them. In fact maybe they expected ACA to be another quick fix.

If we use all the tools the way they're meant to be used, ACA can heal us and change our lives. By attending meetings, working the Steps, reaching out to others, and finding a Higher Power, we can recapture our True Selves – the person we were born to be.

On this day I will have the courage to use the tools of the ACA program, especially the one that's hardest for most of us – reaching out to others for help.

Recovery Message

"Hearing the message of recovery and hope from someone else fans the dim spark of aliveness we keep buried inside." BRB pg 359

When we got to recovery we may have been a mess. We may not have even known it then, but many of us were broken and on our last leg. We may have even tried to kill ourselves with drugs and alcohol at some point, or had unprotected sex with someone we didn't know. We may have buried all our light because we felt we did not deserve to experience it.

We work today to dust off the source of light inside us that is a gift from our Higher Power. We pray and meditate, finding the lifesaving value of doing so. We learn the message of the Twelve Steps and the value of this amazing fellowship that is available to us, just for the asking. We are grateful for the tools of recovery. If we need to get abstinent in some way, we do that with the help of the Steps and a sponsor. We are no longer alone.

On this day I will reach out to whomever I need to help me remember and work through the trauma of my past. If there is something that is blocking me, I will do my part and then ask my Higher Power to remove it from my path.

Trait Two

"We became approval seekers and lost our identity in the process."
BRB p. 11

"Yes, Sir! Anything you want, Sir! Whatever I can do, Sir!"

"Maybe if I do the dishes faster, Mom won't drink so much this weekend."

"I'll keep the little kids quieter, and then Dad won't get so mad."

Many of us feel we have to do for others so they will like us, so the alcoholic won't hit us, so people won't get mad at us. As adult children, we get so good at doing for others that we end up believing we're only okay if we have their approval. Those others can be bosses, friends, coworkers, spouses, and children.

In ACA, we start to see this pattern of approval-seeking. As a result, many of us find that we don't know what we want, or how to make a decision for ourselves. Some of us can't even name our favorite color, but we sure know the favorite colors of others!

As we begin to discover ourselves, we learn to separate the idea of a simple act of kindness from that of sacrificing ourselves in a way that destroys our self-worth. We begin appreciating that we are okay and can affirm ourselves for who we are, not what we do.

On this day I clearly see the difference between seeking false approval and doing a good deed because it's the right thing to do. I am grateful for that realization as I live my recovery.

Letting Go

"In ACA, we learn to let go of control in stages. Our parachute is the Twelve Steps and a Higher Power of our understanding."
BRB p. 40

While growing up, we may have felt controlled by our parents and the palpable dysfunction that surrounded us. As a result, in adulthood we found ways to take control, whether we did it directly or passively through covert manipulation. Being in control made us think we could determine our own destinies.

But trying to control people and situations is exhausting work. If we are truly honest with ourselves, we realize that the control we *think* we have is an illusion. Many of us learned this the hard way, as things began falling apart around us.

By working the Twelve Steps with the help of a Higher Power and our fellow travelers, we come to believe that our focus on gaining and maintaining control leaves little room for the healthy things in our lives, like positive self-esteem, balanced relationships, spontaneity, and a world full of possibilities.

We also learn that letting go of control happens in stages. After all, we are trying to change an ingrained behavior that took a long time to 'perfect'. The key is to be gentle with ourselves.

On this day I will practice letting go of the control I have worked so hard to have over the people and events in my life. I will forgive myself if I slip.

Humor

"We often lost our creativity, our flexibility, and our sense of humor." BRB p. 333

"I always keep my sense of humor tucked in my hip pocket – available at all times," the old man said. "Where do you keep yours?"

When we first walk into ACA meetings, the last thing in the world we think of is a sense of humor. There's just too much pain. In many dysfunctional families, what passed as humor was really a form of sarcasm. For some of us who were the mascot or clown in our family of origin, utilizing humor was second nature. But it was the role we played for survival.

Rediscovering our true sense of humor sometimes begins in ACA meetings. Many times laughter erupts when certain things are said. That laughter isn't meant to poke fun; it's recognition of a shared experience that unites us. Fellow travelers understand what we're talking about.

Opening up to our sense of humor allows recovery to thrive. We discover that laughter can be a wonderful tool in our tool bag. We can watch funny movies or internet snippets to encourage our belly laughter. It feels wonderful to make healthy humor part of the healing process.

On this day I will keep my heart open to the things that make me laugh. Laughter brings me joy and makes everything better. Life is good!

Authority Figures

"Authority figures scare us and we feel afraid when we need to talk to them." BRB p. 417

As children we may have been terrified to voice a thought about anything to the authority figures in our lives. We learned to keep quiet because we usually didn't know what reaction we might get.

As adults, we may still have found ourselves reacting to authority in the same manner, whether it was in a work environment or even a social group or organization that resembled a workplace structure or purpose. We may have tried to avoid authority figures, but they're everywhere. Being self-employed didn't insulate us from these interactions, either.

Even in ACA, some of us place others in roles of authority where we find ourselves recreating our family structure. But recovery is where we can become aware of our reactions and practice new ways of acting. Before we talk to an authority figure, we can stop and perform a reality check. Are we imagining the worst? Is this person going to respond like my dysfunctional parent did years ago?

If we are fearful, a very successful technique many of us use is to write a script and role-play with a trusted friend. As part of this process, we give ourselves plenty of affirmations. Growth happens when we find that the more we actually *do* talk to authority figures, the more our confidence increases. At last we begin to see ourselves as recovering adults, not fearful children.

On this day I will use my recovery wisdom and strength as I interact with authority figures. I am no longer frozen by fear.

Dreams

"We thought we had forgotten these dreams, but our Inner Child remembers." BRB p. 430

As children we had an innocent wish to be heard, held, and protected. But in most of our homes, that didn't happen. When we spoke, it was usually the beginning of trouble. When we tried to cuddle or show affection, we were ignored, laughed at, or flirted with. Most of the time we were alone. The idea of being protected was non-existent. We grew up in a world where the norm was "anything goes, anytime." It was almost impossible to keep up with what was going on, but we did our best.

We fantasized about having a different family where we could be ourselves and it would be okay. We wished for a place overflowing love, a safe place where voices were soft and sweet, and where everyone just talked, laughed, and played together. It is so sad that we didn't get that. We deserved a bright and happy childhood, didn't we?

Our Inner Child is still waiting for this dream to be made real. This desire is still as strong as it was long ago. Who is going to be the person to bring this dream to this child?

In the ACA program we find that dreams can come true. Here, we are able to begin again, one day at a time. We can give our Inner Child all that we weren't given. Recovering dreams is what this program is all about.

On this day I know that I deserve my dreams. I am willing to work to make them come true with the help of ACA.

Affection

"Our false self constantly seeks outward affection, recognition or praise, but we secretly believe we don't deserve it." BRB p. 7

Many of us spent 'forever' trying to portray an image of having it all together, seeking approval by acting or dressing a certain way. We looked to those who seemed more confident to tell us how to think and feel. By doing so, we learned not to trust our own intuition. We were completely at the mercy of others. We were disconnected from our physical and emotional selves.

When we finally received some recognition, perhaps on the job after working nearly around-the-clock, our sense of satisfaction was short-lived. Deep down we "knew" we didn't deserve that recognition because our inner critical voice was saying, "If they saw the real me, this wouldn't be happening."

But as life changes in recovery, we now look for our self-esteem within ourselves and in our relationship with our Higher Power, not other people. We let the peace of the ACA program grow inside of us, one day at a time, through rigorous honesty, striving to know and understand our Inner Child. We stop people-pleasing because it deeply damages us. We have finally become the center of our own lives with an inner loving parent who won't abandon us.

On this day I put myself first and let others think what they will. I am enough just where I stand right now.

Adult Child Defined

"An adult child is someone whose actions and decisions as an adult are guided by childhood experiences grounded in self-doubt or fear." BRB p. 302

Before finding ACA, we didn't have the opportunity to learn any other way to live except from the standpoint of the dysfunction with which we were raised. As children, most of us quickly figured out what we needed to think, say, and do in order to avoid the most pain. We survived the best way we could, relying on only ourselves to get by.

As adults, often our automatic reactions to situations involve extensions of the behaviors we learned as children. We are adults by appearance, but have yet to mature past our childhood reactions. We are haunted by unresolved trauma that easily wreaks havoc in our lives. It is not our fault that we didn't come away with better life skills; we could not have turned out any differently. With the help of the Twelve Steps, we now have a Solution to our Problem. Through ACA, we have the love and support we need to grow through our childhood pain into the confident and secure adults we were meant to be.

On this day I release all negative self-judgment of my identity as an adult child. I am filled with the hope that the promises of ACA offer me.

Promise Five

"ACA recovery is challenging, but the rewards are immense. We must put forth effort and feel the uncomfortable feelings that might come. At the same time, the goal is self-love and knowing that we are good enough just the way we are. This is an ACA paradox." BRB p. 438

In our program, we need a lot of courage to face a great many things. Facing how we were abandoned requires us to summon all the courage we can muster. As we "keep coming back," memories and feelings float up from our subconscious to the mind's eye, and we acknowledge the losses we buried.

As children, many of us wanted or needed to idealize our caregivers. In ACA, we take off the rose-colored glasses and see them as flawed human beings who were unable to be there for us emotionally, physically, psychologically, or spiritually. Facing this abandonment means looking at it honestly with the help of our Higher Power, our inner loving parent, and our Inner Child. This is how we begin to reparent ourselves so that we can become whole.

On this day I continue to seek the courage to face my abandonment issues, resolving to take the steps to make myself whole, so I can bond with others from this consciousness-centered space.

Good Enough

"As we face our abandonment issues, we will be attracted by strengths and become more tolerant of weaknesses." BRB p. 591

For years, our critical inner parent continued to remind us that we were not good enough. It was a replay of what we were taught about ourselves as children. We didn't realize it, but that critical part of us was also saying we would never have enough to satisfy our needy Inner Child. At some point we may have asked ourselves, "What is enough?"

With the help of the ACA program, we began to see that we were making inroads into the healing process that would quiet our critical inner parent. In doing so, we knew we could begin to meet our Inner Child's needs.

As life continues to move forward, bit by bit, we let go of the "enough" of our childhood and learn to accept who we are – that we have so very much to offer. We recognize that our Higher Power helps us fulfill our needs, and occasionally our wants.

On this day I remember that I am and have always been more than good enough.

Promise Two

"Our self-esteem will increase as we give ourselves approval on a daily basis." BRB p. 591

The promise of self-esteem is very attractive, especially given that if we didn't have a negative self-perception, many of us would have no self-image at all.

By showing up regularly at ACA meetings, we increase our "True Self-esteem" in a positive way. We find a safe space to interact with others who are on the same quest. This act of showing up for our True Self gives us a positive view of ourselves, most likely for the first time.

By participating in the meetings and identifying ourselves as adult children, we are sending a signal to our Inner Child that we are aware of the work we have to do, and we are willing to make a commitment to realize our spiritual awakening. More True Self-esteem will come from regularly affirming our current state and our future mission.

By our showing up and participating, we give our True Self approval: approval to get well, to belong, to share, to believe, to hope, to care, to cry, to laugh, to grieve, to live. These simple expressions of our humanity are True Self-esteem of the most precious and rewarding kind.

On this day I will practice doing the things that build True Self-esteem and give my True Self the approval to trust, feel and talk.

Service

"The sincere adult child working an ACA program of meeting attendance and selfless service gets results with Step Seven. This is the sure path when we struggle with a troublesome shortcoming." BRB p. 222

How can giving service and attending meetings produce results? In giving "self-less" service, we must be able to manage our inner critical parent's dominating and controlling nature. As a result of working the Steps, we find that we are no longer as angry or scared to allow life to unfold as it will. Here lies the best answer to what has ailed us. The Steps, when worked with a fellow traveler, help us gain peace of mind and a sense of calm that allow us to feel alive.

This realization is exhilarating. Our joy can overflow, and we realize that this is a very valuable and healthy experience for us. While some of our shortcomings may still have a hold on us, we know that our path to wholeness is clearly marked and attainable. On our journey, we share our new-found sense of purpose with others in the program. With gratitude, we are able to share how the program has transformed us into vibrant human beings engaged in a life-giving program.

On this day I will continue to work on my defects of character and shortcomings and share my personal progress and the results I have received with those who will hear me.

Family Roles

"We are making a statement that we will no longer be loyal to denial and dysfunctional family roles." BRB p. 123

We each grew up playing a role in our families: hero, scapegoat, mascot, or lost child.* Our role may have been related to birth order, or perhaps to how we innately reacted to our situation. If we had several siblings, we probably shared these roles; if we were from a small family or were an only child, we may have had to play multiple roles.

Each role carried certain expectations. Even if the role appeared positive to the outside world, like the hero, it likely turned into a negative as we attempted to wear it while navigating through our adult years.

ACA helps us learn how to shed these shackling roles. We begin to set limits. We act in healthier, "unexpected" ways around our dysfunctional family of origin. We choose to no longer react to events that once set us emotionally spinning out of control. The process is not easy and may take time, yet through it all we learn to live life on our own terms. When we're successful, we release fear, chaos, control and rigidity from our lives. We find new freedom, which is an amazing reward.

On this day I release the role assigned to me in childhood. I embrace my new role, "Recovering Adult Child."

---

* Roles by Sharon Wegscheider

Abandonment

"If the family withdraws support, this might feel new, but in reality the abandonment has always been there." BRB p. 406

On our journey in ACA, at some point we realized we were alone again. We had always felt this way, but never allowed ourselves to face the truth. As we make space for our Higher Power, we allow the fear and pain to pass through us. We begin to see that the universe is a safe place for us, and that by facing our loneliness, we can become whole. We take this inward journey with the help of our sponsors and fellow travelers who have done so before us and who can share their experience, strength, and hope.

We let our dysfunctional families fade in the distance, and we move into new, healthier relationships where we get our needs met. We stop trying to replace our parents with people who wear different masks. Although such relationships might temporarily feel good, they soon come crashing down as we see them for what they are: ugly, messy and codependent.

We realize we may slide back once in a while, because recovery is rarely a straight line. But we are learning to pull out of our nosedives faster and with more grace. There is no need to go down with the ship anymore.

On this day I will allow that which is dead to be what it is. I will take whatever time I need to fully grieve and then move on.

Isolation and Grieving

"Isolation is our retreat from the paralyzing pain of indecision. This retreat into denial blunts our awareness of the destructive reality of family alcoholism and is the first stage of mourning and grief." BRB p. 82

Isolation is a way of protecting ourselves from the grief of our childhoods. We were alone and we had no one who "got us." Protecting ourselves through isolation is common among ACAs. Whether we attend meetings, do Step work, go to retreats or just hang around meetings, we can do all of these things and still protect ourselves from the conscious, deeper knowledge of our losses. In an effort to avoid grief, we can share superficially or not at all. We can get to the meeting late and leave as soon as it closes. So even in recovery, we can remain alone as a way of not allowing ourselves to get in touch with the pain of our grief.

Yet, this isolation can be a part of the grieving process, and we are entitled to stay isolated as long as we need to in order to feel safe. Though it seems contradictory, as fellow travelers, the best that we can do for someone who is isolating is to allow them to grieve in the way they need to as long as it doesn't create an unreasonable distraction to the meeting. There is no timetable.

On this day I will give myself permission to grieve in my own way. If I'm isolating, I will be gentle with myself and be where I need to be until I'm ready to reach out.

February 20

Change

"Change has been difficult in my life, but absolutely essential."
BRB p. 410

As children, we clung to our dysfunctional families, praying that they wouldn't abandon us because that, of all possible changes, would be devastating. As adults, we continued to cling to life as we knew it. We resisted change because it brought up so many issues and questions for us.

Eventually, we realized that our families left us long ago, both emotionally and spiritually, even if they didn't do it physically. With this knowledge came a shift in how we wanted to live our lives and we made way for change.

In ACA, we see our separation from family as a new opportunity for growth. We may still attend get-togethers, but when we understand that our changing selves are no longer welcome in the same way, our longing for the old times lessens.

As we learn to take personal inventory on a regular basis, we allot more space for positive changes and more room for our Higher Power. We view our past with a clearer lens, and we recognize the awesome benefits we reap from our new ACA lives. We gratefully acknowledge that our Higher Power is doing for us what we could not have done on our own. We begin to see life as an adventure. We credit change as the motivating device that brings joy, the greatest of human feelings.

On this day I will see that when I no longer resist change, happiness and serenity will follow.

Strengthening My Recovery • 53

Solution – Gentleness

"We learn to reparent ourselves with gentleness, humor, love, and respect." BRB p. 590

How do we reparent ourselves with gentleness if roughness or even cruelty was a staple of our childhoods? As we grew, we may not have felt capable of kindness toward ourselves because our critical inner parent was always in our heads saying things like "You fool! Your life's a mess! And you're to blame!"

But we knew we wanted to treat ourselves better; we wanted desperately to have an inner voice shift to something kinder, like "Have a cup of tea with me and tell me what's wrong."

In ACA we learn that if we can catch our critical inner parent at work, we can shift gears and try to do the opposite. When we feel criticized, we can hit the "Whoa!" button and stop ourselves from joining in the frenzy. We can tell ourselves "I can't do better than my best, so I will simply do my best right now." We can even teach ourselves techniques that help calm us down in these situations, like changing our visual image of another person from someone who is menacing to perhaps a kindly cartoon character. Something this simple can help us get through the critical patches.

On this day I will treat my Inner Child and myself to twenty minutes alone over a fresh cup of tea or a glass of juice so we can just listen to each other.

Progress

"To make progress, we must want the ACA way of life and all that it has to offer." BRB p. 33

Many of us faithfully go to our weekly meeting and feel we are working our program. We recognize that ACA has helped us make positive changes in our lives, but our enthusiasm isn't the same as it once was and there doesn't seem to be much change happening anymore. Yes, there are certainly other things we'd like to fix in our lives, but it's just not happening. While we appreciate the honesty that happens in our meeting, we're starting to think the program is no longer working for us, that it might be time to move on to something else.

If we find ourselves thinking these thoughts, it may be time for an inventory. Do we have an active relationship with a Higher Power? Do we have a sponsor/fellow traveler we talk to regularly for support and guidance? Do we go to other meetings, maybe even phone or internet meetings, to get a fresh perspective? Have we done service work to step out of our comfort zone? If we answer "no" to these questions, maybe it's not the program that's not working. Maybe we're not seeing the full potential of the program.

On this day I will re-evaluate my commitment to how I work the program because I know it works for me when I work it. And I'm worth it!

One Day at a Time

"We learn to restructure our sick thinking one day at a time."
BRB p. 590

Recovery happens, sometimes whether we're completely conscious of it or not. We just have to keep coming back and doing the work, "One day at a time."

It's amazing when we find we've been thinking about a type of situation that used to bother us, and "Poof!" It no longer has the same power over us. Maybe we encounter something that reminds us of the past, perhaps from our childhood, like how we looked at some classmates and wondered what it felt like to be in their shoes, envying them their seeming smoothness and ability to do everything right. This same "one-down" mentality was what we carried into adulthood, substituting that popular kid for someone we worked with or a neighbor or another parent. What we didn't realize was we were judging our insides by other people's outsides.

With the help of ACA and giving ourselves the time to work at our recovery, we realize that the sick thinking we carried around for so long is evaporating; we no longer look at things the same way. We think about that kid or those other people and suddenly understand the shift in our thought process. We see reality – that not everything is as it appears to be on the outside. We learn to look deeper, especially at ourselves.

On this day I know that I am not now, nor have I ever been, less than anyone else.

Isolating

"Being adult children, we have learned to endure colossal amounts of abuse and aloneness that only we understand." BRB p. 68

As adult children, we often forget that isolating is as natural to us as breathing. We may not even realize that we are doing it. Our first reaction to pain is usually to hold it inward, waiting until we are in agony before we tell someone else or reach out for help.

The tools of the ACA program help us to come out of our isolation and begin to form new habits. When something scares or upsets us, we can go to a meeting or call our sponsor. When we share how we feel in meetings, we look around the room and often see heads nodding in agreement. The feelings we were too ashamed to admit become not so bad after all as we realize we are not alone. Our black-and-white thinking may even be causing us to see things as much worse than they really are.

We have felt alone for a long time, but we don't need to feel that way anymore. By working the ACA program, we can place our trust in a Higher Power and know that we will be safe in turning our pain over. We can let go of the need to isolate.

On this day I will remember that I don't have to suffer in silence. I have a program that is helping me learn to break my habit of isolation.

Recovering Victim

"If we overstate our wrongs and beat ourselves up, we tend to drift into an attitude of martyrdom, or we assume the victim posture." BRB p. 197

Without the leveling perspective of Step Five, many of us would either minimize our wrongs or overstate them. By choosing the second option, we tell ourselves that we deserve the abuse for the wrongs we did. But that statement is a carryover from our childhood abuse.

A part of us had lived with both excitement and fear at the possibility of getting beaten up emotionally again. The feeling of helplessness was familiar because we had only felt loved when negative attention was heaped on us again and again as children.

Some of us only got attention while we were being sexually abused or beaten. We needed to believe we deserved this treatment to survive. There was no other option but to lie about what was really happening in our families.

Today we learn to accept our reality, both past and present. What happened to us as children was not our responsibility, but what we do today is. However, we do not have to take abuse to right the wrongs. With the help of neutral third parties, in the form of our ACA fellow travelers, we change to new rules. If others become angry, we let them take care of themselves. We choose to love ourselves and to be loved by those who have the capacity to do so.

On this day I am no longer a victim. I put myself first and make healthier choices that keep me grounded.

*Blame

"The principles of ACA are not about blame." BRB p. xxiii

Some of us may have heard the saying that "a man without arms can't hug you." Our parents/caregivers were not able to give us what they did not have. The disease of alcoholism or other family dysfunction affects generations and did not start with our immediate family.

By working and living the ACA Steps, we realize that we too were unable to give what we did not receive as children. We were not shown how to have healthy relationships, how to raise children or how to avoid feeling "less than." Many of us vowed not to repeat the patterns of our parents. But knowing what not to do does not automatically give us the knowledge of a better way. This is our legacy, but it does not have to stay that way.

We learn to focus on ourselves instead of being lost in blaming those who couldn't give us what we needed. They could not give us what they did not get themselves. Today, we are led in the direction of reparenting ourselves, taking measures to erase the old tapes in our head and honoring our True Self.

On this day I choose not to blame others or myself for being unable to give what was never given to me. I feel grateful knowing that I can break the cycle of dysfunction and live a better life.

Our Truth

"Denial is the glue that holds together a dysfunctional home. Family secrets, ignored feelings, and predictable chaos are part of a dysfunctional family system." BRB p. 22

As we celebrate our willingness in ACA to look at the difficult parts of our lives, we can find ourselves surrounded by those who deny our reality, perhaps in the same way they always have. It can be family members who say "I don't remember it that way." or "It wasn't that bad – we're still alive, aren't we?" Or it can be people we thought were our friends who say "Can't you just live in the now? Why do you even have to think about that stuff?"

These messages can be powerful and can often temporarily convince us we're on the wrong path. But when we look inside, we know what we feel and we know the impact of our childhood. We know we've felt fragmented and crazy inside, trying to figure out what was wrong with us. We know that we want something better.

The Promises of ACA are what we want. The deniers in our life often can't give us anything but more pain. This is why we choose to separate from them and continue to make room for recovery.

On this day I will listen to what's in my heart and know that I am on the right path. I will no longer listen to those who want me back in my old role that makes them more comfortable.

Tradition Two

"Our group conscience is a spiritual method by which a Higher Power is expressed in our discussions and our decisions. Most of our decisions are based on what is best for the most, instead of what is best for the few." BRB p. 501

Our families were not spiritually focused, and the decisions they made were rarely, if ever, reflective of a Higher Power's loving presence. We may not be much better in our personal decisions. We can be driven by our false selves that react to seemingly small provocations.

In ACA, we collectively learn to gather the wisdom and strength to be courageous about group decisions, taking the necessary measures to ensure safety while not stifling creativity. At the beginning of a group conscience or business meeting, we say the Serenity Prayer to invite a Higher Power into the process. We try to keep our individual egos out of it, sometimes feeling the need to repeat the Serenity Prayer as a way of staying Higher Power-centered.

As opinions are expressed, we may see the group making progress for the greater good while valuing each other's participation. If the group conscience process is working well, we may not even notice that we have become a group of actors rather than false self reactors. What a wonderful experience.

On this day I will remember that I am only part of a group's conscience. I will seek the greatest good for the group while trusting that our decision is an expression of our Higher Power's will and that we have the required spiritual strength to carry that out.

Guilt

"The critical inner parent gives us that guilt feeling when we think about asking for what we need." BRB p. 49

In childhood, we seemed to have gotten lost in the shuffle. When we had needs and voiced them, we were often told we were being selfish and self-centered. Or we were told to take care of ourselves with words like "grow up!" that meant we were on our own. So we stuffed our wants and needs and moved on.

We usually took our survival mechanisms with us into adulthood. Oftentimes they turned on us, though, and we found ourselves in still more dysfunctional relationships, mimicking the same words and behaviors that were used on us as children.

When we reached the safety of ACA, and with help and support from our fellow travelers, we started sorting through our feelings and took an honest look at some of our people-pleasing or aggressive behaviors. We began to find a way to dispel the unearned guilt of our childhood that comes to us through our inner critical parent's voice. We now face only the consequences of our present day actions.

In working the Steps, we are given a chance to discover self-forgiveness and forgiveness of others. Through it all, we humbly ask for help from our Higher Power and it is there as we need it.

On this day I will look inward, ask for help from my fellow travelers and my Higher Power. I will forgive myself if I'm less than perfect. My critical inner parent's voice is losing its power over me.

March

"However, the process of recovery takes time and patience. This is not easy."
BRB p. 72

The Steps

"The Steps sometimes work even if a person picks at them like a finicky child forking a lump of unwanted spinach. Such half measures often create the personal discomfort that motivates the adult child into greater action and personal growth." BRB p. 93

Many adult children join ACA and keep coming back for years. But it seems like there is little change in their lives because they talk about the same things each time they share. They may even complain about certain aspects of the program, seemingly as a reason for things not changing. Those of us who are unable to rid ourselves of our judgmental nature think these people are just not working the program "correctly." We wonder why they even bother coming.

But we've seen it happen time and again: people who hang around long enough start making a shift in how they think and respond. It's as if they suddenly realize that they've been stuck and now it's time to do something about it. Maybe they finally get uncomfortable enough with the way things are, and because they've actually been listening all these years, the switch is turned on. In cases like this, it can be wondrous to see the power of the program at work.

On this day I will not judge how another person works or doesn't work their program. It is not my job. I will focus on myself and my own recovery.

Trait Three

"We are frightened by angry people and any personal criticism."
BRB p. 11

It's insidious – the abuse we experienced. For many of us, our caregivers didn't just get mad, they got angry and enraged. And it could be over something simple. Maybe we were out doing normal kid stuff, but because we had an angry parent waiting at home, we were never sure what to expect. We were repeatedly blindsided with accusations that said we were no good, selfish, irresponsible, uppity, or a whole host of other shaming language. Or maybe it happened to a sibling, which was just as bad because we knew it could be turned on us at any time.

Is it any wonder that as adults we almost visibly flinched when we were faced with angry people? We carried the fear of being criticized with us like a banner that said, "I'm an easy target. I won't even argue with you because I don't have a voice."

But as we start to find our voice in ACA, we begin to separate the anger from the words, and the words from reality. We do not deserve to be talked to 'like that.' And we didn't deserve it as a child. We were innocent! And now, as we learn to reparent ourselves, we can tell our Inner Child that we will protect them when someone is angry or critical. We can do for ourselves what others should have done for us.

On this day I will remember that another person's anger is not mine. If I hear criticism, I can separate truth from fiction.

Step Three

"It is a well of grace we can return to again and again and dip out self-acceptance, self-assurance, and love. Each time we take Step Three, we drink down God's love." BRB p. 142

Step Three reminds us there is unconditional love available to us. By giving our will and our lives over to the care of a Higher Power of our own understanding, we trust that this love and presence will remain in our lives. In times of fear, we can imagine our Inner Child resting in warm, loving arms – feeling the comfort we did not receive as a child.

Throughout our recovery, we use our challenges to propel us to a higher level of peace, understanding, and self-love that would not have been possible otherwise. We trust that we are being led toward our greatest potential. When we accept ourselves for who we are, and feel the love around us, we know we are inherently worthy. We learn patience with ourselves as we continue to grow, knowing we're being guided with love by a strong program, and by a Higher Power of our own understanding, who is always with us.

On this day I will accept the challenges that are placed before me, knowing that I have both the support of my fellow travelers in the program and my Higher Power, who is ever present.

Emotional Sobriety

"A long-time member of our program, when she was new in recovery, said she felt liberated when her sponsor told her she 'could walk away from crazy.'" BRB p. 628

It used to be anything goes in our dysfunctional families. We learned from our parents that it was okay to call each other names and to manipulate through hurtful sarcasm. We didn't learn how to praise each other for our talents or to nurture each other through love and kindness.

No wonder emotional sobriety is such a puzzling term when we finally read about it in the Big Red Book. If we work our ACA program by getting a sponsor, working the Steps, and doing service work, life opens up. We can begin to experience what the program promises: peace and serenity.

The dysfunctional situations we've lived through can be likened to watching water drain in the bathtub – there's a whirlpool at the end. In recovery we learn to identify reoccurring situations that pull us into the current of chaos and keep us stuck. We begin to step away from caustic situations and avoid being sucked back into insanity. We start to make better choices and learn to walk away from "crazy."

On this day I practice emotional sobriety and let go of trying to change other people and things. I remain centered in the peacefulness of my ACA program.

Start a Meeting

"Starting a new meeting requires determination and work, but the reward of watching others find the ACA way of life is worth it." BRB p. 560

As children growing up in turmoil, confusion, and despair, many of us had no anchor, no sense of belonging. We survived from day to day, sometimes hour to hour. We hoped we could outwit, or sweet talk, or hide from our perpetrators. All alone, we relied on our ingenuity, our wits, and our child selves to survive.

When we found out about ACA and read some of the literature, we were surprised. Someone knew what had happened to us. We looked for a meeting. We were very disappointed when we couldn't find one in our town. Again, life just didn't seem to want to work for us.

But we then found telephone and internet meetings on the website, and we worked our program hard. We found great recovery, but the itch to have a face-to-face meeting just wouldn't go away. After enough time went by, we gathered the courage to start a meeting in our town. We contacted WSO and they guided us every step of the way. It took a lot of work, but it was the greatest gift we ever gave ourselves. We finally had an anchor; we finally found our home.

On this day I will remember how life was before I found ACA, so that I can see how much better it is now. If I am able to help start a new meeting, I embrace it as a way to both enhance my own recovery and make ACA available to others.

Buried Memories

"Healing begins when we risk moving out of isolation. Feelings and buried memories will return." BRB p. 590

Did it really happen? Did it happen the way I remember? Am I crazy or are they?

Some of us have few memories of our childhood because of the trauma we experienced. As a result, we may question what we do remember, or even why we feel the way we do when we can't attach specific memories to the feelings. But our body knows something happened because it stores our trauma from both physical and emotional abuse.

As we move out of isolation into recovery, one of the first things we learn to recognize and honor is our feelings. By continuing to talk to and trust the people in our groups, and often a therapist, we gradually gain clarity. The buried memories start to return. Even when they don't, we honor our instincts when we realize we feel unsafe around family members and others. We don't question ourselves. We honor our feeling, knowing that it is real and that we're not crazy. And we take steps to keep ourselves safe.

On this day I will trust my instincts and feelings, even if I can't attach a reason for them that will satisfy others.

False Self

"The false self is the adult child personality expressed in the 14 traits of the ACA Laundry List." BRB p. 7

While growing up, we unknowingly used the survival technique of developing a false self, a disguise, the mask we used to cover the codependent and addictive traits we learned from our dysfunctional families. We feared and were controlled by other people. We based our feelings on our parents' behaviors. We did so because we were not allowed to express our personal feelings; there were consequences for doing so.

The Laundry List is an important tool we use to identify our ACA characteristics. It guides us in taking our blameless inventory, thus revealing our True Self and affirming our worthiness. We learn what behaviors we want to change in order to move from our false self to our True Self.

In recovery, we begin to understand that in order to grow it is important to accept, and not deny, all of our feelings. Some of us use the slogan, "There is no healing without feeling" almost as a mantra. Gradually, our True Self emerges as we reach out to others in the fellowship and as we learn the language of ACA.

On this day, as I remove the mask of my false self, I am free to make healthy decisions about the revelation of my True Self.

Intimacy

"What many adult children have described as love or intimacy before reaching ACA was actually codependence or rigid control."
BRB p. 6

Before we came to program, we thought intimacy was that secret word that pertained to sex and making love. We thought it was about taking care of the other person, doing for the other person, and losing ourselves in the other person – because we loved them so much!

Sure, we all want to be close to our partners, but before recovery many of us lay in the same bed with them and felt a million miles away, starving for affection. We settled for crumbs, and we didn't even realize it. We did everything to convince ourselves we were that happy family portrait on the wall.

Today, in recovery, intimacy has developed into what it was meant to be. We have honest conversations with our partners and close friends and are not afraid to express opinions. We surround ourselves with people who care about us, people we don't fear. We have healthy conversations about money and other important issues, and we don't coerce or manipulate people through shame and guilt. We fill our cup with the freedom of choice. We have healthy partnerships and understand what real intimacy is about. We feel joy.

On this day I will trust myself enough to be open to true intimacy in my relationships.

✳ *Freedom*

✳ *"We seek the power we need to live in freedom each day."*
BRB p. 116

As we listen to story after story of neglect in meetings, we may get angry *for* those around us. Then, if we listen closely, we hear the voice inside that says, "What about me?" We start to pay attention and create space with our words and actions to let that voice finally say what it needs to, what was denied for so long. This process extends into our Step work and then into our very lives, at work and in play.

Perhaps for the first time we begin to feel free. We start to play and learn what that means for us. We learn to slow down, because being over-scheduled is acting out against our True Selves. We see that when we have too much to do, it's harder to get in touch with how we feel. This is no longer ok.

We take the actions we need to for our Inner Child, the same way we would for another child placed in our care. In this way, we cultivate an inner loving parent and free ourselves.

We are no longer waiting for our tormentors to wake up and stop abusing us. The conversation is over. We now know how to nurture ourselves.

On this day I will do something playful and fun. I will feel the freedom that my Inner Child deserves to experience.

Personal Power

"We move out of the victim role and claim our personal power by taking this path." BRB p. 158

We let parasites into our lives, trusting those we shouldn't have. We ended up a victim over and over again. We were exhausted of our vital resources, financially and emotionally, and had no idea why. Spiritually we were bankrupt. Our heads throbbed as we raged at those who couldn't hear us or who swore they wouldn't do it again.

In ACA we got off the treadmill we hadn't noticed we were on. With the help of our sponsor or fellow traveler, we did our Fourth Step and saw that our lives were insane, that we had swallowed poison and not known it. We now felt heard for the first time.

We became ready to go to any lengths to protect and nurture our Inner Children. Leaving no stone unturned, we rooted out the problem. We couldn't remember all that happened to us because we had to forget so we could survive. But recovery becomes a safe place for the memories to begin resurfacing. We stop going to the inner drug store for a dose of fear. We release the trauma in our bodies and walk away different people: confident and alive.

On this day I will choose to go the distance and deal in a healthy way with whatever comes up for me emotionally and physically. If I can't do this alone, I will get appropriate help.

Autonomy

"Autonomy does not mean that an ACA group is isolated and beyond the scope of the fellowship at large. We do not use autonomy to justify changing ACA or its message to fit our own personal desires." BRB p. 608

The focus of ACA is working the Steps and following the Traditions. If they are never, or rarely, mentioned, the impact is that those who attend the meeting are deprived of the essential tools to help them recover.

Likewise, if the meeting requires a specific spiritual or religious belief, the basic freedom to choose is removed, and the meeting should not be called ACA. We are a spiritual program where each person is free to choose a Higher Power or not. There are no mandates.

Meetings are more likely to stay on track when each person has the ability to ask for a group conscience, which provides attendees with a feeling of safety. There is no replay of our childhoods where "because I said so" rules were laid down. No one individual or small clique of people should make group decisions. Business meetings are meant to be open to all meeting attendees. This is the type of healthy guiding principle we didn't have growing up, but we have it in ACA.

On this day I will give myself permission to respectfully question how my meeting is run when something seems uncomfortable, including where the money goes, and if we seem to veer from the Steps and Traditions. In ACA, each of us is as important as the person next to us.

Overly Responsible

"We see how we took on too much responsibility for others' thoughts and actions." BRB p. 115

Some of us were the overly responsible ones in our families. We learned that it was our job to control others, whether actively or passive-aggressively. Our goal was to prevent Dad's anger or Mom's depression; then maybe there would be some peace. Even though we failed time and again, what seemed like small successes "proved" that it was possible and kept us going. We told ourselves that yes, we could control the dysfunction.

As adults, when we took on too much responsibility for others, we were often eventually met with resentment and anger. Who were we to be telling others what to do and think? As a result, we may have lost important relationships and even our livelihoods.

In ACA, we learn that the most important thing we can do is take responsibility for ourselves first. This can be difficult, because our preoccupation with others may have left us with little sense of who we really are. But with time and the help of our program and fellow travelers, we see that this is the path to the peace we were always after.

On this day I will remember that I am not responsible for the thoughts and behaviors of others; I am only responsible for myself.

Change

"We become open-minded to the idea that we can change with time and with help." BRB p. 9

Most of us have heard the saying, "If you always do what you've always done, you'll always get what you've always gotten." In other words, nothing will change until we make a change.

We may have read all the books and made attempts at change, but nothing stuck for long. A big reason it didn't work is that we were probably trying to do it alone. We told ourselves that we didn't need to talk to others about anything; we just had to try harder. And when we hit a wall with whatever new thing we were trying, we found some justification for quitting.

So nothing really changed until we gave ourselves permission to walk into our first ACA meeting. That is where we discovered the power of the group – a mix of new faces with familiar stories. We listened to some say how difficult it was to work on change, and that change takes time. This might have made us run the other way, except that it was followed by talk of how rewarding it is to make even baby steps of change. Because we want that same experience, we keep coming back. Not doing it alone makes all the difference in the world.

On this day I will remember that I deserve my own change and that I never have to go it alone again.

Cross Talk

"In ACA, each person may share his or her feelings and perceptions without judgment from others. As part of creating that safety, we ask that group members avoid cross talking." BRB p. 342

When we start attending meetings, we may be confused about the reasons for the "No Cross Talk" rule. This can feel like a difficult rule to follow, especially when someone is crying. Don't they need to be helped and comforted? But we're told that this is "fixing," which is a skill so many of us mastered as children.

In ACA, we learn that the no cross talk rule is a sacred element of what makes the program work so well. By honoring one another with our full attention when we share, we are all getting something we didn't have access to growing up in dysfunctional families: attention. This is a great gift, being allowed to express ourselves without reserve. When no one interrupts or tries to comfort us, we can feel respected – no one is judging us. And when others are speaking, we listen and learn from their lessons. If we're uncomfortable and want to "fix" them, we stop and think about why we're feeling that way.

By showing up in meetings, sharing our honest experiences, and listening silently to others, we participate in the heart of what makes the program successful. This practice makes us stronger together.

On this day I will listen quietly in a meeting when someone else shares their experience, strength, and hope. I feel good knowing I will get the same respect from others.

Promise Three

"Fear of authority figures and the need to 'people-please' will leave us." BRB p. 591

As children, from infancy through our teen years, we were surrounded by authority figures. This included our family, babysitters and teachers – those who traditionally deserved respect. But many of these people took advantage of our respect for authority by intimidating us into a submissive role. Our natural tendency to please was exploited by the unreasonable demands placed on us.

As adults, our need to people-please took a darker turn and robbed us of our ability to enjoy life. Always seeking to please others, we were left waiting for our turn at getting our needs met.

In ACA, the edges of the puzzle of how we became people-pleasers slowly start to become clear. We begin to free the roots of our people-pleasing habit from the soil of our childhoods. In its place we plant brand new seeds of hope.

Consistent work in our program allows our insight, clarity, and freedom to flourish. No longer fearful of authority and under the compulsion to please, we are emancipated to decide for ourselves whom we need to fear and whom we choose to please.

On this day I will continue working the ACA program to further unearth the deep roots of my fear of authority and people-pleasing. I choose to be free of any hold they still have over me.

Fear of Authority

"We came to see our parents as authority figures who could not be trusted." BRB p. 11

In healthy families, authority figures are parents who are loving, nurturing and supportive. In our families, they usually put fear into our little souls. We endured physical, verbal or emotional abuse. And unfortunately, what we see and experience, many of us learn, and often practice. No wonder our relationships may be chaotic at best when we get to ACA, whether we had become a rigid authority figure or not.

When we admit that the only way we know how to deal with life's challenges is to slam doors, shut down and isolate, or say hurtful things to those closest to us, we take the first step towards being ready to change.

By working the Steps with a sponsor or fellow traveler, we discover the triggers that cause us to react negatively or to isolate. We cry for our little kid who faced the terror and heartbreak when these triggers were implanted. Wounds are reopened as we discover the damage, knowing we often couldn't trust what was going to happen from one minute to the next.

As we sit in meetings, we listen to the experience, strength and hope of other ACAs because they have what we want. We are tired of running – we want healthier ways to communicate so we can trust ourselves and be trusted by others.

On this day I open my heart with courage to find help to work the Steps. I love myself enough to do this.

Step Ten

"We learn to take a balanced view of our behavior, avoiding the tendency to take too much responsibility for the actions of others."
BRB p. 251

We didn't learn balance in our families of origin. Most of us became either super-responsible or super-irresponsible. There didn't seem to be much of a middle ground.

Those of us who were super-responsible often believed we were in charge of everyone else. In the process, we didn't learn to focus on ourselves.

In Step Four we identify our problematic behaviors. As we continue to work the Steps, we increase our awareness of those behaviors and how they affect our relationships with other people. We examine our demands, our criticisms, and our negativity. We inventory our past feelings and motives so we can separate our own dysfunction from that of our family of origin. We begin reparenting ourselves to replace the lack of nurturing and the imbalance we grew up with.

When we regularly practice Step Ten, we are able to stay current. Learning to keep the scales balanced, we acknowledge our feelings and act purposefully in situations, thereby gaining emotional sobriety. We celebrate our lives as they become more sane and manageable.

On this day I will identify my feelings and focus on my own needs, I will practice balance with my responsibilities to others and my responses to the situations I face.

Service

"We give service just by being present to support and encourage other members of the program as they make the transition from frightened adult children to whole human beings who are capable of acting with the spontaneity of a child and the wisdom of a mature adult." BRB p. 354

As adult children, we inherently have the gift of being sensitive and present for others. Yet many of us weren't taught to cultivate this gift in a healthy manner. Because our inherent value wasn't nurtured and was basically forced or punished into hiding, the gift of service was distorted into codependent behavior that caused us to look for love and acceptance through people-pleasing, caretaking, and approval-seeking.

Now, in ACA, we can direct this gift into healthy service. Being present, supportive, and encouraging of others in their ACA work contributes exponential momentum to our own recovery. We experience exhilaration when we feel the release of our fears and restrictions, and naturally feel and act on our inherent spontaneity and wisdom. In turn, this enthusiasm motivates other recovering adult children to share this momentum and exhilaration. As we pass it on, we all receive the benefits of our shared gift.

On this day I will attend an ACA meeting or have a one-on-one interaction with a fellow traveler. I will be truly present, supporting and encouraging another adult child as they release the fears and restrictions of the false self, and feel the exhilaration of their True Self.

Apologies

"When I first came into the program, I would apologize to everyone and everything at the drop of a hat." BRB p. 250

Everything was always our fault. In our family, our very food and shelter were earned by our being the doormat. By taking the abuse year after year, month after month, day after day, and hour after hour, we learned to be invisible. We were containers that those around us filled with their poisoned words and actions. But we mistakenly believed there were some benefits also – a sense of belonging, except that we didn't even know who we were outside of this role.

As we grow and begin setting boundaries where there were none, we find our True Selves. We learn to connect more fully to our Higher Power by going on this journey. We accept that when we don't please people, they are not pleased – so be it. We allow those angry stares to live with the person who gives them. We slowly learn not to internalize the fear we grew up with. We cultivate new, loving relationships as we work the Steps. We remember our past and move through it to a new freedom, a freedom we never knew existed.

On this day I will respond when I know what I want to say, and not because I feel like I need to make someone else happy.

Trust

"These adult children rarely stop to think that self-sufficiency is covering up a fear of rejection which they think could come if they ask for help." BRB p. 102

Most of us had no one we could consistently rely on as children. Everyone seemed to be caught up in the dysfunction, and we were left to manage things ourselves. We became very self-sufficient and were sometimes even praised for that ability.

As adults, our self-sufficiency became a way of controlling things around us. If we did it ourselves, then we didn't have to rely on anyone else, especially because experience told us that most people weren't trustworthy anyway.

Even in recovery, some of us clung to our self-sufficiency, not asking for help because we found it hard to believe that we'd get it. And we would simply not allow ourselves to feel rejected yet again.

But as we continued to go to meetings, we gradually heard the truths we needed and became stronger. We learned to allow ourselves to feel vulnerable and trust that there was help available if only we would ask for it – help in our recovery, help in our work life, and help in our personal life.

On this day I will give myself the gift of asking for help, whether it's in my recovery or anywhere in life.

Self-Protection

"We learned to block or deny our feelings as children to protect ourselves from our unhealthy family." BRB p. 343

Many of us were raised in homes where there wasn't enough love. We weren't encouraged to be ourselves and realize our true potential. We weren't allowed to have normal feelings, so we became numb. We may have been shamed when we felt sad or angry, ridiculed when we showed fear, or shunned when we sought love and understanding from our parents. What we took away was that there was something wrong with us.

And there was some truth to that, but not in the way we thought. We knew how to feel shame, guilt, sadness and fear, but the main problem was we felt them when we didn't need to.

Now, with the help of ACA, our meetings, and our sponsor or fellow traveler, we are given the chance to reparent ourselves. We learn how to feel without letting our feelings control us. We grow in self-confidence.

As our feelings surface, we begin to make decisions about how to handle them. Shall we speak our truth to those around us and try to work things out? Or shall we remain silent, either because the atmosphere is not safe or we don't want to upset the apple cart? There is no one right way. We give ourselves permission to choose what's best for us at the time. If we're uncomfortable with our choice, we ask for help.

On this day I ask for the courage and honesty to recognize my true feelings and deal with them honestly and safely.

Emotional Intoxication

"The third Identity Paper examined the steep cost of surviving by hiding the vulnerable and wounded child in a prison of isolation, the high price of using the myriad methods we employ to protect the vulnerable self by staying emotionally intoxicated and numb."
BRB p. 628

When we came to ACA, many of us had experience with other programs that dealt with sobriety. We may have even heard about emotional sobriety before, but when we learned it was the focus of this program, it really got our attention. We knew we felt out of control a lot of the time, unable to think clearly. Our minds went 100 miles an hour, and many of us had trouble turning them off at night to go to sleep. We couldn't sit still with our feelings. We used activities as a drug to numb ourselves when we were uneasy.

Understanding that we were dealing with emotional intoxication made sense. And we were tired of living that way.

Our journey to free ourselves helps us come out of isolation and relate to others who are finding success. We work the Steps and reach out to our Higher Power and our fellow traveler for help. We practice sitting still with our feelings and let it be okay. We ask our loving parent to speak words of encouragement to our vulnerable self so that we don't get busy to avoid our feelings. We no longer have to walk around numb; we can make it.

On this day I will remember that being alive comes with feelings, and my feelings are all okay! I am entitled to a rich life of emotional sobriety.

Stuck Grief

"My ACA counselor understood what I was trying to do. She helped me understand my loss or the pain of my 'stuck grief' through the Fourth and Fifth Steps." BRB p. 150

The "stuck grief" is very difficult to dislodge because we keep up an endless array of defenses to keep it stuck. We can experience an overabundance of anger, sadness, food, shopping, underachieving, sloppiness, procrastination or cleanliness – a list that only skims the surface of how many ways we can keep our grief embedded.

Difficult as it may seem, the defenses and resistances we have deployed to protect us can be addressed and lowered and lessened after being in the program for a while. With regular attendance at meetings and the use of a fellow traveler or an ACA counselor, we find the strength to allow ourselves to become vulnerable.

As we continue on this new path, we develop greater trust and lessen our fear, which allows us to delve into a Fourth and Fifth Step and dislodge our "stuck grief." Like an un-stuck jam of logs, our grief begins to flow again down the river of our daily lives. We let the natural currents gently and slowly release it into the ocean of our Higher Power's love for us.

On this day I will work with my fellow traveler or ACA counselor to develop trust and lose the fear of dislodging my "stuck grief," knowing that the flow will be set by my Higher Power in whom I have developed trust.

Isolation

"We learn that we cannot recover alone or in isolation."
BRB p. 516

We recover together, sharing the risk of sharing our stories. We risk rejection. We risk humiliation. We risk being afraid that our words won't make sense. We risk crying. We risk being angry. We risk healing.

When we witness one another's pain and shame, those feelings lose their power over us. We break the chains that kept us dispirited, disempowered, disenfranchised, and isolated. Our group carries the collective grief that must no longer be borne alone.

When our loss is brought to the meetings or to the telephone, we no longer cower in silence. We begin to grow wings. We create room in our hearts for hope and trust. We find our power, our center, and our compass. We create space for love, joy, peace, serenity, and our True Selves. We find our Higher Power. We embrace our fellow travelers. We stand shoulder to shoulder, heart to heart, spirit to spirit, and bow our heads in gratitude to a Higher Power for giving us this program. We honor our courage to give the gift of recovery to ourselves.

On this day I choose to co-create a healing sanctuary in my group, which gathers its strength from a power greater than our individual selves.

Disease of Alcoholism

"Looking back, things seemed simpler when Dr. William Silkworth wrote his opinion for AA's 'Big Book' in 1939, including his naming alcoholism as a disease." BRB p. xxvii

Today we understand that alcoholism is a family disease, but Dr. Silkworth's opinion was a very bold statement in 1939. Back then it lifted alcoholics from their deep pool of shame. But their children were left to labor under the effects of the disease. They received no help and were usually not even thought of as part of the equation. Parents often excused the effects on their children by saying they were resilient and would "get over it." But today we know that's not true – it isn't nearly that simple.

Like the courageous young adults who led the way for us in the mid-1970s, today we in ACA continue to break new ground in uncovering the effects of the family disease of alcoholism. We are discovering solutions that work. We start by acknowledging that for most of us, the damage done to us in childhood was like the trauma soldiers suffer in battle. Then, along with the Steps, we use the sure-fire tool of reparenting ourselves to build our own road to emotional sobriety.

As we make our way, we applaud each other's growth and empowerment. We encourage each other as we face the painful memories, learn to stop reacting and work on healing ourselves.

On this day I will continue to admit that the disease of alcoholism infected me in the past. By also acknowledging its effects on me today, I find my way on the road to recovery.

Patience

"However, the process of recovery takes time and patience. This is not easy." BRB p. 72

Looking back to the first ACA meeting we went to, most of us remember the anguish, hopelessness, or turbulence we were experiencing. We never understood our addiction to excitement, but we knew our lives felt out of control and something had to change. We kept hoping the other people in our lives would make the changes so we could experience instant relief, but that wasn't happening.

As we began our recovery, we realized that change wasn't going to happen overnight and that it was okay to take it at our own pace. We learned that change takes patience – to keep coming back, to find a sponsor, to work through the Steps, and to get to an understanding of how important forgiveness and love are. It can take time for us to allow ourselves to feel the calm of serenity.

Some of us have said we pray for things to be boring. That's because we want to end our common love affair with the adrenaline that gets released through excitement and drama. But with practice, and yes, patience, we understand how valuable being in the present moment is. We get there by simply slowing down and trusting in our Higher Power.

On this day I will be patient with my recovery process, acknowledging that I am giving myself a wonderful gift.

Learned Helplessness

"From the nonalcoholic parent we learn helplessness, worry, black-and-white thinking, being a victim, and self-hate." BRB p. 24

Many of us grew up with one parent who was an abuser and one who was our caretaker. The first abandoned us in the midst of their addiction, whether it was alcohol, sexual acting out, workaholism or something else that took them from us. The other parent seemed to hold things together, and we were grateful. But we were often drawn into *their* addictions, including their extreme points of view, worry, and playing the relationship victim. We had to participate in order to survive.

As adults, we saw that some of our learned behaviors kept us from owning our own power. Many of us were still afraid of aggressive people. We worried constantly, seemingly about everything. We played the victim at work and in our relationships; we were naturals because our codependent/caretaker parent modeled that behavior for us for years. When we finally realized how we hated ourselves for these behaviors, we knew it was time to get help.

We learn in ACA that our self-destructive behaviors come from both parents. New feelings surface with our realizations, although we aren't always sure where they come from. It can be startling. But we honor those feelings and don't push them away.

As we continue to make progress, we release our self-destructive patterns, recognizing their origins. They no longer have a place in our lives.

On this day I now choose my own role and how I respond to the world around me.

Connection

"As adult children we have lived a life of isolation for too long. Recovery is about connection." BRB p. xxiv

We often hear in meetings that the program "works when you work it." And we do work hard at it. But sometimes we find ourselves, suddenly it seems, relapsing. We're worried about saying the wrong thing, not feeling connected with those around us, feeling overwhelmed, procrastinating, and wasting time on our escapes instead of doing something good for ourselves. When we realize what's going on, we may ask ourselves, "How can I pull myself out of this?"

But that question misses the point of how the program works. The better question is "Who can I reach out to?" We remind ourselves that we are no longer alone. Being compulsively self-reliant keeps us stuck in a place we no longer want to be.

In understanding that we have options, we learn that the simple act of picking up the phone or going to a meeting can make all the difference. It just takes a little trust. What have we got to lose? Perhaps just our feelings of worthlessness, self-pity, shame, and self-loathing that can seem to lurk just around the corner. And how good it feels to work through these feelings, one day at a time! We find that the program works. We now have enough evidence.

On this day I trust that the simple act of connecting with a fellow ACA is what the program is all about. It can keep me on a positive path with my Higher Power and my recovery.

Workplace Recovery

"We have a high tolerance for workplace dysfunction and tend to stick it out in an unhappy job because we lack the self-esteem to leave." BRB p. 419

Many of us were trained to be numb, so we were. We didn't speak up for ourselves at work or anywhere because it made us feel guilty. When we were abused, we stayed way past respectable limits. We were prone to being bullied. When put on the spot, we usually crumbled, even though we knew in our gut we were right. Underneath, we seethed with anger and resentment.

As we change and grow with the steps, sponsorship and meeting attendance, we take our recovery with us everywhere. We see direct results as we leave destructive self-abuse behind in our personal life and detach from those we are addicted to, oftentimes our parents. In our work life, it can seem as if a spell has been broken. People who used to push us around or take us for granted now begin to respond differently as we set healthy limits. We are changing the rules, and it has a ripple effect.

We are more than our jobs and now give ourselves the gift of free time to enjoy the things we like. This builds our character and self-esteem, one day at a time.

On this day I will begin to stand up for myself at work and elsewhere when I need to. I will gently say no to what is not right for me and celebrate my successes. I will ask for help to deal with anything negative I may get in return.

Tradition Three

"Adult children who are codependents, addicts, debtors, overeaters, sexually compulsive, alcoholics, and gamblers are members if they have a desire to recover from the effects of a dysfunctional family. We cannot turn away anyone seeking help from the isolation and madness of the effects of a dysfunctional upbringing." BRB p. 505

The all-or-nothing thinking that most ACAs have before recovery would have us draw bold lines about who is a bona fide ACA member or not. Time has shown us that the people coming to a meeting are the only ones who can say they are members, and once having claimed a seat, and with rare exception, no one can force them to give it up.

Our fellowship welcomes anyone from a dysfunctional home, whether alcohol was present or not. Adults brought up in foster homes usually lived in dysfunctional situations and can also find a safe place with us to share the effects of their childhood experiences.

There are some occasions when a member creates such fear that the group's conscience has to step in to set up appropriate boundaries. Fortunately, these instances are extremely rare. The scarier idea is that an adult child may be turned away from our door, usually by well-meaning ACAs who unknowingly let their own biases get in the way. Just because someone doesn't talk, or they yell, curse, pout, or cry does not disqualify them from membership.

On this day, unless someone is creating a hazard to others or to the meeting property, I will do what I can to ensure that all members are free to express their experiences as best they can.

Trait Four

"We either become alcoholics, marry them, or both, or find another compulsive personality such as a workaholic to fulfill our sick abandonment needs." BRB p. 12

When we first heard this Trait, we may have reflected on all of the relationships we'd had – those we supported financially, or those where we were supported, but which kept us "under lock and key." There were broken people we tried to mend who "had such potential" – why didn't they use it? Some of us had dangerous partners, but when they seemed to love us, the world was momentarily a happy place.

Many of these relationships mirrored our childhood. But we didn't know we were reliving the past. We thought we chose these people out of normal attraction like anyone else. But that *was* our normal, because we were only taught how to relate to compulsive, dysfunctional people.

In ACA, it is comforting to find different people to relate to – those who have also had rough-and-tumble relationship experiences, but who are choosing a different life. We begin to see how it is possible to relate to them in a new way. We see boundaries being set and maintained. We hear vulnerabilities shared, and we start to feel comfortable doing the same. We begin to trust others and our Higher Power, knowing we are now capable of changing our pattern of self-destructive relationships.

On this day I will focus on my Higher Power and myself to find my center. This will keep me focused so that I can relate to others in a healthier way.

April

"To ask an adult child to surrender control is like asking someone to leap from an airplane without a parachute. Without recovery, an adult child can live in terror of letting go of control." BRB p 39

Step Work

"If we are diligent in working ACA's Twelve Steps, miracles occur that we could not imagine." BRB p. 156

As we began our Step work, we may still have found ourselves thinking about others much more than ourselves. We looked for places to plug in to get the excitement we were used to. We hit up the inner drugstore and binged on the fruits of our crime. It was fun…until it wasn't fun anymore.

As we have become more grounded in ACA, we are more relaxed in how we see things. We know we are not responsible for the world.

We have patience with ourselves, knowing that we won't do our recovery work perfectly. We lighten up on our perfectionist attitudes; we release the unrealistic goals that may have been set for us long ago, either by ourselves or others.

As we cruise through the Steps, trusting our fellow travelers and ourselves, we also experience our Higher Power's love unfolding in us one day at a time. We know we are not alone. This profound gift of recovery allows us to see the abuse that we tried to deny for so long. We value this process of self-discovery as we learn to reparent ourselves with the love and understanding we have always needed and deserved.

On this day I will acknowledge and appreciate my progress in each Step of this journey, whether I am on Step One or Step Twelve.

Wholeness

"We start with the premise that we are whole and that we had a normal reaction to an abnormal situation of being raised in a dysfunctional home. Our normal reaction to protect ourselves has created survival traits, compulsions, and self-harming behaviors, which respond to the ACA Steps and spiritual remedies." BRB p. 143

When we hear we are whole at our core, we wonder, "If this is true, why do I feel so unworthy or defective? Why can't I seem to live from the truth of my wholeness?" The ACA recovery program brilliantly, gently and progressively unravels this dilemma and gradually returns us to our birthright of being whole, of being our True Self.

As we apply the program in our lives and awaken, step by step, to our True Self, we start to feel compassion for all the dysfunctions we used to judge and feel ashamed of. "Of course," we say, "it's completely understandable that I reacted the way I did." We cut ourselves some slack and feel mercy for ourselves. We did the best we could under the circumstances.

It's totally "normal" that we reacted the way we did to the dysfunctional conditions in our upbringing. It's not our fault. We were powerless. We coped as best we could by developing survival traits, compulsions and self-harming behaviors. We weren't bad or wrong for doing that. As we practice the Steps and reparent ourselves with our Higher Power's solution, we forgive ourselves for our shortcomings and reclaim our birthright to wholeness.

On this day I will feel compassion for myself, recognizing that my dysfunctional reactions were "normal" – I did the best I could.

Step Four

"Made a searching and fearless moral inventory of ourselves."
BRB p. 150

When we do our Step Four inventory in the Yellow Workbook, we see that so many of our childhood experiences still seem like fresh wounds. Things that we may have talked about endlessly, even in therapy, take on new meaning when it all suddenly comes together. We notice patterns.

We begin to see a way out of the madness. We breathe a little deeper as the pain begins to subside. We trust in the process. We see that others who have gone through this seem lighter and have a flexibility we want. We trust their experience.

We notice that this inventory is going deeper than the Step work we may have done in other 12 Step programs. We are examining issues that we may have minimized before, especially surrounding our feelings.

We try to be as fearless as possible. Even though we try not to hold back, we also do not push our Inner Children to recount what they are not ready to see. We know we can do another Fourth Step for the next layer of the onion.

On this day I allow myself to be honest and thorough, welcoming the fact that I am always learning more about myself.

Critical Parent

"Judging ourselves harshly for mistakes is the Critical Parent."
BRB p. 307

The criticism we heard growing up, whether it was from our parents, teachers or others, even other children, became so internalized that we learned to let it define us. This wasn't a conscious decision. It's something that happened gradually.

As adults, we carry these shaming messages with us in the form of our own personal inner critical parent. This is why we continue to 'beat ourselves up' when we miss the nuance of a situation or make even the smallest error in judgment. These 'mistakes' might be as simple as walking out the door in front of someone and accidentally cutting them off. Or maybe we're having trouble following a conversation. Our critical inner parent jumps right in with, "How could you be so stupid?" or "What's wrong with you?" When we allow this voice to rule our thoughts, we can second-guess almost everything we do.

As we learn in ACA to silence that critical voice, we replace those messages with more loving thoughts that tell us we haven't done anything wrong – we're okay! If we accidentally cut someone off, we apologize and move on. And we realize there could be many reasons why we're not following what someone is saying. Maybe they aren't painting a complete picture, so we can ask them to explain or rephrase.

Our new responses show strength and they empower us.

On this day I will practice silencing my critical parent and affirm for myself that I am human, and it's okay to be imperfect.

Separate Identity

"As we struggle to form an identity separate from our 'parent' programs, we are also becoming aware of the need to separate emotionally from our alcoholic homes. Only in complete separation can we find the freedom to express who we are and to create the experience of intimate closeness we so desperately needed as children." BRB p. 85

Before many of us came to ACA, our other programs helped us start the journey, but they may have also led us to believe we shouldn't separate ourselves from our abusive families. So we continued to show up for those who were emotionally unavailable, giving them love and support while our own inner resources dwindled.

As our Inner Child develops a voice in ACA, we hear the pain. And we begin to acknowledge the depth of our family's dysfunction. We give ourselves permission to miss family events and let go of the fantasy of what we wanted life with them to be. We are no longer willing to be controlled by them.

In return, we gain dignity and healthy pride; we start to become sane and whole. Even though it is difficult, we realize it is worth it. We find that we are resourceful and have a tremendous capacity for self care, because we have survived our childhood trauma. We seize our own destiny and live our lives from a position of wholeness, no longer operating with one hand tied behind our backs.

On this day I will not look back. I will continue to do what is best for me – creating an identity that is separate from my dysfunctional family.

Progress

"One day at a time we make progress in our emotional, physical, and spiritual lives." BRB p. 255

Many of us have experienced a sense of the unreal when it comes to our bodies, either pushing them beyond the true limits of endurance or completely neglecting our physical needs. Some of us have a natural talent for winning physical contests, while others sit on the sidelines thinking to ourselves that we could do that, but we just don't feel like it.

Whatever our past situation, learning to take care of ourselves means understanding the value of appropriate physical activity that doesn't make us vulnerable to unnecessary injury or illness. We begin to allow ourselves to truly appreciate our place in the universe.

It may seem difficult to learn moderation in all things as we find what good, balanced health can mean for us, but gradually it gets easier. We start to establish routines that become habits that eventually become second nature to us.

The accompaniment to our physical care is our emotional nourishment, which we find through prayer and meditation. This can be done silently or be accomplished by experiencing nature, dancing to our favorite songs, or simply reminding ourselves to breathe deeply. It is part of our progress in recovery – how we help ourselves heal.

On this day I live in the moment by taking care of both my mind and my body. I breathe, move, and ask my Higher Power to be with me.

Sexual Compulsivity

"Many adult children have struggled with sexual compulsivity that has brought great sorrow and a hellish isolation from society." BRB p. 247

We isolated ourselves, even when we were with others. Our bodies did not belong to us, even though we didn't think of it that way. We found ourselves in sticky situations, being sexual with people we didn't like. Afterwards we felt sick. The feeling of being raped again came up but we didn't know where it came from. We were sure that nothing had really happened to us because when we were children our protectors said that it didn't, or it was no big deal. We wanted to believe them. We wanted to hold onto the fantasy that we were loved and cared for.

As we recover, we learn to treat ourselves, including our bodies, with respect. We don't let others touch us when we don't want to be touched. We realize that having sex outside of a committed relationship may be unsafe for us. We know that we can stop being sexual at any time with our loved one when feelings come up that need attention.

On this day I realize that healthy sex comes from trust and respect with a person that I love and who loves me back. I know they love me, not just because they say so, but because they show me by how they treat me.

Family Disease

"Many of us have children who will possibly qualify for ACA one day due to transferring our disease of family dysfunction to them." BRB p. 156

We remember wondering as we were growing up why life was so bad for us and not for other kids. We fantasized about how differently we would treat *our* children. *They* would never feel like this because we'd be the best parents – the parents we always wanted.

However, most of us weren't able to fulfill that fantasy. We wanted to act like loving parents, but often found ourselves doing the opposite. What was wrong with us? These were our little children, why couldn't we do things better? And the guilt began to plague us. We didn't yet realize that the effects from our childhood were so ingrained in us. No matter what we promised ourselves, no matter how sincere we were, we repeated the same behaviors.

In ACA, we are relieved to hear others speak about the same guilt, about their inability to be the parents they want to be. It's a relief to know we aren't alone.

We learn that the way to heal the relationships with our own children is to first heal ourselves by recovering from the baggage we've carried from our childhood. As we do so, we begin to lift our heads and free ourselves from the guilt that is keeping us stuck. We begin to change the way we do things.

On this day I will focus on my own recovery and heal myself first, knowing this is how I will have the most positive impact on my loved ones.

Hypervigilance

"Most ACA members have some form of PTSD, which is often expressed in our hypervigilance of our surroundings or our acute monitoring of comments or actions of others. This behavior is a carry-over from growing up on guard much of the time." BRB p. 160

In recovery, many of us become very aware of how we feel strong emotional and physical triggers by certain things and we don't always know why.

Through our discovery process, we find the underlying trauma that causes this state of hypervigilance. The strong, deep emotions that surface may overwhelm us like a raging sea.

To soothe ourselves, we learn to lie under warm blankets, drink hot tea, and take long baths. We activate our inner loving parent, doing whatever it takes to honor our hurt Inner Child. Our motto has become, "I will take care of me first!"

We dialogue with the wounded parts of ourselves that need love. At first, our Inner Child may seem to scream with rage, "Where were you all these years? How do I know you won't abandon me like everyone else?" But we have the courage to listen to this wounded part, no matter what the cost. We let go of abusive relationships and rearrange our lives to give ourselves more space for healing. We know we are worth it.

On this day I put myself first. When I am in a PTSD tunnel, I will not minimize it to look good for others while I am suffering inside.

Emotional Pain

"Our experience reveals that there is value in emotional pain. With support, and with gentleness, we can find our healthy pain and its healing release, just as we reclaimed our tears."
BRB p. 212

Recovery brought us many new realizations. We came to understand that to protect ourselves during childhood, we had to shut down. This didn't happen for just one event or one day; we had to put a clamp on ourselves for years.

Our reactions to pain were normal under the circumstances. Just as our bodies protected us by recoiling from a hot stove, they protected us another way. When we received the maximum limit of emotional pain tolerable, our bodies distanced us from that pain: healthy recoil. We were most likely unaware of this shutdown. Over the years, so many moments, hours, and days were lost, and eventually, we lost ourselves. We may have even wondered, "How does a normal person feel stuff?"

In recovery, as we begin to uncover the pain, we sometimes feel overcome with an indistinguishable number of emotions. We might think something is wrong or something bad is happening. But we are told by those we trust in ACA that getting in touch with our healthy pain is a good thing.

Thank goodness we have our meetings. We sit together like children who have all escaped a fire. There is comfort in going through this together. We recover our pain by talking about it to others: a great way to heal.

On this day I embrace my healthy pain, remembering that I have a lot to release and process. I feel myself gradually being becoming healed.

Body Shame

"Body shame is not reserved for our weight or shape." BRB p. 441

As children, many of us were cruelly mocked by our families for how we looked. Fodder for jokes were our facial features, body parts, voice, hair, nails, ears, teeth, ethnicity and more.

In order to survive, many of us acted as though this didn't bother us. But secretly we hung our heads in shame. To find a way to fit in, we ate differently, wore bangs, covered our ears, washed our faces relentlessly, and wore clothing to cover up the parts they laughed at. But it usually didn't work – shame and abandonment were the bookends for each day. We lost everything when they abandoned us, because it taught us to abandon ourselves. Our bodies were just another part of ourselves that didn't belong to us.

During the recovery process, we begin to see brief glimpses of our True Selves at meetings as we hear ourselves in others' stories. We finally start to feel acceptance, one hug at a time. Reading the ACA literature confirms that we aren't crazy. Our childhoods may have been stolen, but we survived, somehow. It is with that survivor strength that we doggedly work our program. Gradually, as we look at ourselves, we start to do the most important thing imaginable: we accept our own appearance.

On this day I will look at my whole self in the mirror, smile, and say, "I love every part of you. I am proud of how hard you are working to break the cycle of shame."

Family Roles

"Such survival roles tend to have a hardy life and remain fixed in our personalities long after we have left our unhealthy homes.... There is the 40-year-old sister, living out the lost child role by avoiding holiday meals and rarely calling home." BRB p. 98

Roles adopted to survive our childhood experiences are our default positions in life, unless we become conscious of the underlying causes.

Before ACA recovery, we may have avoided our families because we were overwhelmed with fear, anger, sadness, ambivalence, or mistrust. Not participating in the false cheerfulness of holidays was one way of protecting ourselves.

As we make progress using the tools of the program, we may continue to stay away from our families, but now it's because we realize the interaction is not healthy. We may hope for a time when we are able to care for our Inner Child well enough to re-establish contact. And if we do so, it will be with the full knowledge of what we may or may not get in return when we no longer play the role that makes our families comfortable.

Recovery is a process that ebbs and flows like the waves on the sands of our life. With the help of our ACA support group, our Higher Power, and the compassionate witnesses we find along the way, we can delight in the awakening of our spirit that can bring us joy every day.

On this day I will keep track of my changing family role as a way of noting my progress on this positively exciting spiritual journey I am on.

Relationship Anorexia

"Many lost children practice 'relationship anorexia.'" BRB p. 135

Adult children learn a lot of things growing up in a dysfunctional home. Unfortunately, one of the primary things we learned was not to trust. We learned to place a wall around us for protection from pain.

This wall follows us into adulthood and shadows all of our relationships with acquaintances, friends, co-workers, and most importantly, our intimate relationship with a partner/spouse. We find that, unlike our family of origin, a healthy relationship calls for a degree of trust, something so foreign to us that our safety feels threatened.

When given the choice to let down our guard and allow someone to breach our protective wall, some of us choose to either prevent or end a relationship. We fear failure but sabotage our own success.

As we get emotionally stronger in our ACA recovery program, we start removing the bricks from our wall, knowing that now we can accept what life brings us with the love and support we have for ourselves, as well as from our Higher Power and fellow travelers.

On this day I will continue to grow emotionally with the knowledge that ACA and my Higher Power will guide me in gaining the strength to trust others.

Higher Power

"…many of us are uncomfortable with the word 'God' and can recoil at the word's mention…. These members often find relief in the thought that G-O-D could stand for 'good, orderly direction.'"
BRB p. 78

Many of us were harmed as children in the name of religion and God. Perhaps we grew up with teachings that showed us a punishing God, or in a home where there was no tolerance for other beliefs. We still may not recognize the depth of the damage done to us by the shame and emotional abuse we experienced in the name of God.

When we found ACA, we may have had trouble with the use of the word God in the Steps. Then when others talked about their belief in God and mentioned their religion, it was a huge button that kept getting pushed. If we stopped attending meetings because of this, we rejected a program meant for people of all belief systems, whether they call their Higher Power "God" or not.

If we stay, we can do a number of things. During a share, we can affirm our own belief by saying, "This program works for me because it's spiritual, not religious." Or when someone says "God," we can think of it as the acronym for "good, orderly direction." Either of these choices, or a number of others, can help us find a way to "take what we like and leave the rest."

On this day I will not "throw the baby out with the bathwater." Just because some people believe in a Higher Power that makes me uncomfortable does not mean the program isn't right for me.

Promise Four

"Our ability to share intimacy will grow inside us." BRB p. 591

One casualty of our dysfunctional families was our ability to share intimacy. In our oftentimes dangerous families, intimacy led to vulnerability, which became an open invitation to be hurt and hurt again. We learned to protect ourselves by shutting down our natural need for intimacy. Our false self took charge to protect us from the harrowing pain of a multitude of unmet needs.

As we engage in the process of recovery, we begin to feel comfortable with other ACAs, learning to express our needs at meetings. We may need to be discerning in deciding with whom to share our most treasured hurts, but share them we must if we are to regain our ability to share intimately.

 The process of recovery requires us to become our own loving parent, relieving from duty our most ardent defender, our critical inner parent. Only then will our Inner Child begin to feel and express all the hurt inside.

As we grow comfortable with the uncomfortable absence of our critical inner parent, we build trust that our loving parent will guide us in knowing when and where to share intimately. Our internal intimacy translates into outward intimacy, and we are made whole once again.

On this day I will help my Inner Child feel safe so that my freedom to share intimacy can grow. I will practice sharing intimately with others I have learned to trust.

Critical Inner Voice

"We can secretly tell ourselves that we cannot recover, or we cannot experience the benefits of the Steps. This is the subtle but critical inner voice, attempting to disqualify us from recovery."
BRB p. 49

We have all heard it said that humans, by nature, are creatures of habit. It doesn't seem to matter whether those habits are good for us or do us harm; they give us a certain level of comfort.

Recovery brings change that is often looked at suspiciously by those around us who are used to our dysfunction – it's a known quantity. Some of these people may feel threatened by our change and try to interfere with it. This is not uncommon and others in the program make us aware of this possibility.

But we also become aware of our critical inner parent that can try to sabotage our recovery with phrases like, "Maybe this is the wrong thing to do." "Will I even know who I am if I change?" "Maybe I'm too old to be doing this." When this voice surfaces, it's time to reach out to our ACA fellow travelers for help and support.

On this day I will be aware of how my critical inner parent can try to plant doubts. To stay grounded, I reaffirm for myself that I am now on the right path.

Letting Go

"To ask an adult child to surrender control is like asking someone to leap from an airplane without a parachute. Without recovery, an adult child can live in terror of letting go of control." BRB p 39

A counselor once said the reason adult children have such a tight death-grip on everything is because we're afraid if we let go, things won't be okay. Fear holds us in bondage. We learned it so well growing up from those we loved most. As children we were afraid to go home, afraid to leave home, afraid we did something wrong, afraid we weren't good enough, afraid somebody was going to get hit or kicked, or we feared for our lives...and the list goes on.

In the past, when things happened in our lives, we felt guilt or shame. We learned how to hold our breath and expect the worst. Today, in our recovery program, we learn many new behaviors, including letting go with the help of our Higher Power, our support group, our sponsor, and the roadmap of the Twelve Steps.

In ACA we learn to love and accept each other just the way we are. When conflict arises – and we know it will – we, as adult children, have the opportunity to practice each and every day how to become actors, not reactors, until we feel safe and comfortable.

On this day I will remember the slogan, 'Let Go and Let God,' asking my Higher Power for the strength to relax and reflect on the things I am powerless over.

Trait Twelve

"We are dependent personalities who are terrified of abandonment and will do anything to hold on to a relationship in order not to experience painful abandonment feelings which we received from living with sick people who were never there emotionally for us." BRB p. 17

Many of us wish we did not perpetuate certain family disease traditions like abandonment, but we do so anyway. We may have abandoned someone on purpose as an outlet for our anger, or as a form of retribution. No matter what the reason, we are now in recovery to break the cycle of this multi-generational family disease the best we can.

The idea of *not* abandoning others may feel like a foreign concept. Maybe we just don't know how to stay, how to feel safe long enough to be intimate. It can feel terrifying to get close to others.

Being with fellow travelers in this program is a first step in practicing what it's like to tolerate intimacy. It's also where we can learn to communicate, resolve problems and forgive in ways we were never taught.

We perform a real act of courage when we do things differently in recovery. We can practice; we can do it. This is our living amends – a gift to ourselves and others in recovery, and perhaps to our families as well.

On this day I will practice new, trusting behavior with my ACA friends. I will continue to learn healthier ways of communicating that will keep me from leaving others for the wrong reasons.

Service

"But before we can serve one another, we must first be willing to love and serve ourselves." BRB p. 354

Many of us find such wonderful answers in ACA that we want to spread the word and help others before we understand what ACA is really about, and before we understand that we need to *have it* before we can give it away.

We're all encouraged to offer service in our meetings as a way of giving back. And that's all that's expected of us for awhile.

If we choose to provide service beyond our meeting, it's essential for our personal recovery that we examine our motives. Anything we do, whether it's getting involved in an Intergroup or starting other meetings, must come from a place of love and gratitude for what we've received. If not, we may get mired in control issues, inserting ourselves in situations where we don't belong. Or we may feel victimized if we think we're not appreciated enough. If these things happen, and we're working our program and using the ACA tools, we'll be able to take a step back and see that service is a gift we give to ourselves and others. It is full of opportunities for growth that we might not otherwise have.

On this day I will balance the service I give with my own recovery needs.

Critical Parent

"The critical inner voice is that part of us that judges others and ourselves harshly." BRB p. 337

As children in dysfunctional homes, many of us took on difficult family responsibilities that should not have been our burdens to carry. We were then criticized for not doing things "right." This led us to become hard on ourselves whenever we thought we made mistakes, developing our own critical voice that started playing in our heads. And that led us to apologize for things that were out of our control.

As we recover in ACA, we work to replace this critical inner voice that became so ingrained in us with a new, loving voice that nurtures and supports us. When we take our personal inventory on a daily basis, we learn to sort out what is really ours, versus what has nothing to do with us. We learn to set healthy boundaries, asking our Higher Power for the strength to continue this healing journey.

It takes patience and time to cultivate this loving voice, which is our inner loving parent. We find strength and hope when we listen to other ACAs as we follow a new path where we replace the negative with the positive in all aspects of daily recovery. We become more independent and able to trust our own decisions.

On this day I take responsibility for myself. I give myself positive messages and feel comfort knowing that my Higher Power is with me at all times.

Step Two

"One purpose of Step Two is to introduce the idea of keeping an open mind on the possibility of a Higher Power who can restore sanity." BRB p. 107

For many of us, the wounds are deep when it comes to trusting anyone, especially a Higher Power that is often referred to as God. We have a history of feeling deeply disappointed by most of the people and resources in our lives, including the God we were taught to believe in and pray to.

As a result, when some people in our meetings refer to their Higher Power as God, we have trouble identifying with them, or maybe even accepting that such a concept is real. But Step Two is meant to show us that we have a support system available to us; that we have different options besides going it alone. We can find a Higher Power to help us, and that Higher Power can be whatever we want it to be. There are no rules. However, if we are going to recover from our childhood dysfunction, we are going to have to learn to trust someone or something to help us.

On this day I will learn to trust that I have a Higher Power willing to help me. It may be the group, it may be a feeling of calmness when I experience nature, or a traditional God of my understanding. It's entirely up to me.

Persistence

"Recovery takes patience and persistence. We are naturally impatient to reach the end without delay and skip the hard work of the program." BRB p. xxx

Whenever we think we should be doing more in recovery, doing better, or going faster, it could be our disease talking to us. We might think we're behind, we'll never be good enough, or we'll never get through the Steps. Such thinking can lead us to overexertion, or by contrast make us feel like giving up instead of keeping a balanced, steady approach to working our program with actions coming from love.

There's a great slogan in 12 Step programs: "Just show up." This means simply to be present, here and now only, and do the next right thing in front of us. It means to be at peace with our actions instead of pushing, forcing, expecting, or "futurizing." It gives us permission to be human, be relaxed, and just show up for ourselves. This is how we develop perseverance and balance, one day at a time.

On this day I give myself permission to suit-up and just show up for myself to the best of my ability.

Grief and the Older Member

"Many older members will speak of finding their grief by working the Twelve Steps or by sitting alone quietly and feeling the feelings that arise." BRB p. 200

Older members with years of experience attending meetings, sharing, fellow traveling, and giving service from a space of love may have reached a point where they're able to just sit quietly and allow feelings to arise. Their daily practice over time has afforded them this wonderful gift.

Because for many long-time members the use of the program's tools has become second nature to them; as their feelings arise they allow them to flow out, like hot air naturally rises into the infinite sky. The continuous daily work of taking the Steps draws their grief work out from the depths of their psyche in a gradual and gentle way.

They are worth listening to as they recount their experience, strength, and hope. But they will also be the first to admit that they don't know all the answers; that they learn each day from newer members who can be wise beyond their time in the program. That is the nature of this fellowship. Grief work is part of the healing process that spans all ages and periods of longevity in the program.

On this day I will work a daily program of recovery. As I am ready, I will receive all the gifts of my grief work arising to meet me.

⚜*Connection*

"This connectedness in relationships is characterized by expressed feelings, trust, mutual respect, and an acknowledgment that a Higher Power is real." BRB p. 265

One of the worst things we may have felt as kids was a sense of aloneness, feeling connected to nothing and no one. We then became adults who were aching inside to find a connection to *something*. Often we found this with people who weren't good for us, or we found a temporary sense of connection through food, drugs, sex, alcohol, serial relationships, our children, our spouses, and others who maybe seemed to "have it together." Most things we tried felt good for awhile, but soon we felt lost and empty again.

In ACA we realize that this lack of connection is not our fault, and we aren't unique. To survive our childhoods, we had to disconnect to protect our hearts. But the longer we're in this place now, the more horrible is the pain we experience.

We find recovery from this pain by working the Steps and uncovering our real identities. We learn that the answers are inside us, and that connecting with a Higher Power helps us find those answers. We begin relating to our True Selves as we learn to express our feelings. This helps us finally start to feel connected to others in a healthy way.

On this day I will remember that I am a real person who is capable of having true connections with others. I do this by believing in myself and my Higher Power.

Own Person

"I became stronger as a result of the efforts I made to protect my Inner Child and because of the strength he gives to me when we now work together. We are both flourishing." BRB p. 399

When we were honest, we realized that we had never taken a clean action in our lives. This is when we started to move beyond denial and walk in integrity. We recognized that our behavior had been tainted by the lessons learned in our childhood. Although some good followed us, we needed a fearless inventory to find out and separate what we did *not* need for the rest of our journey.

We did this with the help of a sponsor or co-sponsor and the Yellow Workbook. We gained strength through due diligence. We slogged through the early days of pain, trusting we would one day act with true autonomy. We saw our way through perfectionism to the other side. We were showing up for life, however imperfectly, even when we felt less-than.

Our future began to unfold, unfettered by the desires of other people. We were no longer tied to our abusers. Like a butterfly from its cocoon, we finally were emerging as our own person.

We never knew this level of feeling existed, and we welcomed these changes. As we became more willing to fight for our lives, we understood that we had value deep inside of us all along. It had been calling out in the dark for us to hear and see.

On this day I will embrace my inner truth and my Inner Child. I am my own person.

✳ Trait Five

"We live life from the viewpoint of victims and are attracted by that weakness in our love and friendship relationships."
BRB p. 14

This Trait was hard for some of us to relate to. "Don't call us victims," we thought. "We made it through hell and back. We were tough." The idea that we marched through the world choosing sick people was almost offensive.

It took awhile to come out of our denial. We learned about para-alcoholism and codependency and that, without help, we were destined to continue recreating the past.

We started seeing the truth in our daily lives – how our feelings of hopelessness very often had come from thoughts like, "The world is too big for me to handle," and "I just can't make it." We recognized that we felt like victims who were being taken advantage of. We noticed how we habitually avoided people who seemed self-confident because we didn't know how to talk to them, and they didn't seem to "need" us. We'd felt uncomfortable around them but didn't know why.

When we understand that we are truly powerless over other people, but not ourselves, we discover our willingness to change. The 12 Steps give us a blueprint to follow to become self-confident and assertive – the very type of person we had always avoided but secretly wanted to be all those years. We begin to attract others who are self-confident.

On this day I will be aware when I feel unequal to others. I will stop and affirm that I am just as important as everyone else.

Amends

"Many of us peep ahead to Steps Eight and Nine and sense that we have amends to make to various people, including our parents, who have harmed us as children. Oftentimes this harm is the vulgar act of incest, physical abuse, or mental and emotional abuse by sick parents or caregivers." BRB p. 109

When some of us looked ahead at Steps Eight and Nine, we couldn't understand how we owed amends to our perpetrators. The very idea was unthinkable.

But what we didn't realize was that we were not going to be asked to make amends to unsafe people, and we certainly were not going to be asked to make amends for things we had no control over.

In ACA, we learn that the amends we are responsible for are the things we've done as adults, which usually have their origins in our childhood abuse. However, whether we actually make direct amends is a personal choice, because it is not always a safe thing to do. This is why we look for guidance from those who have already been on this road. If, with their help, we decide we cannot make direct amends to some people, we learn that indirect amends can be made, which includes becoming the person we were meant to be.

On this day, before I make amends to potentially unsafe people, I will first seek the guidance of my sponsor or my other fellow travelers. An indirect amend may be more appropriate in many cases.

Willpower

"We must shatter the illusion that we can reason out a painless solution." BRB p. 123

Adult children do not lack willpower. We have relied on our iron willpower to carry us through the most difficult of times. Sometimes, we may convince ourselves that in order to heal, we simply need more inner resolve. Even after we're in ACA, some of us try to will our Laundry List Traits away, thinking if we only had greater determination to get better, we could make different, healthier choices. Our desire is in the right place, seeking healing and recovery, but the method falls short. We may think we can read or learn about an easier solution and get better on our own, but we need the Twelve Steps of recovery and the fellowship to truly heal. There is no painless solution to our problem.

Throughout recovery, we will feel emotions and pain we may have suppressed. Grief over our childhood will surface, but it will not consume us. Our inner strength, once relied on for survival, will now give us the courage we need. We turn our determination not toward fixing ourselves in isolation, but to committing to our recovery in a supportive group setting.

On this day I accept the emotions that arise during my recovery journey, knowing any pain is temporary, and joy is possible as I continue to heal.

Tradition Four

"The groups are given freedom to make mistakes. In other words, every group has the unabashed right to be wrong. And when wrong, their decision then becomes part of the growth process, both for the meeting and, more especially, for the meeting members." BRB p. 511

The intrepid members who start a meeting may wish someone would give them the thumbs-up sign whenever they make a decision. Should we open with the Serenity Prayer? Should we read the Laundry List or does the Problem have more impact? Do we time the shares? Do we pass the basket at the end? The variables are endless. Each group is autonomous so long as their actions do not affect other groups or ACA as a whole. The group is at liberty to establish its own flavor and meeting style. Some will favor a style that is laid back; others may want more structure. The choice is a group's to make.

ACA cooperates with all other 12 Step programs, but we do not dilute our message in the process. Our focus is on recovery from the effects of being raised in an alcoholic or dysfunctional family using the 12 Steps and reparenting. Whatever choices a group makes, above all, we remember who we are. We are our own program, not an extension of other 12 Step programs.

On this day I will respect the group's autonomy in my effort to carry the ACA message to the adult child who still suffers. I will help keep the focus of ACA on recovery from the effects of being raised in an alcoholic or dysfunctional family.

Disease of Alcoholism

"Since alcoholism is a family disease, all family members are affected without having to take a drink. With an amazing predictability, the children grow up to be addicted or to marry an addicted or compulsive person." BRB p. 13

We may have been conscious of the effects of the alcoholic on our lives. Or more likely, we denied that their disease had any effect on us.

Slowly the veils of denial were lifted as we saw how, like it or not, we had been impacted by the disease, even if the alcoholic had been removed from the home. We may have unconsciously found a new and improved alcoholic personality type with which to continue the crazy-making game of dissociation.

When we attend ACA meetings, we seem to have an innate sense that the meeting space is safe as we speak honestly about what we are feeling and experiencing. We begin to see the patterns and habits in all of our relationships – that the dysfunction can spring from our lips without us even noticing it. We become more aware of the unhealthy choices we make, both consciously and unconsciously, and we choose different options.

On this day I acknowledge that I was affected by the family disease of alcoholism. I will pay attention to the patterns and habits I had denied so that I don't continue to repeat them.

May

Fellowship/Rivers

"By taking the action of responding to one another with love, we simultaneously allow ourselves to give and be given to in a way that heals the wounds of our childhood and meets our simple human requirements for attention, love, and respect." BRB p. 363

Gifts and Talents

"Each of us comes to ACA with many talents. As we grow in our recovery, we discover even more talents within us." BRB p. 515

Many of us come to ACA not knowing what our unique gifts are. We may have always measured ourselves against others and decided we came up short.

But then someone we trust in our meeting pays us a compliment that we believe. With the support of such people, we learn to see, develop and express our special talents, large or small. Maybe our gift is the ability to provide encouragement, even a small amount, to another person that helps them stay on their path. It may not take much effort on our part, yet it can be huge to the other person. Sometimes we may never learn the positive impact we may have had.

Or maybe we have other gifts, such as the words to write a book that inspires millions. Whatever the case, we remember that each talent we possess is tremendously valuable, no matter whether it helps only ourselves or others.

Freeing ourselves from our cloudy thinking is what makes room for our ability to see, develop, and express our talents. That's part of the beauty of ACA: as we feel understood and appreciated, it frees us to express our gifts, becoming whole, well-rounded, recovering adult children.

On this day I recognize that I have unique talents. I am now willing to develop and express them as I learn how valuable I am to myself and others.

Attraction vs. Promotion

"Attraction is different. Attraction is making information available about ACA without strings. There are no pitches and no grand promises." BRB p. 546

Many of us felt the rush of belonging when we started attending ACA meetings. We found so many answers. We wanted to give Big Red Books to everyone because we wanted them to know what we now knew. We may have even been tempted to wear an "ACA Rules!" t-shirt.

But we soon learned to slow down. We found out why this is a program of attraction, not promotion. It's more about actions and not so much about the talking. We allow our Higher Power to work magic in and around us.

We take things as they come. We no longer stay up at night thinking how to put ACA in the local water source. We are sad when newcomers come and then go, but we learn to let them go. We grieve as we watch people die from the disease of family dysfunction all around us while we get healthier.

We trust that there is an abundant source of love for us and for anyone else who is truly willing to walk the walk. We do our part and enjoy the results. As we keep the focus on ourselves, we see better results for us, and that's what positively impacts the world around us.

On this day I will remember that I can't force anyone to get this message. I can make the information available and let others make their own choices. The best message is the personal change I see in myself.

Step Five

"Admitted to God, to ourselves, and to another human being the exact nature of our wrongs." BRB p. 190

In Step Five, for the first time we came clean about our real feelings and walked away from it more whole than before. We were not perfect and that was okay. We allowed our Higher Power to guide us through our histories with new insight. We were validated by our fellow travelers in the process, and we now knew definitively that we had been wronged and that we no longer need to accept abusive behavior from others.

This Step took a lot of courage. We paused before going forward to reflect on how far we had come and to enjoy the view. In a sense we had been reborn into self-awareness on a level we didn't know existed.

We started to put ourselves first because we were worth it. No one could take this new foundation away from us, because it was built on rock-solid pillars that could not be torn down by others anymore. We were gaining the inner strength necessary to face whatever was put in our paths. We were becoming free from those things that plagued us because we had been honest with our Higher Power and another person.

We looked forward to connecting with our Inner Child as we progressed. That child was awakening and knew it would never ever be alone again. We were there to provide the nourishment, giving everything we had.

On this day I will be honest with the most important person I will ever get to know: Me.

Solution – Humor

"We learn to reparent ourselves with gentleness, humor, love and respect." BRB p. 590

The great advantage of teaching our Inner Child to look at life with as much good humor as possible is that it relieves tension. Think for a moment about the last time we heard someone say, "I'm right and you're wrong." Did we automatically assume a defensive posture and scan the speaker's throat for their jugular?

With the help of ACA, we can teach our Inner Child that instead of reacting, it's possible to reach instead for humor and say something like, "Even a stopped clock is right twice a day, so who knows who's right or wrong? What time is it, anyway?" Learning to smile in the face of criticism is an important skill. It helps when we learn that going to war isn't always required if we can sometimes use our wit instead.

Using humor to ease tensions is good for us. On days when we feel unlovable, silly good humor can be just the remedy to lift ourselves out of a funk. Maybe we can tell ourselves "Go find a mirror, look at your wonderful self and give yourself a kiss." That person in the mirror is our Inner Child who will be grateful for our attention. When we find the humor, we're helping our Inner Child's urge to have fun, something that didn't happen nearly enough while we were growing up.

On this day I will remember that humor has a purpose and I can use it to my advantage in the care and nurturing of my Inner Child.

Sanity

"One of the keys to being restored to sanity involves surrendering our need to harm ourselves or to run from our feelings."
BRB p. 137

It is not sane to have a battle within ourselves to keep feelings from surfacing. By running from our emotions, we lose out on the valuable lessons they may teach us. When we deny or stuff feelings, they continue to hide just under the surface. They become jumbled and confusing and tend to come out with the slightest trigger.

When feelings are experienced rather than denied, they lose their power. By learning to sit with our feelings and acknowledge them, we practice self-love. As we start to love ourselves more, we will want to harm ourselves less and begin to treat ourselves with genuine kindness and compassion.

But we don't just stop the behavior of self-harm all at once. Part of the process is to surrender this need to our Higher Power, knowing that we will be shown how to love ourselves. Whether quickly or slowly, we come to have faith in the Promises of ACA.

On this day I will nurture myself by accepting my feelings as they arise, knowing they hold opportunities for me to grow and love myself more fully.

Disease of Family Dysfunction

"Family dysfunction is a disease that affects everyone in the family. Taking a drink is not necessary to be affected. This is an ACA axiom, and it serves as a basis for our First Step." BRB p. 22

Whether we are teetotalers or "self-made" alcoholics, our perfectionist and risk-taking attitudes and behaviors far outlast the seemingly temporary effects of alcohol and other dysfunction in the family body.

In Step One in ACA, we admit that we are powerless over the effects of alcoholism and family dysfunction. Those effects seem infinite in number, just as with the stars in the sky. No matter which effects we start to work on in recovery, we will most assuredly uncover more subtle effects each time we do the Steps. It is a process of discovery – that we are all affected by this disease of family dysfunction.

As we keep coming back, we experience the ever-expanding foundation of our recovery as we continue to admit the effects over which we have no control.

On this day I will remember that I am powerless over the effects of alcoholism and family dysfunction. However, I am not powerless over myself. I now have the willingness to face the impact my childhood has had on me.

Worldwide Fellowship

"ACA is a worldwide fellowship.... New groups are established each week somewhere in the world." BRB p. 350

We suffered such confusion and chaos as children. Feeling horribly alone, on display, hunted, in danger, and lost, we wondered when our world would ever look like other kids' worlds. What was wrong with us that made our world different?

Many of us grew into adults who became jaded and numb and shut down. We gave up on our world becoming like others. We were just hoping to get by without too much drama, too much pain. We did little things daily to hang on, but we were aware that our lives were a struggle and very disappointing.

When we got to our first ACA meeting, we discovered that we were not the only people who felt like this – we weren't alone after all. When we heard that ACA was a worldwide fellowship, it was exciting to know that so many people were finding help. Sadly, this disease of family alcoholism and dysfunction exists everywhere.

Now that we know this is a global problem, we also know it wasn't created by our particular parents, and we must admit they weren't the only problem. It's bigger than that. Knowing that we're part of a world of people who are now recovering together as adult children gives us great hope and a feeling of comfort.

On this day I join hands with the world of adult children as I remind my Inner Child, "We were never alone."

Inner Child/True Self

"During these years of family dysfunction, our Inner Child or True Self went into hiding and remained heavily fortified under addictions or dependent behavior." BRB p. 106

Before ACA, we might have heard about and even had glimpses of our Inner Child, or True Self – the part of us that hungers for the unconditional love and support we didn't receive in our families. This is the part of us that is most often buried pretty deep behind defense mechanisms and addictive behaviors that we thought were somehow protecting us from further harm.

But in recovery we learn the reasons why our True Self went into hiding. It finally starts to makes sense why that part of us can be elusive and hard to access on a regular basis.

As we identify and release our childhood trauma, we come out from behind our addictions and self-destructive behaviors to make it safe for our Inner Child. We reparent ourselves and give ourselves what we didn't receive. We begin to blossom inside and make ourselves whole with the help of our Higher Power, our fellow travelers and the tools of ACA.

On this day I will welcome and nurture my True Self. With the support of my Higher Power and ACA, I am able to provide for myself the unconditional love I've always deserved.

Relapse

"In ACA, we have stories of relapse and the importance of getting back to the program if relapse occurs." BRB p. 391

We may have thought that relapse was only for others with more serious, life threatening addictions, not those of us in ACA. We had been abused. We were the ones in the right. If we let our character defects get out of hand once in a while, we were entitled, weren't we? That wasn't relapse. That wasn't even life-threatening.

By taking an honest look at ourselves in the Fourth Step, we see that emotional relapse can be just as life-threatening as anything else. We realize how we may have relapsed when we've gone back to our family of origin too often, hoping things would be different. But instead, we watched them tear each other to shreds and found ourselves participating, even a little bit. Maybe we've ignored our screaming Inner Child as we practiced other self-harming behavior, ignoring our Higher Power in favor of our old compulsive self-reliance.

Seeing how susceptible we can be to relapse, just as those who deal with substance abuse, we become more vigilant, but not in the way of our childhood hypervigilance. This vigilance is an awareness of how "awake" we are. We are mindful about maintaining conscious contact with our Inner Child and our Higher Power through our daily inventory. We create the time and space we need to move forward on our journey, no longer abandoning ourselves.

On this day I will maintain daily contact with my Inner Child and my Higher Power to help me stay focused so that I avoid emotional relapse.

Family Relationships

"At an appropriate time, we review the relationship we want to have with our families. We will choose to avoid some family members because they are draining or abusive." BRB p. 123

Even though we lived through the same experiences as others in our families, we may have reacted differently and developed different scars and ways of coping that often divided us much more than it united us.

When we begin our recovery in ACA, this divide makes it more difficult to be around the circus that is our extended family. With practice, resolve and support from other ACAs, we give ourselves permission to avoid situations that can drain us of all energy and even cause us to revert to our own dysfunctional behaviors.

If we think some family members are too toxic and abusive, we can disconnect. We don't have to participate because we know how emotionally draining they are. We have a choice. We don't have to go down with a sinking ship.

This separation doesn't have to be forever. Many of us eventually get to the point of reintroducing our True Selves to the family, and we let them make the choice to interact with us on our terms, or not.

On this day I give myself permission to separate from my family's dysfunction. This gives me the opportunity to become who I am meant to be, not who I am expected to be.

Change

"The more I change, the more I get these little hints from people around me to go back to my prior behavior, because that's when they felt safe with me." BRB p. 411

As we started to break out of our old patterns, others became unhappy with us. They felt betrayed and abandoned as we became more self-sufficient. We were no longer taking care of them, and our healthy detachment put a distance between us that was uncomfortable for them.

Taking care of ourselves is new behavior because we were taught to always placate others. Our new reactions are helping us gain ground for the first time. We are no longer bludgeoned and bullied by the silence of others as they try to manipulate us. We have begun to trust our own feelings over the desires of other people, no matter how much we think we need those relationships to be okay.

We allow others to own their own feelings. When someone is angry, we no longer assume it's our fault, and we don't let their anger control us. We move forward.

If others break off relationships with us as a result, or act wounded, we don't try to fix things; we are no longer willing to throw ourselves under the damaging tires of shame. We have learned to walk around those spiky pits of guilt and move on.

On this day I will trust that if one relationship ends, a healthier one will take its place when the time is right.

Responding with Love

"By taking the action of responding to one another with love, we simultaneously allow ourselves to give and be given to in a way that heals the wounds of our childhood and meets our simple human requirements for attention, love, and respect." *BRB p. 363*

Taking action coming from love challenges the family of origin belief system. As children, our ability to love and trust was forced into hiding due to either abuse, or neglect, or both. Deep in the recesses of our soul, our Inner Child knows the truth and waits for the right opportunity to give and receive love.

Once the space for an inner loving parent opens, our Inner Child emerges and engages us in a loving, caring, discerning manner that often may surprise us.

As we grow, we give service in our meetings and within the fellowship. We come from a place of love and gratitude, which reinforces our commitment to our Inner Child and inner loving parent. We feel the effects of our changed responses; so do other ACAs who witness our growth.

On this day I open a space for my inner loving parent so that my Inner Child can emerge, feel loved and show gratitude, especially to other recovering adult children.

Sense of Purpose

"Our experience shows that the Steps are a proven way of life, yielding new meaning and a sense of purpose in one's life." BRB p. 95

Did we save a life today?

Did we smile or have a kind word for a stranger? We might not know if that stranger was in the midst of despair, wondering if life was even worth living. Could our simple act of kindness have brought even the smallest spark of hope to that person?

We are not responsible for what others do, but we can consider the possibility that our recovery brings us new awareness of what is happening around us and the positive impact we can have in seemingly meaningless everyday contact.

We go through each day deep in our own thoughts. Often, we unwittingly avoid eye contact with others.

Even if we are not having the best day, smiling at a stranger and perhaps seeing a smile returned feels good. Maybe we let the person in line behind us go ahead when we have a basketful and they have one item. Or we take a few extra seconds to make eye contact with the clerk and wish them a good day.

These random acts of kindness can brighten someone's day and help us feel connected. We may never know the impact we make through our actions, even if we only spread a bit of joy in the moment. But it is worth the effort to carry this message of hope.

On this day I will remember that what I learn through ACA and the Steps is not just for me. My progress can affect everyone whose life I touch.

Letting Go

"Recovery is not about perfection. It is in the becoming that we experience the promises of recovery." BRB p. xxiv

Some of us thought we had to figure out how to work the ACA program perfectly. We grew up in homes where that was the norm, and we expected nothing less of ourselves. We attended meetings and just "knew" everything would suddenly fall into place because we showed up and did the homework. However, in the rote process we followed, we missed the vital step of discovering and nurturing our Inner Child.

We didn't make room for our feelings and for the process that helps us uncover who we are truly meant to be. As a result, when we finally experienced a different bottom, one we didn't expect, we found our Higher Power waiting for us to reach out.

Now we accept that we are a work in progress, letting ourselves be where we are. We don't know all the answers and discover that we might not find them soon. We are learning to let go of perfection, and that's a hard nut to crack. We live with unsolved problems because it's part of being human. This is part of the freedom we are discovering. The promises of recovery are now being fulfilled.

On this day I let go of my own ideas of what recovery should look like and open my heart to what it is – a series of unfolding experiences that I welcome with gratitude.

Promise Five

"As we face our abandonment issues, we will be attracted by strengths and become more tolerant of weaknesses." BRB p. 591

Being left without a means of finding our way back is the essence of our abandonment. As a child in an alcoholic or dysfunctional family, we were required to leave our True Selves behind. Our false selves took the lead so that we could try to avoid the inevitable pain and disappointment. This gave us a long-lasting impression that anyone we cared about would leave us too.

Drawn to people who also want to recreate the abandonment drama, our lives seem to be an endless loop of attraction, distraction, and abandonment.

We face our abandonment with the tools of recovery. The challenging 12 Step work we do brings with it an ability to find our way back. Able to realize our powerlessness, our thorough inventory reveals the source of our disconnection from our True Selves.

In our meetings, we learn to nurture our Inner Child by understanding the role of our inner loving parent. We make better choices and see that the strengths and weaknesses folks have are but an expression of their humanness. We can decide to whom we will be attracted.

On this day I will use the tools of recovery, meetings, telephone calls, and fellow travelers to face my True Self abandonment, and find a way back to wholeness with consistent use of the Steps and Traditions.

Dissociation

"Because we shut out our parents when we were children, we tend to shut out people as adults." BRB p. 187

Surviving childhood in a dysfunctional household required many of us to use a number of coping mechanisms to maintain any semblance of sanity. One was our ability to dissociate (separate mentally or emotionally) from what was happening around us or to us. Although dissociation helped us survive then, as adults it closes us off from the possibility of having healthy relationships.

Sometimes fear of rejection motivates us to dissociate, so we distract ourselves because if we don't feel, then we hope we won't experience any pain. But dissociation also deprives us of healthy joy.

Sometimes our hypervigilance causes us to constantly monitor our surroundings for signs of trickery or slights. But it can also deprive us of the opportunity to make good friends.

With these dysfunctional filters, we can misread the words or actions of others as an assault, causing us to become defensive, go on the offensive and shut down completely.

In ACA, as we peel back the layers of our childhood survival traits, we learn to sort out what no longer works in our adult lives. We leave behind traits that no longer serve us. We gratefully see how this program gives us the strength to change and the courage to be open to others. We no longer wish to be alone.

On this day I will be kind to myself if I find myself dissociating. I will be open to people and new experiences.

Authority Figures

"We realize that life today really is different than when we were children without a voice." BRB p. 73

The authority figures we grew up with were scary. They got angry when anyone questioned or challenged them. There didn't seem to be any logic to it, so we did what we could to avoid having the anger directed at us.

As adults, we often felt our bosses' behavior resembled that of our parents. The potential authority they wielded made us feel like that little kid again. We avoided asking for help because we expected to be belittled. From our experience and that of our friends, that was a very real fear because, like our parents, many bosses are good at pouncing on the weak. So, rather than risk confrontation, and because we became adept at figuring things out for ourselves as children, we decided that was the way to survive at work. It was exhausting.

We realized early in recovery that we wanted and needed to find our voice. But the stakes seemed too high to experiment at work. So we role-played situations with our fellow travelers. We practiced what we could say, or what we might have said. We gradually started to gain self-confidence. And when the time was right, we spoke up. The elation we felt when it worked was indescribable. We were becoming who we knew we could be. We were making a difference – to ourselves!

On this day I will practice finding my voice with someone in the program I trust so when the time comes, I'll be ready to speak up for myself.

Service

"Meanwhile, those who are spiritually awake accept Twelve Step work with an attitude of service rather than sacrifice. By the time we reach this Step, we know the difference between being a rescuer and giving service with love." BRB p. 289

Placing the Solution and Problem on the walls does not a meeting make. Reading the opening script and closing down the meeting doesn't make a meeting either. What makes the meeting is the spirit with which these tasks are done. Giving service from a space of love in ACA is a spiritually-enhancing experience for all involved. By the time we have been in ACA for awhile, after having taken the Steps and being graced with a spiritual awakening, our ability to do service from love has also been established.

We know the difference between control and service. We know of tolerance and boundaries. We know how to be thoughtful, realizing we are only seeking to follow the group's conscience in furtherance of our primary purpose – to carry the message to the suffering adult child who is seeking recovery.

Adult children are attracted to spiritually-awakened ACAs and groups, and wish to help keep the doors open. We realize that were it not for the meeting, we might have little hope of recovering, and we trust each other since our service comes with no strings attached.

On this day I will give service to the ACA fellowship from love, realizing that I am supporting my own progress when I help make another member's progress possible.

Unique Journey

"We find that a difference in identity and purpose distinguishes Adult Children of Alcoholics from other 12-Step Programs and underscores the need for our special purpose." BRB p 81

Our first ACA meeting may have seemed almost overpowering for many of us. From our war-zone childhood homes, we brought with us our hypervigilance, anxiety, and anger. We were on high alert as we scanned the "weirdos" sitting around us.

Some of us entered these rooms after finding that our other Twelve Step programs weren't giving us the emotional sobriety we needed. Some of us came after chance encounters with people who saw how troubled we were and asked us if we'd grown up in an alcoholic home, or with some other severe dysfunction. It may have felt embarrassing to be so easily diagnosed, but knowing there was a place where we might be heard felt hopeful.

In spite of our anxiety at our first meeting, we were hooked. We heard laughter and secrets from others that convinced us we weren't unique or insane, only sick from overexposure to parental addiction.

As we kept coming back, we found a sponsor and other fellow travelers we trusted who helped us through our Step work. We learned how shame and guilt had controlled our adult lives, and how we were conditioned to take responsibility for other people's problems. We were now on a unique journey to reparent ourselves.

On this day I will appreciate who I am, knowing that going to ACA and practicing its principles can take me home – not again, but for the first time.

Step Three

"We don't release some things to a Higher Power and hold onto others." BRB p. 142

The Steps and Traditions mention Higher Power and prayer for a reason. They are part of learning to rely on someone or something else instead of continuing the compulsive self-reliance many of us learned in childhood.

Our belief system is a personal choice. How we pray or whom we pray to is part of that personal choice. It's even up to us to determine what prayer is.

In meetings, we hear many examples of the power of prayer. We learn that it is communication that can bring answers when we are fearful, confused, or need help making decisions. Prayer and meditation can calm us so we can feel a conscious contact with *our* Higher Power.

When we let go of problems, the Steps show us how to care for ourselves and recover from the effects of our childhoods. But if we pick and choose what we let go of, we hold on to things that can continue to drag us down.

Connecting to a Higher Power helps us know we are not alone and defenseless. Turning our problems over helps us release the burdens we have been carrying around. We now have faith and trust in something greater than ourselves.

On this day I choose to make prayer part of my daily ritual. I see how it can benefit me to turn all of my problems over to a Higher Power and ask for a new direction to be revealed.

Feeling Understood

"My sister and I don't communicate any longer since she doesn't understand who I am." BRB p. 407

We used to make excuses for people when we said things like, "Oh, they don't know any better." There may be a lot of truth in that statement, but it feels like we were saying, "They just didn't see me when they ran me over, so it's okay." Just because someone is a family member doesn't mean we should accept the unacceptable, including subtle things like them not really hearing us, or less subtle things like having them label us as over-reactive.

Through ACA, we can now tell whether we're being heard or not. We realize that others don't have to agree with us, but they may not disrespect us. We recognize our needs and start to speak up for ourselves. We are learning to live a healthy emotional life, no longer wishing to be around denial and shame. We let go of those who can't journey onwards with us because we cannot carry them while we are climbing to the heights we need to keep our heads above water. We may reconnect with them later, but that will be our choice.

Before recovery, we may have spent all our energy on our families because we thought that was what we were supposed to do. Now we give our "gifts" to those who can appreciate and actually understand them.

On this day I choose to spend my time and energy on those who wish to make this journey with me. I deserve to be heard and loved for who I am.

Learning to Thrive

"We learned to keep our thoughts and desires close to our hearts."
BRB p. 431

As we grew up, it was not safe to share any part of us. When we risked being vulnerable and letting people know what we wanted, we were shamed and ridiculed, made to feel stupid for having needs at all, let alone dreams. Our struggles may have been as basic as having to keep our own clothes clean or finding food to eat. We put all our energy into surviving. By the time we were done, we had no energy to claim our birthright, the ability to dream.

Today, we nurture ourselves by deciding what we want the universe to send us, because we're open to the possibility that we can have those things. We allow ourselves to swim around in the scent of promise. We deserve it. We realize that wanting something is not bad; it's a healthy part of being human. We allow our minds and hearts to wander because this is how we learn what we want and need. We no longer stifle ourselves with negative images and thoughts. When we are blocked, we talk about it with our sponsor or share in meetings. We don't keep it to ourselves and allow our souls to wither with isolation. We now put our needs first and are not waiting for anyone to rescue us.

On this day I will show up for myself by allowing myself to think of what I want and not just what I need to survive and thrive.

Stored Loss

"This sharing of our story with our sponsor or informed counselor reveals destructive patterns in our adult lives while illuminating abuses from our childhood. We also begin to see our grief or stored loss lying beneath our decisions to wrong ourselves and others."
BRB p. 110

Some of our shares with our fellow travelers are about the deeper, self-destructive patterns we have been acting out. We may have assumed that we were helpless to change these patterns. Hope seemed to have vanished from our lives.

ACA restores the hope that we can change. The program teaches us that our destructive patterns are learned in childhood and continue to affect us as adults. The knowledge that we, ourselves, aren't self-destructive gives us hope to change what we thought was an unchangeable aspect of ourselves.

It slowly becomes clear to us that unexpressed grief is at the root of all the decisions and actions that resulted in hurting ourselves and others. Finally, relief from these habits can be seen as we raise our sights and see Step Two as giving us the hope we thought was forever lost.

On this day I will share with my fellow travelers my deeper self-destructive patterns in order to help release them. I will express the grief and loss that underpin these habits as I look to Step Two with a renewed sense of hope.

Trait Six

"We have an overdeveloped sense of responsibility, and it is easier for us to be concerned with others rather than ourselves; this enables us not to look too closely at our own faults." BRB p. 14

The tendency of most of us is to own every problem around us. We are the fixers. It doesn't matter whether or not we were asked to help – we will give everyone's problem our full attention.

It's not difficult to assess where this tendency came from. Being responsible for the chaos in our family of origin was repeatedly put onto our small shoulders as children. We were placed in the middle of adult dysfunction at a very young age. We learned it was our job to focus on others and make things better. We also learned that our needs and wants were not important. It became a habit we carried into adulthood that also kept us from looking at ourselves.

In ACA, for perhaps the first time, we are asked to focus on ourselves and own our own part in our dysfunctional lives. We acknowledge our character defects. As we do so, we are gently guided through the process of reparenting ourselves with love and kindness.

We learn that our needs are important. Our feelings are worthy of attention. The strong pull to fix others lessens. It was never our job in the first place. We start to get used to this new freedom.

On this day I know that if I did not create the problem I am not responsible for the solution. I focus on myself.

Resistance

"Pushing down and holding back the history of a lifetime of injury and hurt from consciousness is painful, not metaphorically or psychically painful, but physically agonizing. It's a matter of blood, tissue, nerves and bone." BRB p. 623

Our bodies ached. We woke in the night. We sat there sweating, our pulses racing. We saw dark figures coming to get us, only to realize we were safe. During the course of our day, when people hugged us or shook our hands, we could tell they felt more relaxed than we did. When we tried to touch our toes or perform other physical tasks, we struggled. We often got sick because we carried the trauma in our bodies.

Slowly we come to realize that we need more to recover than just talk. We need to find ways to relax our physical selves as well. We need to unknot ourselves, physically as well as emotionally, mentally and spiritually. We gradually, patiently find ways to accomplish this by trying new things until we learn what works for us. We embrace this process on our path to a better, healthier life. We seek outside help when we need it, and share our progress in the safe haven of ACA.

On this day I give attention to my physical health. I will make a doctor's appointment if I need to. I will also explore different ways to release trauma from my body, trusting that I will find what works for me, one day at a time.

Fear

"ACA is for people who can make the connection between childhood neglect and an adult life of fear and loneliness." BRB p. 33

Living in fear can be addictive. Healthier people can feel fear about things occasionally, but they deal with it constructively. But many of us can be driven by fear in everything we do. We grew up in uncertain conditions that caused feelings of intense fear while we waited for the next blow up, for the next piling on of emotional pressure and stress, or even for the next silent treatment that left us wondering if we even mattered. Our childhood fear was real. So how could we not become fear-based adults? We were left with a sense of loneliness, of feeling that we might never escape.

But ACA came to our rescue! It may sound simplistic, but this is where we *are* rescued – not by someone else, but by our own willingness to seek change. We learn that we can release the grip that fear has on our lives. We leave the sense of loneliness and isolation behind. We know we have choices; we're no longer a captive audience.

We examine our reality and understand that most things we fear can't hurt us unless we let them. Our fixation on these things is what does the real damage. As we experience recovery, we learn to replace fear with love and compassion for ourselves.

On this day I will ask other ACAs and my Higher Power to help place my fears in their proper light. I have compassion for myself as I do this work.

Self-Forgiveness

"Self-forgiveness is an elusive concept for adult children. We ask that the adult child keep an open mind and consider that God has already forgiven the person." BRB p. 113

Forgiving others was tough enough, but for some of us, forgiving ourselves seemed a monumental task. We carried the shame and guilt passed down from generation to generation, from one hurt person to the next in a chain for maybe hundreds of years. We may have found that we needed to act compulsively to stay numb to the pain: maybe we chose drugs, alcohol, food, gambling, approval, cutting, video games, power, rules, or spending. We lived in fear because deep down we thought we were unlovable.

In ACA, we learn that we can have a relationship with a healing Higher Power that we can define in any way we want. If our families were abusive and perfectionistic, we no longer bow down to them. We reject the feelings of despair and hopelessness because they no longer belong to us.

As we begin to forgive ourselves for real or imagined wrongs, we become ready to reparent our Inner Child. In doing so, we make room for a new outlook, one that allows us to believe that part of us is already whole and sane, already with our Higher Power, and already forgiven. As we continue to heal, we will come to understand that we were forgiven all along.

On this day I will hold my head high and act as if I am forgiven, even if I don't yet fully believe it.

Sincere Effort

"Each of us must make a sincere effort to make progress in the program whether working on one or many compulsions or addictions." BRB p. 51

Many of us have the tendency to make things a lot more complicated than they need to be. But we've all heard the slogan, "Keep It Simple." If we keep telling ourselves that recovery is too complicated, we may be giving ourselves a good reason not to work very hard at it or make much forward movement. Sadly, that means we could sit in the rooms of recovery waiting for a miracle to happen for decades. And if nothing changes, nothing changes.

But recovery is not measured by time spent in the program, but how we work and live the program. Our Higher Power is not going to do the recovery work for us.

The choice is simple – either occupy a seat in the meetings and keep the same dysfunction in our life, or step out of our comfort zone and try the path that has been proven effective by so many others.

ACA sponsors and fellow travelers are available to help us along our path. We couldn't do it alone before we came to ACA, and we can't do it alone now. If we've just been floating along, it's time to swallow our pride and make some forward movement.

On this day I rededicate my efforts to use the tools of recovery. I will pick up the phone and the BRB and learn something new about myself.

Awakening Spirit

"In ACA we carry the awakening of the spirit down to the deepest level where the Inner Child is paralyzed by fear." BRB p. 360

When we attended our first ACA meeting, the Twelve Step language may have intimidated us. What the heck were these people talking about? Was this part of some cult? Was it safe to keep coming here? Could these people really be happy, even with all their problems?

As we kept coming back, we learned to explore recovery slowly and start to become an inner loving parent to those wounded parts of ourselves that hurt for longer than long. We found the pain and the shame that was deep within us. But we also found that beneath those things lay a wellspring of life, the energy to carry us through anything and everything. We discovered a path inside ourselves, a path that could lead us home should we have the courage to follow it. We no longer had to do it alone.

On this day I have faith that by consoling my Inner Child, I also get closer to my Higher Power.

Tradition Five

"When carrying the ACA message, we stick to our story and to the principles of recovery. We don't proselytize, bully, evangelize, or manipulate the person we are attempting to help." BRB p. 516

The focus of a single purpose guarantees that we are never going to be distracted by other tempting glittery objects. We do one thing only – we carry the message to the adult child who still suffers.

We may be tempted to run into our communities and raise an ACA banner proclaiming the virtues of the program and the obvious need for the 12 Steps to address many social ills. We know there are more people who need the program than those who truly want it.

However, Tradition Five does not require us to "convince" anyone. Experience has shown that if a person lacks the willingness to change, they are unlikely to receive the ACA message well.

So we carry the message to those adult children who still suffer and we move forward, living the principles of the program. We do what we can to ensure the meetings are available to all who want them. And we learn to let go of those who don't respond to the message.

We humbly realize that each person has a Higher Power available to them, which is the only thing that can help them find the willingness to hear the message.

On this day I will carry the message in a manner that follows Tradition Five. I will remember, above all, that I carry the message in my daily life through my own recovery.

People-Pleasing

"We believe that we will be safe and never abandoned if we are 'nice' and if we never show anger." BRB p. 11

We went overboard to give to and care for others. No one asked us, yet we expected that in return they would nurture, praise, and acknowledge us. But why should other people be expected to go out of their way to fulfill our needs? When did they sign the contract we carried in our minds?

We learn in recovery that the praise, confidence, and caring we need must come from within ourselves. Being too nice eventually leads us to feel angry, resentful, and anxious.

As we begin to express our true feelings, we focus on ourselves and direct our energy toward identifying and correcting our character defects. Instead of getting stuck in our *niceness*, we follow the ACA Steps in our daily lives. As a result, heartfelt peace and contentment heal us and our relationships, one day at a time.

Relying on our Higher Power enables us to become stronger spiritually. As we no longer depend on others for our happiness, our self-confidence increases.

On this day I will stay mindful of how easy it can be to fall back into my people-pleasing mode. To help me move forward and avoid burnout, I will rely instead on my Higher Power and my sponsor to guide me.

June

".... we do not have to participate in their dysfunction. We are free to live our own lives." BRB p. 123

True Self

"We begin to see that we can bring our True Selves to a relationship. We have something to offer that is different than unhealthy dependence. This is what ACA recovery looks like."
BRB p. 265

Discovering our True Selves – what a journey! When we look back at our first ACA meeting, we thank our Higher Power for getting us here. Maybe we hoped for a quick fix to stop the insanity and to have a better life, or a miracle answer about how to fix other people. But that's not exactly how things turned out.

As we keep coming back, we find that working the Steps is not always easy, nor is it pretty. But the key to freedom is courage, vulnerability, and the willingness to shed our tears while we follow this quest. We work with a sponsor or fellow traveler who has walked this walk before. We discover our ineffective behavior patterns and become willing to change. We don't get stuck on blaming our parents and the generations before them.

Slowly, the ACA Promises come true. As we work our program, we develop those characteristics and learn to breathe and love life. We play again. We become healthier and have healthier relationships with ourselves, our families, our friends and community. We become sponsors and help others through the swamps, gently and tenderly, the way we were shown. With the help of our Higher Power, we discover we had the "ruby slippers" all along!

On this day I continue to do the work that helps me discover more aspects of my healthy True Self.

Humility

"True humility is willingness to seek and do God's will with our best effort." BRB p. 223

In ACA, we move from wanting and being willing to actually finding the passion that begins our journey into recovery. We look for that passion because without it we merely talk recovery, we do not live it.

We look past our desire to heal ourselves and we develop the humility needed to seek our Higher Power's will for us. With that humility, we surrender ourselves to the spiritual seed that's blossoming inside of us. We move toward that essence, and the closer we get, the more in touch we are with our own spiritual being. We begin to live in the present.

And in that *now*, we see the world differently. We notice the spiritual essence in others and the beauty around us. We begin to feel the peace. We begin to shed our past, including the person we thought we were, and we are at peace with the stillness. Further down the path, we realize that the stillness is our Higher Power working inside us.

On this day I seek the humility needed to accept my Higher Power's will, knowing that it is the basis for my journey to recovery. The miracle of ACA has begun.

Step Six

"Were entirely ready to have God remove all these defects of character." *BRB p. 207*

We may have balked at the words "character defects." Wouldn't a more appropriate term be "character defenses?" Didn't they get us through an unlivable situation? Wasn't the destruction we experienced part and parcel of surviving a hostile environment?

But whether we call them defects or defenses, when we get to ACA we finally realize they don't work in our lives anymore, that we are ready to put them down. We begin to ask our Higher Power to remove these things as we are ready to give them up. The process becomes intuitive as we continue to work the Steps, become sponsors, and see the positive effects the program has on ourselves and others.

We shed our coping mechanisms as we see them for what they really are. We can't believe we haven't seen them before, but now we know and won't go back. This new way of life is based on accountability. We cultivate our inner loving parent and show our Inner Child we can be trusted. Just as a healthy parent sets safe boundaries for a child, we set boundaries for ourselves. Our hurt parts no longer run the show. Our Inner Child walks into the love and flourishes.

On this day I become willing to examine and remove the next defect that I'm tired of carrying around.

Balance

"We can connect with a power greater than ourselves and find balance." BRB p. 306

As we practice our recovery program, we come to know "balance." We start to learn what we can or can't handle, when to rest and when we can move ahead. As we search for a pace that works best for us, our ups and downs are no longer so wild and out-of-control. "Easy Does It" is now our recovery mantra.

If we get impatient at times, we recognize that it may take time for us to be ready to make certain changes. We learn acceptance.

Although it's important to keep challenging ourselves, we cannot force ourselves to recover faster. Some issues are deeper than others. We look to a power greater than ourselves to find the patience to accept however long it takes to get there. Whether we are slower or faster, it is our reality, and that can change over time. If the nervous person next to us seems to want to race to the finish line, we affirm our resolve to move at a healthy pace.

On this day I practice gentleness and acceptance as a way of finding a balanced recovery. I acknowledge that the pace at which I recover is what's right for me at this moment.

Dissociation

"In some cases the stored hurt creates a dissociative effect in the adult. The adult child has dissociated from his or her body." BRB p. 17

As children we learned to go outside of ourselves to relieve the pain of whatever was happening in the moment. Being the object of our parents' vicious verbal and/or physical attacks hurt terribly, but many of us also experienced abuse at the hands of family "friends" and siblings that continued for years. We learned to be "somewhere else" when that happened. We were afraid to say anything because we feared the abandonment of whatever tenuous relationships we had.

As a result, many of us became adults who feared authority. If we were afraid of our father, we may have become fearful of men. If our mother was the perpetrator, we were fearful of women. In spite of this, we wanted these people to love us. When they were unhappy with us, we became helpless children, unable to verbalize our side of the story. We lost our autonomy.

Today we recognize our patterns. We know what's happening when it happens. We have a choice not to use our childhood survival skills. Instead, ACA affirms for us that we are adults and our feelings matter. We do not need approval from others. We own who we are. We can ask for what we really want, instead of seeking approval and being people-pleasers.

On this day I will listen carefully to my heart. I will speak up and voice my feelings, knowing that no abandonment is more painful than when I abandon my True Self.

Beyond Survival

"By moving beyond survival, we realize that lost dreams or wishes can reemerge." BRB p. 429

We ask our Higher Power to help us realize our true potential by discovering our True Selves – the ones we were meant to be. We live in the moment, finding both the strength to be gentle with ourselves and the insight to recognize when we are being critical of ourselves or others.

ACA's Solution tells us we can restage our childhood by being our own loving parent. What a healthy sounding way to change the effects of growing up in an alcoholic or otherwise dysfunctional home. These beautiful words fill us with hope that there is indeed a way to reparent ourselves out of the shame, fear and emotional pain ingrained in our being.

As we put these words into action, we learn to be gentle with ourselves, alleviating much of our self-imposed stress. We touch base with and nurture our Inner Child, finding that this is time well spent. We come to understand that we cannot truly love others until we can love ourselves. This becomes a recovery goal that we practice daily. We give ourselves gentle positive affirmations. We know the seed of love was planted in our souls by our Higher Power, and our True Selves will allow that love to grow and flourish.

On this day I will connect with my Inner Child to recapture a positive memory or dream, and live it as an adult. However small this dream or memory seems, I recognize its impact on making me a new person.

Reparenting

"The first step in reparenting ourselves involves recognizing the loving voice inside." BRB p. 298

Growing up in a dysfunctional family was chaotic. We walked on egg shells, waited for the other shoe to drop, or held our breath and waited for the war to start. In the morning – after a brutal night – everybody pretended like nothing had happened.

When we first came to ACA, many of us were angry, defensive and at the end of our rope. We were either in the middle of chaos or in deep isolation. We knew full well what it felt like to be on this emotional roller coaster of life: one minute up, the next minute down.

What we learn in this program is that showing up and doing the work is critical. As we learn the value of surrender, acceptance, love and forgiveness, we begin to build a strong foundation for a better way of life. We learn to reparent ourselves, which means we become our own loving parent who provides our Inner Child with what we didn't receive from our families. It's like starting fresh, almost like being reborn.

On this day I am grateful for what ACA has taught me about the value of my choices and how to reparent myself. Each day I start fresh and give my Inner Child only positive messages.

Workplace Roles

"To get help, I would manipulate my co-workers by playing a role, such as being overly nice, being the victim, or volunteering to do something for them." BRB p. 420

We pandered to others at work, just as we had in our abusive families. Sometimes we didn't even know we were doing it until it was too late, and then we had to live with the consequences of having given away our power. This was a familiar scenario. We were re-creating our childhoods.

As we find our voice in ACA, we are no longer satisfied to play the same roles we've been used to. Even though we are sometimes afraid of what comes next, we are learning to walk into the unknown, one day at a time. Whether or not our path is the same as others in our meetings, we are united in our common bond – our desire to heal with the help of the 12 Steps. They give us a structure for living that we never had before.

We begin to carry the Steps and the program with us to work where people can find themselves in meetings without even knowing it. We are setting boundaries and approach situations calmly and directly. As we uncover triggers that can still be activated, we work with our fellow travelers to discover their roots so that we no longer act out. We teach others how to treat us in a far different way than we have before.

On this day I choose to be my True Self with everyone I come in contact with.

Step Twelve

"Spiritually awake adult children understand the spiritual axiom which states: 'We must give away what we have to keep it.' This is one of the most selfless acts of love we can offer a confused world; however, we must love ourselves first to have something to give away." BRB p. 288

We who felt terribly lost and hopelessly confused, or bitterly angry and very sad for most of our lives experience a deep and lasting peace of mind from working the ACA program. Using the Steps, reparenting ourselves, and achieving a spiritual awakening feel so good. We are full of joy and want to share the wealth!

Our daily lives feature endless ways to share our True Selves with our families, co-workers and neighbors: everyone can potentially enjoy our recovery. Perhaps newcomers to our meetings benefit most from our spiritual awakening. They hear our emotional sobriety and sense our joy. Many come to meetings from a dark place and may be somewhat bewildered by the terminology and frank talk about deeply-held family secrets. They may never have heard anyone talk openly about these subjects *and* offer a Solution.

We are a very special group of folks whose experience, strength, and hope can light the way for others if we keep coming back and sharing that light. By remembering the slogan "First Things First," we transmit our recovery through a personal act of service – loving our True Selves.

On this day I will recall my early days in ACA and the wonderful gifts I have received: clarity and freedom. I will share my love for my True Self so that others may know hope.

Other Laundry List

"Our experience shows that the opposites [of the Laundry List] are just as damaging as the counterpart." BRB p. 8

Realizing the damaging effects of the Other Laundry List gives many of us our early sense of frustration with the ACA program. Once the elation of finally finding a group of people who get that we were affected by our childhoods eventually fades, we start the slow process of admitting that we may have unconsciously done the very same things to those around us that were done to us. This is a hard reality to accept, but it is the necessary ground breaking that allows our spiritual foundation to be poured on honest footing. With time, we realize we were in denial about our actions. The behaviors that served as a protective way of getting through our traumatic childhoods did not serve us well as adults. We had become used to beating ourselves up and acting out.

ACA suggests that we reparent ourselves and break the harmful cycle we've found ourselves in. With the support of our meetings and fellow traveler, the work we do helps us feel embraced by our inner loving parent and our Higher Power. We can now allow the process of coming out of denial and into spiritual consciousness to slowly and gently unfold as we recover buried feelings and memories that drove our True Self into hiding.

On this day I admit that not only was I affected by the dysfunction, but that I also affected those around me. And I will practice being gentle and loving of my True Self as I continue to awaken spiritually.

Fear

"Adult children often live a secret life of fear." BRB p. 10

Every day individuals use faith to overcome fear. As polar opposites, fear and faith cannot occupy the same space. Fear involves a tightening of the senses whereas faith requires a complete release of them.

The ACA recovery program teaches us to identify and expose our fears to the light of day. We accomplish this with the loving support of others and our Higher Power. We do this in a safe environment where no one judges us for our past, for our fears, or for the ingrained reactions we carry from our childhoods.

Most of us go through life waiting to exhale, waiting to not feel defined by the position we hold, our possessions, or someone else's concept of who we should be. We have given our fear a lot of power to control our reactions. But we are exhausted by all this "work" and want to feel peace and serenity in our lives.

ACA gives us the chance to feel free to be the person we were meant to be, someone who is loved and respected for who we are, not what we do. As we strengthen our belief in our Higher Power, we free ourselves from our fears and stop believing our staunchest critic, our false self. We become our own loving, nurturing parent.

On this day I will be aware of any fear that encroaches on my ability to focus on recovery. With the loving support of my fellow ACAs and my Higher Power I will release that fear and feel at peace.

Shame

"Shame blinds us to the fact that love is inside each of us waiting to be discovered." BRB p. 168

We are often broken when we come to ACA. Through denial, we don't even know what we don't know. It takes time to realize how badly bruised (emotionally and sometimes physically) we were as kids. Shame ruined our sense of self. We had a self when we were born, but it was chipped away day after day until we seemed to be in shreds. There was little left but the reflection of our parents' hateful and frightening words and actions.

Some of us may have felt confused when we started recovery as we were told to reach inside for our self-worth. We didn't know that we had any and we doubted ourselves at every turn. Even though we felt hopeless, we hung onto the words we heard in the meetings. We saw others recovering and it felt hopeful. It helped to read the literature on a daily basis, and eventually we felt a shift happening.

We continued our Step work, going to meetings, relying on a Higher Power and reaching our Inner Child. We began to truly see our value. No longer defined by the shaming voices of the past, we had a new image of ourselves – a true image of the valuable person we always were.

On this day I look at myself through the eyes of recovery, not through the eyes of my caretakers from childhood. I see the love inside me that continues to grow.

Trait Seven

"We get guilt feelings when we stand up for ourselves instead of giving in to others." BRB p. 15

As children, many of us felt we were always wrong. Our parents/caretakers were quick to point out our mistakes, and seldom if ever pointed out what we did right.

As adults, we approach many problems, still with the assumption we are wrong. With that comes the assumption that others must be right. When asked our opinion, we often vacillate, attempting to read the face of the person we're speaking to so we can decide which response matches their opinion. Sound exhausting? It is!

In ACA, we learn about boundaries, that they need to be both communicated and upheld. So we start setting boundaries. But then comes the hard part: enforcing them. When we try to do so, we may immediately feel guilty, start second-guessing ourselves, and fear the other person will now think less of us. That guilt can undermine our recovery.

But with the help of our Higher Power and our fellow travelers, we learn to get past those feelings and stand up for ourselves. It's a process with some trial and error, but as we experience success, we start to feel empowered to be the person we were always meant to be.

On this day I know any guilt I feel for not giving in to others will pass, and my recovery will be strengthened by my ability to value myself.

Service

"Humility comes from God and is a sibling of anonymity, a foundational principle of the Twelve Steps and the Twelve Traditions. Through anonymity, we practice service with love."
BRB p. 223

In our families, humility and humiliation often got confused and led us to either become very passive, aggressive, or passive-aggressive. In working the Twelve Steps and Twelve Traditions, we are given a different definition of humility. In ACA, humility is about being the one we were supposed to be before our families infected us with their dysfunction and before we recycled that dysfunction in our own lives. It is about being our True Selves.

Anonymity is naturally confused with our alcoholic/dysfunctional family's desire to keep secrets. The difference is that in ACA, we don't share what others say or tell who was at our meetings as a way of giving security to each other. Knowing this allows us to feel safe to share our own story. When we are tempted to judge, ridicule, or speak of someone else, we are reminded that through the practice of protecting the anonymity and confidences of our fellow ACAs, we now have a higher purpose, a healthy limit that gives life rather than diminishes it.

The possibility of performing service in ACA flows powerfully from our understanding of these principles in our lives. The newcomer feels it, the old-timer appreciates it, and our Higher Power loves it.

On this day, love for my fellow ACAs, humility, and anonymity will provide me with a positive motivation for the service I may choose to give to ACA.

Promise Six

"We will enjoy feeling stable, peaceful, and financially secure."
BRB p. 591

Chaotic, unsettled, and on the verge of financial ruin. For many of us these were the undercurrents flowing through our families. The river of alcoholism or dysfunction coursed its way through every aspect of our lives, leaving indelible imprints on our makeup. We came to ACA to learn how we had experienced this as children, and how as adults we unconsciously and regrettably had recreated the same conditions, only to feel helpless and bewildered by our current circumstances.

With our Higher Power's guidance, we have been given a program that helps us first understand, then experience the hidden circumstances that set us up to seek out these alcoholic and dysfunctional conditions. Like a dredge boat, the Steps and reparenting allow us to dig out the river bed, change the river's course, and reduce the rapids to a sleepy river, naturally guiding us to soft sandy shores of stability, peacefulness, and financial security.

Though there may still be occasional choppy waters, we realize that the program is like a huge unbreakable inner tube that allows us to ride out most of the daily challenges, so long as we are willing to trust, hold onto, and apply the spiritual principles we have learned and practiced.

On this day I will allow the full remembrance of my childhood conditions, use the program to reset my course, and enjoy feeling stability, peace, and financial security.

Healing

"There is no Healing Without Feeling" BRB p. 52

For so many of us, we learned to feel helpless and even hopeless, like giving up was the only intelligent way to endure our childhoods. This hopelessness is part of what feeds the depression we experience as adults. It may seem paradoxical, but in ACA we learn that we need to experience our grief in order to alleviate our depression. It may only be through first-hand experience that we can understand how this works.

There is a difference between the stagnant quality of hopelessness and the flowing quality of grief work. The former seems like a permanent state. It drags us down and makes us feel like there's no way out. The latter seems more like a temporary phase on the way to acceptance, integration, and peace. One never seems to say goodbye, while the other is about the courage to say goodbye to the losses we've sustained and all the things we cannot change.

The thought of doing grief work, of feeling the pain of our past, may seem daunting, but in ACA we come to know that this is the balm that heals our ruptured souls.

On this day I have the courage to grieve my past in order to say hello to the present and the future.

Step One

"Recovery from the effects of an alcoholic and dysfunctional upbringing is a process, not an event." BRB p. 124

"Read my book and you can change your life overnight!" "Come to my seminar and I'll give you everything you need!" We hear things like this all the time. And many of us have bought those books and attended those seminars because we were looking for the quick fix, one that would cause us to suddenly change our dysfunctional lives into what we always thought they should be. Maybe we also heard people say that if we wanted something badly enough, we could make it happen. But we often missed the part about how things worth having take work.

When we came to ACA, maybe we thought *it* could be our quick fix. We might have seen the 12 Steps as a 'once and done' program of recovery where we'd suddenly be cured.

But as we open our minds and embrace the Promises, we begin to really examine our lives. We need to understand where our dysfunctional behaviors came from. And knowing how long it took us to develop them helps us realize that it will probably take some time for us to change those behaviors. We begin to really internalize the fact that recovery is a process. And the ACA process of recovery works if we work it!

On this day I will look for ways that help me make even small changes. I am willing to give my recovery the time it deserves because I'm worth it!

Newcomers

"There is great joy awaiting you to watch a frightened or foggy newcomer attend his or her first meeting and watch that person open up." BRB p. 293

When we arrived at our first ACA meeting, we weren't sure what to expect. Very nervously, we walked in and found a place to sit anyway. Some of what they read made no sense. Our minds went in and out of focus. The Laundry List got our attention, and people's shares brought up a bundle of feelings. There were rules about sharing, and we were pretty nervous to make a mistake, so some of us didn't share. Silence felt safe and familiar. Some of us did share, either simply stating facts, or like a gushing faucet, unable to turn off.

Timidly we wondered, "Could this be our answer?" We attended more meetings. We got to know a few faces and we learned their stories.

We opened up slowly. Now and then, we chatted with members after the meeting or in between meetings by phone. Before we knew it, these people felt like family. We joined together and supported each other as we all recovered from our childhood effects.

When newcomers walk in, perhaps looking dazed and afraid, we smile and welcome them while remembering we were once in their shoes.

On this day I will remember how I felt when I started ACA. I admire my courage and dedication, just as I do for everyone who walks in the door of my meeting.

Non-Dominant Hand

"After introducing ourselves to the child within, we can ask other questions. We write out the question with our dominant hand and write the reply with the other hand." BRB p. 305

We used to be afraid of our feelings. We *thought* we knew how we felt. We knew all about how others felt at all times, but we never developed the discipline of listening to ourselves because we were punished in our families for doing so. Some of us recreated that same punishing silence within ourselves in our work and romantic relationships.

When the hurt becomes too great, we are willing to go to any lengths to recover. We do things that are scary because we are building trust with our sponsor, fellow travelers, and our Higher Power. We seek the answers to our past, however we can find them. Non-dominant handwriting is an important tool in getting to early memories. We try answering questions by writing in crayon with our non-dominant hand. It has worked for others before us.

Most importantly, we are building trust with those voices inside us that have needed to speak for longer than long. They want to contact us and discharge the poison they have been holding back to save us from pain. We start to feel safer as we begin to heal and become ready to hear "our history."

On this day I will trust the messages I get doing non-dominant handwriting, because what is said true for that part of me. I will listen without trying to push the feelings back down. I will give the words inside me a space to breathe.

Grief Work

"Grief work can take many forms and can bring some of the greatest rewards of the program. Some grief work involves journaling in which we write about incidents in our life and reflect on the feelings we had at that moment." BRB p. 202

We ignored our grief because it did not seem like it belonged to us. For years, we didn't feel we had permission to feel sad or to experience loss. In our families we were taught to not talk, not trust, and not feel. No one ever sat us down and told us that explicitly, but we knew that was the rule.

One of the tools we use in recovery is the art of journaling all of the things we've been holding in for so long in order to help us get in touch with our Inner Child. An effective writing variation is the non-dominant handwriting exercise described in the Big Red Book. It is a powerful way of getting clues to stored trauma in our bodies. We allow that hurt to surface and provide ourselves the space to heal, to cry, to bleed, to sob, to laugh and to experience the joy we were robbed of as children and even adults. It's one of the ways we get to the other side of our grief.

On this day I will make time to journal about my feelings as a way of expressing the grief I hold from my childhood.

Tradition Twelve

"We protect personal anonymity at all costs to keep our meetings safe. By keeping ACA safe, we strengthen our group unity, and we attract new members who are an important life source for the fellowship." BRB p. 552

Perhaps no Tradition means as much to the ACA program as Tradition Twelve. This is where we protect each other by not mentioning who we see or what we hear at meetings. This anonymity is the spiritual foundation that strengthens our program.

We share only our first names for very good reasons:

- It helps newcomers feel more comfortable about sharing intimate details of their lives. Privacy is respected.

- Anonymity is a great equalizer. As garden-variety ACAs, our job title, education, and where we live mean nothing. It doesn't matter. We are all in meetings for the same reason – to recover from the effects of our family dysfunction.

- Those who refer others to ACA can feel comfortable knowing anyone who attends will not be required to give personal information. In fact, they don't have to say anything if they so choose.

By protecting anonymity, we are reminded that we are part of a spiritual program. Anonymity is also related to humility, which is one of our spiritual principles. Humility reminds us we are all equals. The humility we have learned helps keep the doors open.

On this day I will honor Tradition Twelve by honoring the anonymity and confidences of those I see at meetings. This allows the doors of ACA to stay open for all who may follow.

Tolerating the Unacceptable

"We will see how our low self-esteem has us judging ourselves mercilessly, giving others the benefit of the doubt, and tolerating inappropriate behavior." BRB p. xxi

Many of us were taught that it was virtuous to "put up with" whatever was doled out, shut up about whatever was going on, and deny our feelings in the process. This led us to doubt our own perceptions, which led us to doubt our own self-worth. Because we actually survived, some of us interpreted our ability to deal with unacceptable situations as resilience.

Unfortunately, we didn't learn that it was acceptable to set boundaries and limits, and that it was okay to say "no" to unacceptable behavior. This is what we learn in ACA. We don't have to be stoic, or pretend that things don't bother us when they do. We don't have to apologize for stuff that's not ours or feel ashamed when we feel triggered. We have the right to our reality, our experiences, and our feelings.

With the help of our recovery support system, we are now learning to trust, to feel, and to talk; this is a wonderful way to live. We can surround ourselves with people who listen to us and acknowledge our feelings. We can be more human, vulnerable, and safe.

On this day I remind myself that being resilient (tolerating abuse) is not the way I want to live my life. I can relax and trust safe people.

Defects of Character

"You are not a defective character. You have defects of character."
BRB p. 188

Many of us have difficulty hearing the word "defect" and applying it to ourselves because of the way we were raised. First, if we ever said we had a problem, that was usually how we got in trouble. We were criticized for who we were, so the last thing we wanted to do was point out that there was something wrong. Second, most of our "faults" or "defects" became a part of us as adults because a parent demanded we act a certain way. We were not to blame for acquiring these habits, but they really get in our way today.

In ACA, it is important that we acknowledge what is happening in our present lives – the habits we have that perpetuate the family dysfunction. We get honest about their impact to ourselves and others in order to recover from them.

We realize that a defect is something that stops our positive momentum, and we all have them. But that doesn't mean we are defective. Our habits will change as we recover. But first we must see them, admit them, and work them out using the Steps and all the tools now available to us.

On this day I will gratefully and joyously remember that my defects are losing their hold on me as my recovery grows.

Boundaries

"The level of choice we develop in ACA is proportional to the integrity of our boundaries. The more we let go, the stronger our boundaries become. This is an ACA paradox: Letting go creates stronger boundaries." BRB p. 148

Most of us grew up in families without boundaries. It seemed like everyone was in each other's business, passing judgment and telling each other what to think and feel. Even if we had understood the concept of boundaries, we wouldn't have been able to set them for ourselves in the midst of the dysfunction. Yet on some level we often instinctively knew that our boundaries were being violated, whether it was emotional or physical boundaries.

As adults, we were often the boundary violators because of the enmeshment we learned from our families. We simply didn't understand how boundaries worked, and we didn't know how to honor them.

In ACA, we learn that a lack of boundaries is usually about control and manipulation. It's never as simple as it seems, and it takes work to uncover the root of what's really happening. But as soon as we begin to deal with the underlying issues and release the hold they have over us, our boundaries are strengthened; we let go and offer other people the opportunity to find their own way without our help. We learn to separate what's really important and what's not in order to survive as healthy adults.

On this day I will remember that when I choose to let go and not to involve myself where I don't belong, I am creating stronger boundaries for myself.

Emotional Eating

"An ACA relapse can bring a return of self-harming behavior. The behavior can include emotional eating, drug use, compulsive sexual relationships, or other harmful behaviors." BRB p. 391

As children, we were not allowed to feel our feelings. It wasn't safe to say we felt sad, scared, or angry. Ignoring our feelings really hurt us inside. To relieve our pain, many of us turned to an addictive behavior, which for some of us was finding comfort in food. But this emotional eating caused us to gain weight and feel ashamed of our ballooning bodies. Family members and others then made fun of us. It was an unfair cycle: food comforted us, but that comfort caused even more problems than we originally had. We tried everything we could think of, but nothing worked permanently to stop this cycle. We were crippled with self-hate.

The beauty of the ACA program lies in its virtually guaranteed healing of our childhood damage. We find our comfort in the practice of the 12 Steps, work that restores our stolen identities. As we recover, decades of stuffed feelings and buried memories emerge. Our Higher Power helps us handle these emotions and accept ourselves. Our loving parent guides our Inner Child through each emotion with the gentleness we crave and the dignity we deserve.

On this day, when powerful emotions surface, I will remember that I have the right tools ready and waiting. I can use the Steps, the meetings, and the telephone to help me find true comfort.

Conflicting Feelings – Holidays

"We knew our parents would forget or would trivialize birthdays or holidays." BRB p. 296

The conflicting emotional shift of any holiday can trigger a tsunami of pent-up feelings that cannot be reined in by any sentimental holiday movie, song, or festive decorations.

Sorting out our conflicted feelings and perceptions is not easy. If it were, we wouldn't find ourselves attending meetings, going to therapy, and doing Step work. But we know these tools help us unravel the interwoven strands of our childhood experiences so we can understand how they affect us today.

Through recovery, holidays can provide an opportunity to reevaluate our childhood experiences and how they influence us today. We find that the disappointment we felt because of our parents' attitudes back then may have led us to trivialize present holidays to avoid our own pain and loss.

By doing ACA work, we are able to examine not only our dysfunctional attitudes and behaviors, but also those of our families. From an emotionally sober place, we may uncover the roots of the coping mechanisms we created to make sense of the nonsensical. We can now put them into their proper perspective as relics from the past to be viewed in a glass case as a distant vestige of how things were, not of how they have to be today.

On this day I will examine the conflicting feelings I acquired during my most vulnerable years, recognizing how things were and knowing there is now another way to live.

Self-Doubt

"We were taught to doubt ourselves so it became natural to believe that we are wrong, defective, or uninformed."BRB p. 302

Many of us learned early to doubt what we knew we saw because our parents shamed us into believing we were incapable of knowing. At first we knew the difference, but eventually we believed that our hunger pangs and other feelings were our imagination.

When we enter the rooms of recovery, we are ready to release this way of thinking. We begin to see that we no longer need to live in the survival mode of our childhood. We are ready to wipe the slate clean and write a new future.

In ACA, we meet people who will support us as we take a second look at our past. By working the Steps and using the tools of the program, we gradually challenge the stories, roles, beliefs and negative, distorted thinking that has colored so much of our lives. We begin to accept the reality of our childhoods and that we did not cause the problems.

We now get to write our own future. We no longer have to be defined by our original family roles or by the toxic thoughts, words and actions of those around us. We get to choose what we want from life, how we see ourselves, and decide which filters we will use to perceive the world.

On this day I have the courage to face my past and the faith to write my future. I no longer doubt what I know to be true.

Caretaking

"...we do not have to participate in their dysfunction. We are free to live our own lives." BRB p. 123

As children, we may have had to literally be our "brother's keeper" because in the dysfunction we were given responsibilities far beyond our years. And we didn't learn to take care of ourselves in the process because we were so focused on others.

As adults, many of us continued this pattern: ignoring our own needs and being drawn to people we could take care of. We told ourselves we were okay because we were caring, compassionate people. And in return, we often received praise and adulation. People said things like, "Isn't she wonderful?" "What would we do without him?" This fed the hole in our soul for a while.

But then the praise stopped coming unless we asked for it. The satisfaction we thought we were experiencing diminished. We may even have started to blame others for being ungrateful.

When we joined ACA, we began a program of rigorous honesty and learned to recognize what we were doing. Yes, people took advantage of us, but we taught them to treat us that way. And now, with the help of ACA, our Higher Power, and our new family, we have begun to undo that. We are letting others take responsibility for themselves.

On this day I will continue taking care of and valuing myself because I am worth it! I will give others the gift of taking care of themselves.

Tradition Six

"Tradition Six keeps ACA free of outside influences and reminds us not to lend the ACA name to any related facility or outside enterprise. By following this Tradition we also avoid money and prestige issues that would hinder our primary purpose." BRB p. 521

Our program cannot be bought or sold. We deal with spiritual matters that are freely given and freely received. We are each entrusted with keeping the program clear of any financial motives.

There are temptations to affiliate ACA with a multitude of programs that deal with family issues. Some of them may even prove financially profitable. We find that such arrangements may prove so distracting that we forget the focus of our program.

The problems of money, property, and prestige can be very hard to resolve, and the ACA program practices a form of corporate poverty that frees us from the financial strings that would pull us away from our primary purpose. We cannot serve two masters while doing the work that only an ACA can do.

This Tradition also gives us guidance for organizing our own lives so that we can keep our focus on what's important, while avoiding distractions about money, property, and prestige.

On this day I will observe the Sixth Tradition and help my group focus on our primary purpose, turning away from any distractions from outside sources.

Not Alone

"On our journey, we need the assistance of a trusted friend with knowledge of recovery." BRB p. 379

The ACA Big Red Book tells us we're trained with 72 seasons (18 years) of learned survival skills that turned into dysfunctional behavior as adults. Knowing this makes it seem unreasonable to expect total recovery in a few meetings, a few hours with the ACA Workbook or even a cover-to-cover read of the Big Red Book.

In cases of divorce, it's said that it takes a year of grieving to recover for every five years of marriage. If we translate that formula to our circumstances of grieving our ACA "soul rupture," it becomes even more understandable that recovery is an ongoing process. And it can't truly happen without the help of our Higher Power and fellow travelers who are able to lead us away from years of frozen emotion.

ACA recovery has its ups and downs, no matter how hard we work at it. So it's important to know we can relapse, just as in other Twelve Step programs. However, an ACA relapse can take us into periods of sadness and isolation. This becomes less frequent as we continue to give ourselves permission to be human and to make mistakes. We learn to put down the mirror of harsh self-judgment to let life and serenity in.

On this day I will remember that recovery is a journey that I don't have to take alone. I will trust other ACAs who are also seeking the truth to help me.

July

"Our experience shows that you cannot recover in isolation." BRB p. 127

Applying the Program

"ACA is a proven program that can help us in every area of our lives if we apply it." BRB p. 415

As we enter theaters and sport stadiums, we are offered a program. If we attend a conference, we will likely check the program they give us to see if there are topics of interest. Programs occupy a prominent place in our lives; we know they can offer us valuable insight into what we might experience at an event, such as who is on the team roster or whether we will see a star or a stand-in.

For ACAs, there is a program available that offers an anchor for our spiritual and emotional lives. It gives us the 'roadmap' missing from our childhoods that were lost in dysfunction. We've already tried navigating through life on our own. But we've fallen short of our intended destinations and experienced stormy weather with our friends, co-workers and family.

In ACA, we have found the prescription for living the rest of our lives, from the Twelve Steps to the Twelve Traditions, from finding a sponsor to being a sponsor, and from reading the BRB to doing service work. There is no trauma, no misfortune, nor virtually any life problem too great that it cannot be placed in its honest and true perspective by working the ACA program.

On this day I rededicate myself to my program and the pursuit of the priceless gift of serenity.

Asking for Help

"At this juncture, the adult child usually isolates or becomes involved in busy work to avoid asking for help." BRB p. 66

We took care of everyone else for years, learning to be as invisible as possible, both physically and emotionally. Our worth was not based on who we were, but on what we could accomplish or do for others. We became so used to the struggle, that we created it when it wasn't already there. Living in a hurricane of activity was normal for us. We started to avoid quiet because that's when we heard the painful voices, those that cried from deep within and said, "You are not good enough."

As we learn to live in a different reality, we begin to recognize our self-worth. We see that our very existence is a gift from our Higher Power. We learn to reach out to our fellow travelers for help and feel love and acceptance. We allow others to take care of themselves, and we choose those who can do so to be our companions.

We become willing to own all of our feelings, not just the happiness or joy we are feeling, but also the anger and even rage when they come up. We recognize them as gifts that can lift us out of sandpits of grief and shame. We are careful not to harm others with these "gifts," but instead use them as a gateway for healing our woundedness.

On this day I will no longer do other people's work. I will feel the freedom of being responsible for myself, recognizing when I need guidance.

Step Seven

"Humbly asked God to remove our shortcomings." BRB p. 217

As we begin to find peace in ACA, we listen for when the wheels get squeaky and learn to seek appropriate help, knowing that we don't have to do this alone. We see our Higher Power everywhere we go, especially in the people around us in our meetings.

We are no longer fearful. Our shortcomings are being removed and they no longer define us. We are not a collection of wrongs. We realize that recovery is a process – that there is no race to the finish line.

But we don't take the slow route either. We have sobered up to the grim reality of the effects of dysfunction in our families and have decided we are out of their game. It no longer pays any dividends. We have been on that other side for so long and we simply don't want to be there anymore. The way we related to the world no longer works.

We see the results of our efforts in recovery, and we like ourselves better as we allow the process to work within us. We begin to attract healthier people, leaving behind the dysfunctional relationships that show no promise. There is nothing better than this new feeling as we move into the future. We are walking out of the fog of dysfunction towards who we truly are.

On this day I will continue on this journey to work with my Higher Power to remove my shortcomings. I choose to be healthy.

Long-Term Trauma

"Through the first 18 years of our lives, our families had 6,570 days to shame, belittle, ignore, criticize, or manipulate us during the formative years of our being." BRB p. 105

How could we have turned out any other way? We grew up in dysfunction, and it's not our fault we were affected by it. We were just children. All we knew of the world was what we were shown by our parents – the people we were hardwired to trust and emulate. It's not our fault we didn't find a way to stop the abuse. We learned the language of abuse, just as we learned to speak our native tongue – it was automatic.

We're not whining, over-thinking it, or making mountains out of molehills. Our Laundry List Traits are a legitimate reaction to long-term trauma.

The good news is that something magical happens when we accept we are powerless over our childhood trauma and its effect on us. It doesn't mean we give up and let it have power over us. The opposite happens. It loses power over us. We begin to have a choice about how we respond when the dysfunction manifests itself in our adult lives. It's like admitting there's a leak in the roof, and now we can put a bucket on the floor, change out of our wet clothes, and fix the roof. And we can do it without guilt because the leak was already there before we came along.

On this day I embrace the freedom that comes from accepting there is nothing I could have done to prevent the dysfunction I grew up in and the effect it has had on me.

Inner Loving Parent

"Learn to validate yourself by becoming your own loving parent."
BRB p. xxiv

In ACA, we pay attention to how we talk to ourselves in our heads. Mindfulness helps us stop those thoughts that say, "What's wrong with me?" and replace them with, "I have a lot of things going for me. I am amazing!" As we work our program and make progress, we become our own loving parent and learn to take care of ourselves by affirming our growth.

It seems second nature for us to be critical of ourselves – even about our recovery work. We can tell ourselves that we aren't doing it right, or it's taking us too long. But when we see children learning to read, is it okay to criticize them along the way? Or do they need to hear encouragement and support, and have someone say positive things like, "Outstanding! You're doing great. Keep it up." Most of us didn't hear these words in our dysfunctional families, but we can learn to say them to ourselves now.

Our inner loving parent can tell us some of the most wonderful words a parent can say to a child, words a child remembers for a lifetime, words that help a child know they are okay the way they are. "I love you and I am proud of you." This is what we've been waiting to hear.

On this day I will capture positive moments, feel proud of myself for the work I am doing, and tell myself I am loved for who I am.

Change in the Workplace

"By using our program and the support of our fellowship, we learn that we can affect changes in our working lives." BRB p. 425

At work many of us noticed we were extremely uncomfortable. When we talked about our job difficulties, an ACA member asked if we'd ever read Chapter 14, "Taking Our Program to Work."

When we read it, we couldn't believe how true it was. Again, ACA literature told us things about ourselves we didn't know. We started to see ourselves and our jobs with fresh eyes. We learned that we related to people at our jobs as though they were our families of origin. We saw them through the filter of our Laundry List Traits, and we acted accordingly with each person, depending on their mood and/or who they reminded us of from our family.

By relying on a Higher Power, the support of our meetings and fellow travelers, and our continuing work on the Steps, we now notice little changes here and there. We are able to pause and ask ourselves, "Is this big reaction I'm feeling based on the here and now? What does it remind me of?" We use our recovery tools and call or email our recovery supporters during these times to process our experiences. Before we know it, our recovery is present in all parts of our lives, especially on the job.

On this day I will remember that I am safe and important, whether I am home, at work, or somewhere in between.

People-Pleasing

"By transforming our people-pleasing manner, we do not stop caring about others. However, we stop going over the line to ensure that we are never abandoned." BRB p. 112

As children, we looked to others such as our parents or teachers for approval. Doing so often kept us safe. Over time, this practice taught us to abandon our own sense of worth in favor of someone else's external measure of our value. Without others' approval, we felt like failures.

Through ACA, we learn to listen to our own inner loving parent's voice, no longer needing to rely on others to give us a sense of ourselves. We learn to be true to ourselves, acting in ways that are aligned with the core values, beliefs and feelings that are becoming part of us. We seek no one's approval but our own.

We sometimes find that our new actions may cause conflict with others. But with confidence in our new inner compass and no longer fearing abandonment, we hold fast to our beliefs, speak our truths, and strengthen our sense of self. We no longer need external forces to justify our existence.

On this day I will listen to my inner loving parent and know that is all the approval I need for my thoughts and actions.

Willingness

"In ACA we become willing to apply what we learn in the program to our daily lives and to relationships." BRB p. 401

When we first got to ACA, some of us couldn't wait for recovery to be finished. How long was this going to take, because we had better things to do than hang out with damaged people. After all, our story wasn't that bad. We just wanted to fix the little things that were holding us back so we could get on with our real lives.

Now Step work and service are two of our favorite things to do. Creating a safe place for ourselves and others--to acknowledge the wounds we all carry--and then begin to grow is the most exciting adventure we have ever been on. The 12 Steps are a design for living that is better than anything else we have tried up to this point in our lives. We are grateful for those who came before us who kept the doors open.

In our homes and in our jobs we practice what we learn at meetings – like listening. We allow others to speak their truth. We learn not to control others and not let ourselves be controlled or manipulated. We trust that the principles of the program that have worked for so many others will continue to work for us in all our affairs. We are becoming fearless in our pursuit of a healthy life. We now have joy, and others can see that.

On this day I will be real in all that I do. By doing so, I make space for others to own their truths.

Siblings

"We are not responsible for rescuing, saving, or healing our parents or siblings who remain mired in family dysfunction. We can detach with love and begin the gradual process of learning about boundaries." BRB pg 102

Our relationships with our siblings were usually complicated growing up. If our parents were 'at war' with each other, it meant we were often 'at war' with each other. It's what we learned; it's what we lived!

As adults, still caught up in this all-consuming family dysfunction, we were in each other's business and knew what was best for the others, even if they didn't. We often gossiped about each other, formed alliances and competed with each other.

When we began to find a better life in ACA, some of us jumped right to the Twelfth Step and decided it was now our job to rescue our siblings because now we really knew the answers. But the Program tells us otherwise. If we are to find true recovery, we have to do the hard work for ourselves and detach from our family, setting healthy boundaries. If not, we'll continually struggle with ways to save them.

When we stop and really listen to ourselves, we see that doing these things is not what recovery is about. All of these "fixes" are no different than the way we've always operated. We learn to let go, realizing we can't heal them. We must release them to find their own way.

On this day I will remember that my true recovery lies in my ability to detach, set boundaries, and heal myself first

Codependence

"As adult children from various families, we focus on ourselves for the surest results. We gradually free ourselves from codependent or addictive relationships." BRB p. 60

Before we entered recovery, it seemed like our relationships were codependent or addictive. It's what we were used to; it's what we grew up with. If anyone wanted something different from us, we were uncomfortable because we didn't really understand what that "something" was. We could keep up the act for a short time, but the walls eventually went up. We had no role models for healthy give and take.

As we learn to focus on ourselves in ACA, at first it seems awkward. Most of us are not used to taking care of ourselves emotionally. Gradually we begin to see that we can walk away from those who still abuse us and we feel a sense of freedom that's new because we don't feel guilty.

We gather strength from those who have come before us in the program. We hear how they have faced difficult changes with faith and trust in their Higher Power and those they share their journey with. We see the promises of this program being fulfilled in others, and we now have the courage to ask for the guidance that's available.

On this day I release my codependent and addictive relationships in favor of those based on mutual respect. I will learn a new "dance" that fills me with life.

Trait Eight

"We became addicted to excitement." BRB p. 16

For most people, a lot of things can create excitement: seeing a new movie, having a favorite old friend visit, preparing for a holiday, shopping, getting a new pet, celebrating birthdays, and even sex. But the problem for many adult children is our need to create excitement in order to feel alive. Too often, this is done in a negative way that harms us and our relationships.

In adulthood, this addiction to excitement can play out in many ways, including starting frequent arguments with a spouse, having an affair that creates excitement and then pain, playing extreme sports because we crave the adrenaline rush, or using drugs or alcohol to feel "up." If we don't have a certain level of excitement in our lives on a regular basis, we feel like life is boring, something's just not right, we are missing out, or maybe we are just not loved.

In recovery, we can identify the ways in which we create excitement that harms us and our loved ones. We then learn to stop ourselves before we go over the line. This can give us a sense of calm that may seem uncomfortable at first, but we'll get used to it. This is part of learning who we are.

On this day I pray for the wisdom to identify negative excitement that I may create. I no longer wish to harm myself and others by this behavior.

Balanced Inventory

"In ACA we look at our parents' behavior, family roles, rules, messages, abuse, neglect, and how that affects us as adults. We balance the inventory of our family system with a thorough inventory of our own behavior." BRB p. 109

Step Four may be the first time many of us tell our whole story to someone else. This is a remarkable event, one that leaves us with a sense of wholeness we have never experienced before. The idea we may have been carrying around, that we were unlovable, is now slowly melting away.

One of the wonderful things about ACA is that our Fourth Step inventory helps us understand where we truly came from and who we're becoming. We accept all of what we were given so that we can decide what to keep. When we take our inventory we make it balanced, recognizing that we are now making our own choices; we are no longer blindly accepting what others have implanted in our minds. We don't have to carry all the abuse and neglect that were passed down to us generationally.

The balance we learn allows us to see where we need to go. We continue to keep the focus on ourselves and change what we can. We no longer look for temporary solutions to life's problems.

On this day I will trust my direction. I have begun to see more clearly that this new path I walk will give me the freedom I deserve.

Spiritual, not Religious

"We must remember that ACA is a spiritual and not religious program. Faith and religious conviction are not requirements for ACA membership. We avoid dogmatism and theological discussions, yet, a Higher Power is a key part of the ACA way of life." BRB p. 106

It often seems amazing that we can become so close to one another in our meetings, relying on each other for emotional support, and still have disparate views on what constitutes a Higher Power. This is because we have come together for a single reason: we recognize that our dysfunctional childhoods override everything else. We support each other for who we are because we have a commonality that unites us.

ACA does not endorse any religious view. As individuals, if we have our own religious view, we may not use ACA as a platform to try to convert others. If we do not have a religious view, we are not entitled to criticize another member's religious viewpoint. We practice tolerance for others.

All belief systems have one thing in common: they are spiritual in nature. Our personal spirituality and recognition of a Higher Power of our own understanding are what help guide us on our healing journey.

On this day I will remember that my spiritual beliefs are a vital part of my recovery; they need not match those of other people in the program.

Using Others

"As adult children, most of us have used a variety of relationships in an attempt to heal ourselves from the chronic sense of aloneness in our lives." BRB p. 173

We swam inside other people like a fish swims in water. This gave us some relief from the anxiety we felt when we were alone. Other people's problems, no matter how bad they were or how needy those faces became, were a tonic to our existence – a way to get out of ourselves. But we learned that we had become overly focused on others, using their dramas and excitement to energize us in unhealthy ways. This is how we realized we had an unhealthy dependence on excitement.

In recovery, we stop trying to fix others. We replace those relationships where we kept going in circles with healthier relationships with others in the program, recognizing the honesty that is available to us.

When we find an ACA sponsor or fellow traveler, it may be the first emotionally honest relationship we have ever had. From there, we learn to take our recovery out into the world and make friends with people who have the same qualities and integrity, people who have boundaries and can take care of themselves. At some point, we realize we've made the final turn – we now find overly needy people unattractive. We finally understand why people reacted to us the way they did before recovery.

On this day I will seek to connect to my Higher Power and connect through the healthy energy of others who want to heal both inside and outside of program.

Promise Seven

"We will learn how to play and have fun in our lives." BRB p. 591

Just as we learned to fear our alcoholic and dysfunctional families, we can now learn to play and enjoy ourselves. This does not mean playing solitary games on our computers, tablets, or game consoles.

A way that many of us learn to become more light-hearted is by finding real enjoyment in the company of other ACAs. While we maintain a certain structure in our meetings, we can also experience fellowship before or after the meetings and share good times. This may feel weird to some of us at first because we are learning to relate to people differently than we're used to, but as with the rest of the ACA program, daily practice helps us become more comfortable with the idea.

Laughter starts to flow more naturally as we begin to let our guard down. We become less concerned with saying the right thing and more concerned with just being in the moment. Where we once filled every waking moment with activity as a way to keep ourselves occupied, we can learn to become more of a *human being* than a *human doing*. We can now have fun because we are finally free from the fear of showing our True Self. Did you hear the one about two adult children who walk into a meeting…?

On this day I will practice playing and will enjoy having fun with others in a wholesome and positive way.

Service

"We are motivated to get out of ourselves and to be of service to others... We give back what has been given to us freely in ACA."
BRB p. 439

In our early ACA experience, we may have been skeptical, confused, angry, or sad. Certainly no one has ever come to ACA because things were working well. A physical, mental, and spiritual bottom usually brings us to ACA.

Having come to ACA meetings a few times, we may have caught a glimmer of hope that the ACA program may help us. After awhile, we may have asked someone for their number or had a cup of coffee with them to see if we might become fellow travelers.

As we reflect on those early days, we can only imagine what might have become of us had we not found an ACA meeting. Our thoughts may turn to those whose lives are similarly affected, and we would like for them to have the same opportunity for spiritual growth.

So we may decide to participate in the group's business meeting, or accept a service role at the group, Intergroup, or World Service level. Or maybe we feel most comfortable accepting the invitation to chat or have a cup of coffee with another ACA who is about to embark on this wonderful spiritual adventure. We decide our own best way to give back.

On this day I recall my early days and the progress I have made. In return, I will perform service in some way so that other ACAs may find this life-saving program.

Sexual Abuse

"We release the shame we have carried surrounding the sexual abuse." BRB p. 233

Those of us who were sexually abused often gravitate to self-destructive behaviors to numb the pain and shame. With meetings and the help of our Higher Power, we gradually shed some of the behaviors that keep us stuck. If we have acted out sexually, we learn respect for ourselves and others; if the use of pornography has brought us shame and guilt, we look honestly at its effect and let it go, one day at time; if we have numbed ourselves with "socially acceptable" pastimes, like TV and computer games, we learn to find balance.

Some of us who are connected financially to our perpetrators begin to take steps to become financially independent of them, letting go of their control.

In recovery, we honor our Inner Children who survived the abuse by learning how to play again, by giving them a voice and listening to them, especially around sexual thoughts. We let them know that it's okay to talk, to trust, and to feel. We let them know we are there for them, and that they come first – that they don't have to be sexual to be loved.

On this day I will remember that as I work my program, I am rescuing myself and no longer allowing the abuse to control my life.

Stored Trauma

"Clinical research strongly suggests that childhood trauma or neglect are stored in the tissue of the children. The emotional or physical trauma does not go away without an effort to address the original cause." BRB Page 17

"It's in your bones" they might have said. "There's something the matter with the whole family." These statements only beg the question that often gets overlooked, "Why?"

Though the trauma of our forefathers and foremothers is stored in us, then so too must be the restorative part of the body. In fact, when we work the Steps, reparent ourselves, attend meetings, and join with a fellow traveler, we are using some of the most powerful tools know to restore our bodies back to a balanced, natural condition. This is not easy and often takes considerable effort and persistence, and may even include an occasional or even a frequent ACA relapse.

However, there *is* no easier, softer way. The process of recovery involves real work and determination that pays dividends beyond our expectations. If we are willing to stay on this recovery journey, if we trust the Steps and Promises, our bodies can release the stored trauma, which brings us true relief. The miracle of recovery is the destination and we can get there.

On this day I will pay close attention to my body and the clues it gives me about my stored trauma. I reaffirm for myself that by using the Steps and reparenting myself, the trauma energy can be released so that I may experience a wholeness I could not have possibly imagined.

Balance

"We balance our experiences as children with the knowledge that we have a unique chance through ACA to break the cycle of family dysfunction." BRB p. 95

Many of our family members seemed to live from one reactive moment to the next. There was little, if any, thought given to planning ahead for possibilities and/or how best to approach situations. Some of us tried to change this pattern as adults, perhaps as we raised our own families. Maybe we became rigid when planning, to overcompensate for the chaos we had experienced, or we may have found ourselves frequently feeling overwhelmed. We did not seem to have the capacity to look at the big picture and act accordingly, and we consistently berated ourselves for this shortcoming.

When we find a new way to live in recovery, we work to erase old tapes and old ways of doing things. But ingrained habits do not disappear overnight. When we feel ourselves at either end of the reaction spectrum – too rigid or feeling overwhelmed – we open our new tool bag and find a way to center ourselves, whether it's through a phone call or using another tool of recovery. By doing so, we reinforce our resolve to live intentional lives. We find purpose and hope because of the balance we are able to integrate. This leads to the peace and serenity we have always deserved.

On this day I will pause and think about how I want to live my day. I affirm that I deserve to live the balanced life that I choose, not a life that simply happens to me.

Emotional Intoxication

"In his 'Next Frontier' article Bill [W.] wrote, 'If we examine every disturbance we have, great or small, we will find at the root of it some unhealthy dependency and its consequent unhealthy demand.'" BRB, page 628

Growing up in dysfunctional homes meant that chaos was normal. As a result, we may have become adults who could not feel at ease when things were calm. We may have craved drama and excitement on such a subconscious level that we were drawn to it without realizing the reason why.

In recovery, we gain the clarity to see that out of our craving for intensity, we were finding a form of comfort by continually recreating our childhood atmosphere. But even though this chaos felt familiar, recovery teaches us that our vulnerable and wounded child's needs were not being met.

By attending meetings and listening to the stories of other adult children, we learn that we are not alone. When we work the program, we cultivate two essential qualities in our lives: courage and self-esteem. Through the Twelve Steps we learn to let go and turn our will and our lives over to a Higher Power of our own understanding. When we do this, we find that gradually the desire for emotional intoxication will leave us.

On this day I free myself from the cycle of emotional intoxication by listening to my Higher Power's guidance. I deserve balance, which I get by practicing my program in all areas of my life.

Authority Figures

"Abuse from authority figures in childhood has left us on guard as adults about authority figures. We tend to place people in the category of authority figure when they may not be such a person." BRB p. 379

Fear of authority figures in our adult life can add unnecessary stress when old fears get triggered. As children, many of us were always on guard to not displease our parent or to find a hiding place when danger was present. One or both parents may have been experts at creating real or imagined fear in us.

Routinely, we now encounter others who have authority over us, either because of our jobs or theirs. Some of us also allow people to assume an authority role because we are afraid of conflict. It can even feel daunting when a parking attendant tells us we can't park "there," or a sales clerk tries to talk us into a different purchase. Our goal in recovery is to recognize these situations for what they are, and learn to act as adults.

To gain control over our lives, when we interact with someone in authority, we now do a quick internal check. Are we feeling fearful, angry, resentful, or timid? Are we putting our alcoholic parent's face on this person? If so, we stop and examine the situation from a new perspective. The interaction may not be pleasant, but it is *not* our childhood coming back to life.

On this day I will recognize when I am responding to authority figures with childhood reactions. I will now approach things from a new perspective as a recovering adult.

Therapy and the Twelve Steps

"The miraculous combination of therapy and working the Twelve Steps set me free from the prison of my childhood playpen to explore and experience my real and unique self." BRB p. 55

When we first came to ACA, some of us found it confusing and disorienting, but somehow comfortable. We may have taken a while to get started on working the Steps, but when we did, we saw changes in ourselves. It was so heartening that we were finding our True Identity. Sometimes, though, we wondered if we needed help beyond what we could ask of our fellow travelers.

We heard others occasionally mention that they saw a therapist, and that combining therapy with ACA was really helping them. We were surprised when a fellow traveler pointed out Chapter 16 in the BRB, "ACA and Therapy." It seemed clear that therapy could be a useful ACA tool for us. So we took a risk – we made a different type of phone call.

Before long, we realized that because we found a therapist who understood adult child issues, it was all working. Maybe we didn't find someone on the first try, but we had the courage to keep trying until we did.

We now see our recovery process move faster and deeper. Our courage in taking a risk is paying off. We feel gratitude that we love ourselves enough to seek this kind of help.

On this day I will pause to reflect on the value that therapy can have for my journey to help me find my unique True Self.

Grief and Childhood

"Genuine grieving for our childhood ends our morbid fascination with the past and lets us return to the present, free to live as adults. Confronting years of pain and loss at first seems overwhelming."
BRB p. 83

We may have been going to meetings for many years, lamenting the slings and arrows of our recovery life. Perhaps we thought we were "Living life on life's terms," – doing the best we could. But often progress seemed to come in dribs and drabs. This left us with a sense of frustration at the little spiritual progress we had made, despite our best efforts.

But what may have been missing was the willingness to genuinely grieve for our lost childhoods. Grief work is not about just learning to tell our story, but about starting to discover and express the underlying trauma and emotions. Doing this level of work is the true path to freeing ourselves.

When we are no longer held in place by the disembodied stories and the undercurrent of repressed feelings, we can begin to take positive action, change our life's terms, find joy in the present, and feel alive for possibly the first time.

On this day I will tell the real story of my childhood trauma. In doing so, I will free my True Self and enjoy this day my Higher Power has given me.

Indecision

"Children of alcoholics are paralyzed by indecision when trying to separate emotionally from their homes." BRB p. 87

When we started telling our story in ACA, we may have felt like we were betraying everything we had ever known, and we were – but that was okay. Part of recovery is releasing ourselves from the emotional chaos of our family of origin by rebelling, getting mad, and walking out, saying, "I'm not gonna take this anymore."

We are reparenting ourselves when we detach from our abusers and take responsibility for our own actions. We learn to share what really happened to us with fellow travelers and in meetings. We continue to heal when more memories surface and we work through them. We take care of ourselves by journaling, exercising, and learning to eat healthier.

We may still be paralyzed with indecision at times, but we allow our healed parts to nurture the parts that are still sick and wounded – they show up for each other. We rely on those with more recovery to mentor us by observing how they manage times of stress and peace. We walk towards freedom.

On this day I will make forward movement, even when I am afraid of the consequences. I now have a healthy support system that I know will be there for me, including my inner loving parent.

Feelings

"People want recovery, but they prefer it be pain free. That is understandable, but unfortunately, identifying and feeling our feelings is a part of healing." BRB Introduction p. xxiii

"Feelings? What are those?!" As children from dysfunctional homes, if we cried, many of us were told, "Stop crying or I'll give you something to cry about!" If we openly showed our feelings, we risked being told we were stupid or that we'd never amount to anything. When our parents failed to show up at our special school events, we learned not to show hurt or disappointment. The more vulnerable we were, the more we were shamed. When we were verbally or physically abused, we pretended it didn't happen. Our broken hearts shut down.

When many of us first come to ACA, we may have no idea how we're feeling. We've been shut down for so long that numb feels normal. Our tears are frozen. Opening up to our feelings seems threatening and scary.

As we keep coming back, we learn to heal by developing trust in our fellow travelers. This feeling of trust can lead to the opening of the flood gates, an expression of emotion that eventually feels normal. As we release our old pain, we make room for discovering how to play and have fun again. We open our hearts and feel joy in our lives.

On this day I welcome all of my feelings, especially those that are unfamiliar and uncomfortable. I have the tools to work through them in order to mend my broken heart from childhood.

Step Two

"Came to believe that a Power greater than ourselves could restore us to sanity." BRB p. 130

Our parents had been our gods. This is normal for children because parents are their primary support system.

As adults, many of us had not progressed past this stage of growth, no matter how far away we moved. We had believed everything they said for so long that we continued to internalize their negativity and messages without even being around them. Their voices were inside us.

Concerning religious beliefs, some of our families had no tolerance for anything except their religious belief system. Others of us may have been told that only weak-minded people believe in a Higher Power.

In recovery, when many of us seek to identify a Higher Power, we may be confused by these intolerant and abusive viewpoints. To find clarity, we give ourselves permission to step away from those old ideas, even about what the word God means. Many of us may start by seeing our ACA family as the "something greater than ourselves." This is the beginning of our search for spiritual freedom. It may seem foreign at first, because this wouldn't have been allowed in our families.

But we're on a journey. We try things out and see what works for us. We notice we have an inner compass, and we start to follow it fearlessly.

On this day I know there is a power greater than me. I honor the fact that my concept of a Higher Power may continue to change as I grow.

Codependence

"We focus on others to avoid looking at our own behavior and fear." BRB p. 335

Why do some of us want to take care of everyone else so badly? Why do we get so incensed when we see others treated poorly, feeling anger and rage towards the perpetrator?

Yes, we feel deeply that no one should take advantage of other people. But the baggage we are carrying from our childhoods often causes us to go beyond trying to help someone. We can blow things entirely out of proportion with our unresolved sadness and rage.

In ACA, we learn that we cannot be effective in helping others until we deal with our own issues. We do this by getting honest about the true nature of our behaviors. When we fight someone else's fight, aren't we really fighting for that wounded part of us that remains unhealed? When we feel their pain and hang onto it, aren't we really feeling our own childhood trauma?

Often the best way to help others is to let them learn how to stand up for themselves. And the best way to help ourselves is to be aware of what we're doing and why we're doing it. When we focus too much on someone else's fight, we realize that it's because we have unresolved issues.

On this day I will be clear about my motives before I look outside of myself to take action.

Vulnerability

"To withstand the intense pain of living with insanity and to have any sense of control we must deny our feelings and hide our vulnerability."BRB, Pg 356

As we grew up we were shattered into many parts. Because of the insanity around us, we learned to hide our more vulnerable parts in order to survive. Some of us became multiple personalities and others of us were less broken, but we all found ourselves numb in some way. We adapted and adopted whatever survival techniques we needed.

In ACA recovery it can take time for some of our hidden parts to make themselves known – until they trust there is an inner loving parent who accepts them.

We work with our recovery partners and discover how to give *ourselves* the warmth, love, compassion and understanding we didn't experience as children. As we comfort and protect our Inner Child, we make healing our priority as we learn to quiet ourselves to see what feelings come up – what memories resurface.

To help ensure that the rooms of recovery are available for ourselves and others, we can also begin to give service in our meetings in small ways. We see that our honesty can encourage others to face their own fears as we learn together how to experience balance in our lives.

On this day I will listen to and comfort my Inner Child, accepting all of the parts of myself that make me unique. I look forward to who I can become as I heal.

PTSD

"PTSD symptoms can include hypervigilance or the constant monitoring of one's surroundings for potential threat of harm."
BRB p. 345

Many of us have few concrete memories of childhood. We know we lived through amazing trauma, but if we're asked what happened to us, we often have few examples to relate. We may have defining moments that we remember, but we also have years of "blanks." Some memories we do have were related by our siblings.

We repressed our memories as a protection mechanism. But when we arrive in ACA, we try to locate them because they're the key to much of our dysfunctional behavior. Some behavior, such as hypervigilance, seems inexplicable in its intensity. We can even be sitting with our recovery friends, perhaps in a meeting, and we can't seem to let go of monitoring everything that's going on. What we might have previously labeled as a highly overdeveloped sense of responsibility is more likely PTSD.

As we work our program and become willing to uncover our trauma, we begin to free ourselves from the heightened state of awareness that wears us out and causes problems in our relationships. We unbury memories that have gotten us to this state, often with the help of therapy, and by sharing our story and listening to others in meetings.

On this day I will not be afraid to uncover the memories that seem to bind me to my dysfunctional behaviors.

Tradition Seven

"In ACA, we learn to give for the right reason, and we learn the right amount to give. We give our fair share and let others give their fair share, so we all take ownership in ACA." BRB p. 524

At ACA meetings the Seventh Tradition reminds us that we contribute as we are able. There was a time when a quarter was thought to be enough. As times changed, a dollar seemed about right. More recently, two dollars has become more the norm.

As the fellowship grows, the need for financial contributions from members may also grow. Some groups pay higher rents and may ask members to contribute more if they can. However, this is not obligatory and never a requirement for membership.

Financial contributions support not only individual meetings, but also local Intergroup and the World Service Organization (WSO), which spreads our message around the globe. The WSO hires special workers for its literature distribution center. Translations have to be verified, books printed and shipped. Much occurs behind the scenes to make carrying the ACA message possible.

Like other 12 Step fellowships, ACA does not depend on anyone else to take care of our "house." Being fully self-supporting, we do not owe outside interests, so no one else tells us where or how to carry our message.

On this day I will give the financial contribution I can so that the meetings I attend will thrive. I do my part to ensure that the ACA message is available to the still-suffering adult children of my community and around the world.

Isolation

"Our experience shows that you cannot recover in isolation."
BRB p. 127

Many of our childhood memories center around the isolation
we felt in our homes while growing up. We may have had few
or no childhood friends. To have friends could have placed us in
a position where they would want to come to our house – and
we couldn't risk that.

The lack of close friendships deepened the sadness and loneliness
we already faced on a regular basis. That loneliness also affected
us as adults where many of us felt a social awkwardness that
fueled both addiction and isolation.

We experienced the feeling of being alone, even in a crowd;
and we felt lonely, even when we were in a relationship. Fear
of failure, lack of trust, and fear of abandonment compounded
things by leading many of us to choose others who also lacked
the skills to have a healthy relationship.

Attending ACA meetings is the first step in breaking the
pattern of loneliness and isolation. As we keep coming back, we
are amazed to hear our own stories coming out of the mouths of
others in the room. We realize we don't have to be alone in our
despair; we have found people who will love and accept us, even
before we can love and accept ourselves. In ACA we are home,
maybe for the first time in our lives.

*On this day I will allow my fellow travelers to touch my life and
know they will support me through my journey.*

August

"The safe harbor we find in ACA meetings is the starting point for transforming our survival traits." BRB p. 112

Gratitude

"The gratitude we feel is limitless." BRB p. 292

Often we may have said or thought to ourselves at a meeting, "I had so much going on that I almost didn't come, but I am so grateful I did because I heard just what I needed." As our recovery progresses, we are thankful for what may seem to some of us like divine timing. We feel grateful for the right meeting topic at the best possible moment. Often a fellow traveler with just the right message will show up when we are ready, or perhaps the message has been there all along and we're finally ready to hear it. Sometimes we may see a person only once, but what they say or demonstrate is exactly what hits home for us at that moment.

All around us we begin to notice our needs are being met when we're ready to recognize what is being placed before us. We may even be lucky enough to receive something we just want. Whatever we receive, it will be a gift.

If something is presented that we don't want or need, we have the choice to let it go and turn it over. Sometimes we are just meant to have the information so we can pass it on to someone else who needs that very gift.

On this day I am aware of the wonderful gifts that appear when I need them. I am grateful for the opportunities they present for personal growth.

Dissociation

"Another form of not being in the body involves dissociation or 'leaving the body.'" BRB p. 269

As kids, we may have gotten into big trouble when we showed how we felt. So many of us taught our little faces and voices and bodies NOT to show emotion. We may have eventually learned to disconnect from our feelings even before they surfaced. We knew we had to live physically in our bodies, but we could refuse to listen to what our bodies were trying to tell us. Some of us became so dissociated that we even looked at others to know when to smile or frown. We had lost our identities in the process.

When we found ACA, we heard dissociation described as a disconnection from our feelings, thoughts, body needs and other parts of ourselves. We also learned that childhood trauma was the cause.

At meetings, when we heard others say they felt numb, empty or dead inside, we may have identified because of our own trauma and disconnect. We heard that change is possible, but it requires work.

When we make the commitment to ourselves, our feelings start to show up; they may be strong and come in large quantities. It's scary, but we have the support of other ACAs. Working the program, and learning to trust in a Higher Power, helps us restore our True Selves. We accept our feelings and become who we were meant to be.

On this day I will pause, find a quiet place to sit, and breathe whenever I feel disconnected from myself. I will maintain conscious contact with my Higher Power…and myself.

Step Eight

"Made a list of all persons we had harmed and became willing to make amends to them all." BRB p. 227

Making an amends list is part of wiping the slate clean for ourselves and walking into a new way of life. Many of us had been part of physically and emotionally unsafe relationships as adults, and we knew we eventually had to own our part in those relationships.

As we made our amends list, we were told to put ourselves first. In doing so, we thought about all the things we had lost, most importantly our childhoods, and what that meant for us. Even though we missed the stages of child development we were entitled to, we realized we could nurture ourselves and help make up for that loss.

In making amends to ourselves, we acknowledge any self-harm we have done, including not forgiving ourselves for simply being human. Then we move on to amends to others, knowing we aren't being asked to make amends to unsafe people.

Taking Step Eight helps us grow spiritually and emotionally. Whatever amends we eventually make, it's a healing process. As part of this process, we continue to work on the character defects that have placed us in the position of making amends in the first place. We go forward in confidence and love to whatever comes next.

On this day I will stay current with the amends I owe myself, and then work with those I may owe others.

Spiritual, not Religious

"In ACA, we take a spiritual and not religious approach to healing the effects of being raised in a dysfunctional home."
BRB p. 76

The writers of the 12 Steps knew that, even though we claimed to be spiritual, the use of the word "God" could be controversial.

When we hear the word "God" in our meetings, some of us feel comforted, and some of us experience negativity and sadness. No matter what our reaction, it is important for us to remember that in ACA we unite around a spiritual foundation that allows us to believe what we choose.

Many of us grew up knowing a loving, supportive God, and many of us grew up with a punishing God. No matter what beliefs we had in childhood, we often found a different understanding as adults. In many cases, we continue to search for a path that feels comfortable.

Spiritual, not religious means that our fellowship recognizes there are many belief systems, and the cloak of spirituality allows us to be equals in our recovery. No one of us knows the right answer for anyone else. There is no one right way to believe, and we respect each other's differences, even while we unconditionally support each other.

On this day, while I seek to strengthen my spiritual belief, I practice tolerance for beliefs that differ from mine.

Tolerating Pain

"The level of pain that adult children can tolerate without admitting they have hit a bottom is astonishing." BRB p. 68

We learned to live with pain as children and continued to do so as adults. When faced with the pain of toxic relationships, we slip into survival mode to avoid the uncertainty of change.

We know that our lives are in chaos, that we accept the unacceptable from the people around us, and that we have no reason to expect tomorrow to be better. Yet we trudge through each day, often with a pain so deep it feels out of reach.

Everyone who has walked into ACA has felt the apprehension that comes with change. Often, fear of change is so strong that we can still convince ourselves that things aren't that bad.

We are all creatures of habit, even when those habits are harmful to us. ACA is the first step in saying our lives are out of control and we need help. The question is, do we want to live a life that "isn't that bad," or do we have the faith in our Higher Power, in our program, and in ourselves to overcome the fear of change?

We do not have to do this alone. Our fellow travelers are more than willing to take the journey with us.

On this day I will reach out my hand to end the cycle of pain and know there will be someone there to hold onto.

Therapy

"A good therapist should ask you about trauma and abuse, including child sexual abuse, if there are clear indicators of family history, acting-out behavior, records, or other discernible factors."
BRB p. 462

Some of us have been in therapy with people who mirrored our abusive parents. They told us that our childhood sexual abuse was no big deal because what happened to children at a young age doesn't really affect them. We sometimes even allowed them to sexually abuse us in the course of therapy.

We realize that there are a lot of good therapists out there, but not all of them are safe. We do not let this stop us from getting the right help. We learn how to set boundaries with the people who work for us, including those who seem like they are in a position of authority over us. We stop trying to please others. We allow ourselves the space to say what we need, but we check first to see if it's safe to talk.

When a therapist isn't working for us, we allow ourselves to explore other options. When we stop going back to poisoned wells, we are reparenting ourselves with love. We learn to take the power back, the power that was stolen from us in childhood. We trust our instincts because we have created safe boundaries in which to allow them to be revealed.

On this day I will ask as many questions as I need to, no matter what the situation. If I'm not satisfied with the answers, I will explore other options.

Unconditional Love

"The child feels he must perform or do well to earn a parent's love." BRB p. 30

For many of us, we had to perform appropriately to get any feeling of love or acceptance as children. But conditional love was the only love, if any, that we received. Many times the conditions were as dysfunctional as the love, and often they changed from day to day. We heard people talk of unconditional love, but many of us didn't think that it really existed.

In ACA, when we listen to the voices in our heads that tell us we're not good enough, we understand this is our inner critic. It's no longer our parent's voice, but our own, repeating the negative words spoken to us as children. But how did this happen? We weren't going to be like our parents. But here we are telling ourselves the very words that cut us like a knife when we were vulnerable children.

Once we see the harm we are doing to ourselves and know why it's happening, the ACA program helps us replace negative words with positive affirmations. We can give ourselves the unconditional love that was denied us as children. We don't have to please anyone to get it. The cycle of pain is ending. We are now free to face life with a positive frame of mind, getting ready to give the blessing of unconditional love to others.

On this day I give myself unconditional love and acceptance. In doing so, I will then truly be able to accept and love others.

Trait Nine

"We confuse love and pity and tend to 'love' people we can 'pity' and 'rescue.'" BRB p. 12

In many aspects of our lives we are drawn to the familiar, not because it is good for us, but because it is more comfortable than change. The fact is that as much as many of us protest, we are drawn to other dysfunctional people. The reason for this attraction is very likely a deep sense of shame many of us carry from our childhood that we keep as our well-guarded secret. The message of this shame is that we are not "good enough," because as children we did not feel valued for who we were.

Only by entering into relationships with other sick people will our secret be secure in the chaos of the dysfunctional. We can focus on them and rescue them, which often makes them want us more – at least for a while.

As we gain self-respect in ACA, these innate attractions start to disappear because we realize we're not getting our needs met. As we change, and as hard as it can seem at first, we may have to leave some relationships behind if the other people are not willing to change also. In doing so, we learn to reject the notion that this is somehow selfish. That is codependent thinking that is not fair to anyone, least of all ourselves.

On this day, with the help of my Higher Power, I choose healthy people to be part of my life, people who are willing to embrace the new me.

Shame and Blame

"As ACA becomes a safe place for you, you will find freedom to express all the hurts and fears you have kept inside and to free yourself from the shame and blame that are carryovers from the past." BRB p. 590

The cycle of shame and blame was well established in our families of origin. We heard abusive words and/or were physically punished. We emerged from all of this with an established sense of shame that included thinking of ourselves as

- Defective: something is wrong with me
- Helpless: nothing can be done about this
- Alone: nobody else has this problem

As adults, some of us found that if we shifted blame to others, we could hide our own sense of shame. Some of us may have lashed out with extreme anger, not knowing where it came from, or used perfectionism, pride, people-pleasing, and approval-seeking to cover up our sense of shame. Some of us fell victim to addictions.

In ACA, we come to appreciate that there is nothing wrong with us that meetings, a sponsor and consistently working the Steps cannot overcome. Shame and blame give way to an understanding that we make mistakes, but *we* are not mistakes! We claim the identity that we are inherently good, even with all our perceived misgivings, warts and dents.

On this day I will use my courage and honesty to break the generational bonds of shame and blame.

Our Past is an Asset

"Our experience tells us that our past can be our greatest asset if we are willing to ask for help and do the work to find out what happened." BRB p. 153

We sometimes wonder how differently we could have turned out had we been raised without the problems of alcoholism or family dysfunction. While it is normal for us to consider "what ifs," we know that when we work through the abuse and hardship of our childhoods, we can come out so much better on the other side.

But what can possibly make our past an asset? In recovery, we see that all we've been through provides us a unique opportunity to look deeper at our lives than we might have otherwise. We take on the task of untangling the web of our history, knowing that greater peace will result. We revisit old wounds so that we may finally heal the hurt and better understand our thoughts, feelings, and behaviors today. We are able to reclaim our inner strength and learn from our struggles.

In ACA we don't do all of this work alone. We may have been alone as children, but now we have our fellow travelers. We hear them share the same pain, and see the wisdom and knowledge they have gained in their own recovery. This same wisdom and knowledge is becoming part of who we are, also.

On this day I recognize that my past provides a unique opportunity to grow in self-actualization. I look forward to the continual wisdom recovery offers.

True Self

"While the Inner Child or True Self can be the spark of our creativity, we must also remember the child is a deeply hurt part of ourselves." BRB p. 303

Many of us have pursued an understanding of our True Self, awakening our Inner Child and expressing our creativity in hopes of relieving ourselves from suffering. Yet we face an obstacle – a persistent and harsh self-judgment that we can't seem to stop. This underlying thinking compels us to continue dysfunctional and addictive behaviors. We wonder why we can't get out from under this "curse-like" self-sabotage and realize the promise of our True Self.

We learn in ACA to get in touch with and feel the pain and grief of the deeply hurt parts of ourselves in order for the True Self to blossom. We've avoided this for years, usually unconsciously, and we've suffered from the consequences of this avoidance. We come to see that we won't enjoy the fulfillment of living as our True Selves until we face and get free from the roots of the wounded parts from childhood.

With our Higher Power's help, and support from our fellow travelers, we practice a gentle and gradual process of peeling the layers of the onion to find the core of our pain and, paradoxically, to find the joy of our True Self. It's an organic process unique to each of us, yet we're supported in a unified approach that integrates the Steps, our Higher Power, and our Inner Child.

On this day I have the courage to face what's necessary so I can realize the promise of my True Self.

Reparenting

"The need to reparent ourselves comes from our efforts to feel safe as children." BRB, p. 83

Because of our dysfunctional childhoods, we usually see things differently than others. We don't feel all warm and fuzzy when we see a TV commercial where the salesperson loudly exclaims, "Come on in. We'll treat you like family!" In our minds, that doesn't sound like such a good thing, because our families weren't safe. And when we feel compelled to buy a greeting card for a parent, we are grateful we can find something in the humor section rather than choose one that gushes with gratitude. But underneath the humor, there is a deep sadness.

In ACA, we learn to recognize the reality of our feelings. We make a choice that instead of remaining under the layers of dysfunction, we will take positive steps to reparent ourselves using the tools of ACA. These steps and the path we're on may not always be crystal clear, but we keep coming back until we find where we need to go. Along the way, we grieve the loss of what might have been. And we work towards someday getting to a place of forgiveness, which will help us far more than anything else.

On this day I honor my feelings and the reality of what was in order to choose a new way of living and reparenting myself.

Language

"We recognize a spectrum that transcends language and trauma. We recognize the light in ourselves and others." BRB p. 438

In our dysfunctional families, many of us held our heads down because we consistently heard language that was meant to shame us. We were told things like, "I'll give you something to cry about," "Who do you think you are – something special?" "If you can't do it right, don't do it at all!" "What are you – stupid?" and "Can't you do any better than that?" These negatives became so ingrained in us that we still hear them inside our heads from our critical inner parent.

In ACA, we learn to hold our heads high as we hear different, affirming messages, like "One Day at a Time," "First Things First," "Easy Does It," and "Keep It Simple." They remind us to be gentle with ourselves.

As we recover from the hurtful language of our childhoods, we start by acknowledging the harm it has done. We affirm that we are not defined by these shaming words as we tell ourselves that crying is okay, that we are special human beings, that we don't have to be perfect, and that we all make mistakes – it's what makes us human. These positive assurances help us finally explore who we were meant to be. And as we heal, we are able to provide similar assurances to others.

On this day I will make a conscious effort to think only positive things about myself and my abilities as I learn to undo the damage of the past.

Disease of Alcoholism

"If your parents did not drink, your grandparents may have drank and passed on the disease of family dysfunction to your parents. If alcohol or drugs were not a problem, your home may have been chaotic, unsafe, and lacking nurture like many alcoholic homes." BRB p. 18

Great! Granny did it to Mom and Mom did it to us! What chance do we have of being able to get well?

Even though this was passed down through the generations until it finally got to us, and perhaps to our children and grandchildren, who do we blame? Can we really blame Mom or Granny or even Great Granny? Indeed, none of them intended to pass this baggage down to us. But here it is: ours to unpack.

Fortunately, we have the best chance of them all to do something about it. Today we have a much better understanding of the multigenerational nature of trauma transmission. And this understanding is constantly evolving. We are fortunate to be part of a wonderful human experiment to reverse the effects of generational family dysfunction and achieve emotional sobriety.

Like most experiments, we start with a premise: that we can build a life of stability, safety and nurturing. As we toil in the laboratory of our lives in recovery, we find just the right mixture of experience, analysis and spiritual principles, and issue daily progress reports to our fellow travelers and our Higher Power.

On this day I will note the progress I have made in finding my emotional balance, and give myself the privilege of believing I can and will recover.

Promise Eight

"We will choose to love people who can love and be responsible for themselves." BRB p. 591

Prior to coming to ACA, we had been unconscious about a great many things. Perhaps the most painful was our unconscious choice of the people we thought we loved.

As children, we wanted to love our parents. So we overlooked their dysfunction as a way to make them lovable. After all, the alternative was to see them as they really were and leave – a choice that is rarely possible for a child.

As adults, we continued to make unconscious choices to love other dysfunctional people until one day we got it. Something was terribly familiar about the people we had chosen to love. It was déjà vu, all over again.

As we come to consciousness about our childhood experiences and do the work in ACA, we begin to love and accept our True Self. Only then are we capable of having healthy relationships with others. We begin to choose people who are capable of truly loving us, and who take responsibility for themselves. We are now willing to share our True Self, the person we were meant to be, the one who is able to love responsibly in return.

On this day I will examine my relationships, both past and present, to help me understand the choices I have made. I will begin to share my True Self with others in my life so that I may find the love I deserve.

Service and Healing

"The healing we receive by giving service in ACA removes our deep feelings of inferiority in giving and receiving love. Our sense of inadequacy begins to disappear when we see the value of the service we give." BRB p. 363

In a myriad of ways most of us were taught that we were inferior. Our perceptions were challenged. Our feelings were denied. Our thoughts were overpowered by the dysfunction in our families.

As we "come to" in ACA, we realize that our perceptions, feelings and thoughts are being respected because they are true for us. Through regular attendance at meetings, we slowly develop the knowledge that we are not inferior, and begin sharing and working the steps with a fellow traveler.

At some point we notice that others chip in to make this miracle possible by doing service to keep the meeting strong. This is where part of the magic of recovery happens: in one instant we are lost, and in the next we become able to help by doing service work ourselves for the group.

Seeing new members attend their first meetings and then seeing them as they begin to "come to" brings us joy and makes any level of service we can give an act of love that reflects our love of our True Selves.

On this day I will recall my first days in ACA and the comfort I found. As I am ready and able to do so, I will continue the tradition of freely giving service to help ensure that what I have received is available to others.

Choice

"We learn that real choice is God's gift to us for letting go."
BRB p. 155

As children, we may have felt trapped in an unhappy home life because we had no control over a parent's drinking or other family dysfunction. We carry this feeling into adulthood, often feeling like victims of circumstances or of people who trigger in us painful childhood memories.

In Step Three, we may be confused about what it means to turn our will over to our Higher Power – that without our will we will be trapped with no options. We worry that we will be giving away our power. In reality we are giving over our controlling nature to our Higher Power.

As we learn to focus on what is within our control, namely ourselves, and let go of control over other people, places, and things, we open ourselves up to more choice. We learn that we can choose our actions in situations, rather than reacting and feeling like a victim. We can let our Higher Power take over what is not ours to control. This frees us to begin making life-affirming choices.

On this day I give what I am not meant to control over to the care of my Higher Power. In its place I feel a greater freedom of choice than I have ever felt before.

Willingness

"With willingness we are well on our way to recovery." BRB p. 50

In the rooms of recovery, we learn to use the acronym HOW: Honest, Open-minded, and Willing. In ACA, we need to be all three. However, willingness may well be the key to doing the work it takes to achieve the results we seek.

There is a big difference between wanting something and being willing to do the work to get it. Most of us have spent our life up to this point wanting things: higher self-esteem, less anxiety, and a family that loves us unconditionally.

So we enter the ACA program with a mental list of what we want. But are we willing to put forth the effort to recover? We make time for others, for work, for recreational activities, but making time for ourselves may be a foreign concept.

In ACA, the only person we are trying to change is ourselves. The way to make that happen is to make the time for it to happen – to be willing to put ourselves on our schedule, maybe for the first time in our lives.

On this day I will focus on changing my "want" list to include being willing to spend time on myself and my program.

Emotional Sobriety

"With emotional sobriety, reparenting ourselves becomes a reality in our lives." BRB page 265

Our program calls us to recognize the truth within us. A beginning truth is that our families, in their unfinished spiritual states, corrupted our thinking. As young children, we could relate to no one other than our families to 'see how the world was' around us.

This often involved a series of dysfunctional beliefs, such as "I can make it on my own," "I am too proud to accept help from anyone," and/or "We are s-o-o-o-o much better than they are." This led us to a false sense of independence or even superiority that effectively cut us off from many forms of useful information that could have helped us.

As adults, we lived with this corrupted thinking, in a state of confusion and denial, unable to admit that we needed help and unable to trust anyone.

When we find recovery in ACA, we discover that we can reparent ourselves. We learn to see the truth about our parents in a non-judgmental way, which helps us first accept whatever good things they passed to us. Then, without anger or resentment, we firmly reject their dysfunctional ways of thinking. We are now free to chart our own course of behavioral, spiritual and emotional sobriety.

On this day I will focus on using all I've learned in ACA to help me reparent myself. I choose spiritual and emotional sobriety.

Survival Traits

"The safe harbor we find in ACA meetings is the starting point for transforming our survival traits." BRB p. 112

The dysfunction we grew up with grabbed hold of many of us with such powerful claws that we learned to perform to suit the needs of others. We took on behaviors that helped us survive the best way we knew how.

Some of our survival traits were so integrated into our psyche that we felt like two people inside: the person we learned to be and the one who was "emotionally dying" to break free.

But even as adults, we had no clue about what to change and how to change it. We just knew that we had to find a way out if we were ever to have a chance at experiencing a "normal" life.

ACA is that way out! It is a proven path that leads to new ways of thinking and being. But it's not easy. Transformation takes time and energy. It also takes self-acceptance and self-forgiveness because we will inevitably slip and slide. That's why we need to know that we don't have to be on this journey alone.

On this day, if I find myself slipping, I will take a deep breath and pick up the phone. I am no longer alone.

Inner Drugs

"Because we were raised in chaotic or controlling homes, our internal compass is oriented toward excitement, pain, and shame. This inner world can be described as an 'inside drug store.' The shelves are stocked with bottles of excitement, toxic shame, self-hate, self-doubt, and stress." BRB p. 16

Do the following situations sound familiar? We walk into a room full of strangers and instinctively find the most toxic people in the room to befriend. We leave home with "just enough" time so our adrenaline is pumping when we arrive at our destination. We over-commit ourselves so that we can't possibly do everything we promised, and then shame ourselves because we've failed yet again.

Many of us just naturally choose situations that create drama, people who are spinning out of control, and a life that balances on the edge of insanity. It almost feels like we're hard-wired to operate that way.

As we begin to understand the damaging effects of these inner drugs we keep taking, we learn to replace the toxic people and drama with mutually respectful relationships and healthy excitement for our recovery. We no longer need to recreate the familiar conditions of our childhood that keep us trapped in the chaos. We gradually begin to appreciate the peace and quiet of serenity. It takes time, but we now realize we deserve better than the hand we were dealt as children.

On this day I choose healthy people to spend time with – people who also value serenity. I welcome the calm that is becoming my new normal.

PTSD

"PTSD is a condition of the body and mind in which a person stores the memory of a violent attack or life-threatening event."
BRB p. 344

When we got to ACA, we knew our minds and emotions were affected, but our bodies? We saw that the literature talked about how our bodies carry original trauma, so we started to pay attention. We soon noticed something very disturbing: we had a lot of automatic body reactions that happened without our "permission."

Eventually, we realized that our present-day bodies were acting on auto-pilot to safeguard us from perceived threat signals that our child-bodies stored long ago. It was overwhelming to hear that, because how do you change your body?

We found that one way was to keep reading encouraging words in our Fellowship Text. It gave us hope that our bodies could recover when we read on page 621 that "What can be learned can be unlearned..." and on page 626, "We now have gathered the knowledge and experience needed to transmit a vision for healing the injury and hurt caused by childhood trauma."

As we worked the Steps, followed the Traditions, and attended meetings, we saw that our minds, emotions, spirits, and bodies started to heal. We were amazed at this program's power. It was larger than the effects that we carried in our blood, tissue, nerves, and bone.

On this day I will help my body recover by acknowledging when I have a physical reaction to a seemingly non-threatening situation. I will then reach out to try to uncover where the reaction is coming from to help myself heal.

Grief as Freedom

"Experienced ACA members speak of grief with a sense of serenity rather than with sorrow or resentment." BRB p. 200

When listening to ACAs share at meetings, newcomers may at first only hear the recounting of the childhood events and their effects. If they keep coming back, they may experience an extraordinary transformation.

Over time, newcomers may realize that what they are hearing isn't just a recounting of a story: it's an opportunity to be heard. In alcoholic and dysfunctional homes, none of us was allowed to tell our story. We did not feel that we could trust our families to listen to us because our feelings were minimized or dismissed.

With experience, the newcomer may hear our shares as a courageous, insightful, and inspired reclaiming of our lives. When the experienced member shares, the sense of serenity doesn't stem from the story. The serenity is in realizing, most often for the first time, that the meeting allows us to talk, trust, and feel. No longer imprisoned, what is being witnessed is a grieving process that frees a lost soul.

On this day as I begin to free my soul from the prison of my childhood, I will be present for my fellow ACAs as they do the same.

Survivor

"It is my bias that no one deserves to live a life of fear and shame."
BRB p. xviii

Many ACAs go from blaming, shaming, complaining, and condemning ourselves and others to finally learning to name what is really going on. By doing so, we begin to come out of our victim and/or victimizer roles. We ask our Higher Power to help us remove and release our unhealthy behaviors, thoughts, and feelings. We let go of the justifications we created in our minds for our actions, thoughts, and emotions. Yes, we experienced abuse or neglect as children, and maybe as adults, but we know that does not excuse our dysfunctional behavior now.

As we gain strength and recover, we become healing survivors and then thrivers. We gradually and sometimes more quickly, develop new capacities for healthy well-being in our lives. We learn that we deserve a happy, full life. We learn that we have always deserved this. We don't have to do anything to be worthy, we just ARE.

As thrivers, we now know that our Higher Power is there for us. We learn to have unconditional love for ourselves and others.

On this day I acknowledge that I am worthy and deserving of a happy, full life.

Acting Out

"By working the ACA program, we learn to recognize when we are thinking like a victim or persecutor and to talk about it."
BRB p. 9

Since the Laundry List was such an important part of our original identification when we found ACA, we used that mindset (how we were wronged) during our early recovery. To reveal the full extent of our grief and to un-stuff our emotions, however, we needed to reflect on our past through the eyes of the victims we'd become.

Step work revealed how our past not only victimized us, but taught many of us to be cruel, vindictive, and scathing when we decided we were 'gonna pay them back.'

Then we saw the Other Laundry List and found further self-identification. Along with being victims long ago, many of us were angry, frustrated children who learned how to hurt others. And hurt them we did, for many, many years.

Having promised ourselves as children that we would never be like our parents, we stood now as adults with their same behaviors.

But in ACA we soon found we were not alone in this paradox. In our meetings we sat together, each of us victims and victimizers; we lifted our heads, removed our shame, and understood we could not have turned out any other way. We started recovering with our new ACA family.

On this day, if I feel like striking out, I will take a time-out so I can take a "time-in." I will focus inward, reflect and talk about it with a fellow traveler.

Honesty

"With the help of ACA, we are offering our parents fairness as we look at the family system with rigorous honesty. We are looking for the truth so that we can live our own lives with choice and self-confidence. We want to break the cycle of family dysfunction."
BRB p. 27

"What is honesty?" asked the old man.

"Telling the truth," I said.

He raised his eyebrows and replied, "That's only half of the answer. The other part is consistency, which means telling the truth *all the time*."

How many times do we tell half truths? "Yes, I'd be glad to do that," we say, but deep inside we're already shaming ourselves for giving in. "So, what's wrong?" someone asks. We answer, "Nothing," when our hearts are so broken we'd like to end it all. Or the phone rings in the middle of a fight, and we cheerfully answer like all is right with the world.

When working the steps in ACA, we have the privilege of practicing rigorous honesty with a fellow traveler. We want to break the chains that hold us in bondage – to stop repeating the same ineffective behavior. We're tired of failed relationships, verbal abuse, and isolation. If we truly want to find peace and serenity, we courageously walk through the swamps, hand in hand with our fellow traveler, armed with honesty, to face the truth. We want a better life. We make room for the good stuff that we deserve.

On this day I will be mindful in the present moment and be honest. I will make healthy choices and thank my Higher Power for the encouragement that got me here.

Self-Sabotage

"I decided the only way to overcome this self-sabotage was to integrate my critical parent into my recovery process."
BRB p. 207

We tried to ignore our critical inner parent – that compilation of the voices we heard as children and were used to hearing in our heads. If it was too strong to ignore, we tried to fight it, but it always seemed to find a way to win.

In ACA, we learn to uncover why this critic has had such a strong hold on us. By acknowledging the trauma that's behind the voices, we understand and gradually learn to substitute new behaviors so we can silence this tyrant in our heads.

This gives us freedom as we bring new light into our lives in little ways. We begin to trust ourselves, others, and our Higher Power. We have healthier relationships as we find ourselves attracted to the strengths and depth in people who can hold our feelings safely rather than trying to shut us down.

We let go of the dysfunctional people. While they may have taught us the lessons we needed to learn, we know that staying is toxic. In doing so, we feel no shame or remorse; it is time to move on. We are open to the next adventure.

On this day I will be aware of my attempts at self-sabotage because I believe in the promise of the growth ahead of me. I will use my lifeline – the support system that ACA gives me.

Boundaries

"I am more aware of how I overstep my boundaries, and how I try to force things to work the way I want them to work."
BRB p. 414

We were vulnerable as children in dysfunctional homes. We experienced no one who was able to set healthy boundaries and maintain them.

In ACA we learn to see the importance of boundaries by practicing the Steps and by identifying and working on our character defects. We learn to recognize boundaries that have been crossed, including when we do it to others. We feel free when we set new boundaries. Progress happens, one day at a time.

The ACA program also helps us recognize manipulative behaviors, which is usually a companion for those with boundary issues. If we're the manipulator, we begin to see that our attempts to change others will eventually fail; in the meantime, they'll only complicate things. As we grow stronger, understanding boundaries places everything in perspective.

To help us stay focused, we look to Step Ten, "Continued to take personal inventory and when we were wrong, promptly admitted it." It allows us to inventory our thoughts and actions on a regular basis. This keeps our impulsive natures in check so we recognize boundaries in everyday life.

On this day, as my identity and values become more clear, I will work to become consistent in setting my own boundaries and honoring the boundaries other people set.

Therapeutic Ideals

"There are, as well, ways to describe the manifestation of two therapeutic ideals: no excess tension in the body and a neutral reaction to symbolic associations and mental representations of trauma." BRB p. 622

Many of us thought there was no way out, that the process would go on and on like some weird torture game. We had no goals because we thought we didn't deserve them. Helping others achieve *their* goals felt good, but it was not something that we could do on our own. We didn't want that responsibility. It was safer to just stay small, not have any dreams or needs.

We learn in ACA that living in our bodies is a vital part of recovery. We seek ways to relieve excess body tension, perhaps by using trigger point massage in combination with yoga. We discover that we are carrying a lot of trauma in our very muscles that needs a way to work itself out. We collect the experiences of others, both in and out of the program, and we learn through reading the right material.

We worked the Steps so that we would no longer be mentally triggered by the same things repeatedly. We now seek that same relief for our bodies.

*On this day I will be conscious of my physical tension and where I carry it in my body. Acknowledging this connection to my trauma is a way of beginning my journey towards **complete** recovery.*

Tradition Eight

"Sponsorship and Twelfth Step work are free, but the special worker should be paid for his or her good work. All aspects of recovery in general are free." BRB p. 530

We give service from a space of love in ACA so that every adult child seeking recovery may find a safe place. Many of us are truly generous with our time and expertise. And we do not expect or accept any compensation for giving a ray of hope to our fellow ACAs. We know what it is like to feel hopeless, looking for a way out. With joy in our hearts and hope in our words, we extend ourselves while seeking nothing in return.

But some requests are too big to ask members to handle for free day-in and day-out. For those jobs, we hire special workers. They staff our service center and are responsible for sending literature, maintaining our meeting list, answering calls, and otherwise providing information about ACA to anyone who wants it. They help us spread the message.

Without them, most people would have difficulty even finding a meeting. If we didn't have a Newcomer's booklet and other printed information, each meeting would have to create their own materials. These are essential ways the ACA message reaches those who want it. It all fits together nicely – a combination of volunteers and special workers.

On this day I will share freely with the suffering adult child who is seeking to recover. I will also feel gratitude that ACA has special workers who serve the larger fellowship.

Grandchildren of Alcoholics

"More and more people are identifying as grandchildren of alcoholics. Technically, these 'GCoAs' are ACAs. They were raised by parents who passed on the disease of family dysfunction without having alcohol in the home." BRB p. 56, footnote

Some of us have wandered through life wondering why we had so many problems. Our childhoods were not filled with alcoholism or addiction. And yet, there was a dark cloud over our homes. We couldn't talk openly; we couldn't be ourselves. There was a lot of confusing behavior. We received punishments that didn't make sense. We had to watch out for ourselves. Sometimes our parents were available, but often they were full of rage or confusion, or they seemed to mentally "check out."

The first time we heard the Laundry List in a meeting, we related to many of the characteristics even though no one drank or used drugs at home. We felt the need to be there. We heard others share and realized that ACA embraces all of us, simply because we walked in the door.

Working Step One gave us an opportunity to draw a family tree. We soon saw the connection: alcoholism and addiction in past generations. The disease of family dysfunction was like a legacy. This helped us stop wondering if we belonged so we could focus on recovering.

On this day, even if I can't pinpoint where there might have been addiction in my family, I know I belong in this program. I will use all the tools available to me to recover from my family's not-so-unique dysfunction.

September

"Who would have thought that talking, trusting, and feeling would equal a spiritual experience, but it does for adult children. We felt this new spirituality in our breathing and in the sense that we could face life on life's terms." BRB p. 285

Surrender

"We must find a way to surrender and to become teachable."
BRB p. 156

At each meeting, we see ourselves in the ACA Problem as it is read aloud. We identify with the Traits and know the pain they have wrought. We hear the Solution and want to see it working in our lives. We took the difficult step of walking through the door into our first meeting, and gathered the courage to return again and again.

In order to recover we must trust in the process by admitting that we cannot heal alone. By listening to our brothers and sisters in ACA, we learn something new and realize we do not have all of the answers. We can know the Problem and Solution in our heads, but without help, many of us will have great difficulty knowing it in our hearts, where it truly matters.

We learn to let down the walls of isolation we have so carefully constructed and allow ourselves a measure of vulnerability in order to work the Steps. We surrender our old ways of being and trust that our Higher Power is leading us to greater levels of growth.

On this day I practice trust by surrendering to the recovery process. I open my heart and thereby open myself to healing.

Trait Ten

"We have "stuffed" our feelings from our traumatic childhoods and have lost the ability to feel or express our feelings because it hurts so much (Denial)." BRB p. 17

If we came to ACA from another program and were familiar with Step work, we may have felt we had covered all of this ground before. We knew how to speak "program talk," and our lives were already better, right? So why were these people in ACA not focusing on the *Solution*? What's with all the complaining?

In ACA, we don't hide from the pain anymore. To others this may sound like complaining, but we know that's not what it is. We are locating our pain so we can heal. We allow our Inner Children to come out of hiding and flourish. First they may be angry and sad and need comforting. Then they become our best friends and companions in our Step work. We find new vitality as we see where this partnership leads us.

Our lives become the greatest adventure there is, totally unique. We learn more about ourselves each day by integrating the past into our present and seeing that we are no longer stuck. When we visit old neighborhoods of feeling, we are no longer parched and starving for attention. We nourish ourselves with the love and support of our Higher Power, the Twelve Steps, meetings, and fellowship.

On this day I will chip away at the years of denial by being willing to be present for whatever feelings come up in my day.

Step Nine

"Made direct amends to such people wherever possible, except when to do so would injure them or others." BRB p. 235

Amends can be scary. It's hard having to admit we are wrong or that we did something to harm another. We learn that our first amends are to ourselves. But we also must make decisions about when amends to others will harm ourselves or others, or when we're avoiding personal responsibility due to pride.

As we recover in ACA, we learn to trust our instincts. But we also need to be sure that the fear we bring from childhood doesn't get pulled into the mix inappropriately. We're adults, and most amends situations we face will put us in very little danger of being physically harmed as we were in childhood. So it's the emotional part we're worried about, whether we can handle what comes back at us. And even though we may not realize it right away, that eventually starts to make the decision of whether or not to make amends easier.

After we talk it through with our sponsor and others we trust, we'll know whether the amends are appropriate; if so, we'll decide whether we're strong enough to make them. If not, then we'll wait until we are.

It's about keeping our slates clean.

On this day I will make amends to myself first. Then I will prepare for my necessary amends to others, which I will do if, and when, I'm ready.

Generational Grief

"Our search for our grief/loss can begin by asking this question: 'What did I receive from my dysfunctional family and what would I have received from loving parents in the same situation?'" BRB p. 204

We grew up with expectations of normal, supportive behavior, but our expectations were not met. This spawned a grieving process. We didn't realize that previous generations were grieving too, which helps explain, but doesn't excuse their dysfunctional behavior. We often say our parents did the best they could with what they had. Unfortunately, what they had was too often not nearly enough, just as what they had received was not enough.

Unprocessed grief from our childhoods and our ancestors' childhoods can put us in a perpetual state of mourning. The generational nature of this is called "complicated grief." This grief can hold us hostage, undermine our ability to function well, and adversely complicate relationships. It can contribute to medical problems, because grief has friends called shame, sadness, depression, and insecurity – a great prescription for being unhealthy.

In ACA, we uncover the roots of our grief, recognize what we didn't receive as children, and see how we learned to react as a result. ACA teaches us how to stop the grief cycle and become our own loving parents. We do the work for ourselves before we can help future generations have less baggage to carry forward.

On this day I recognize the immense grief I carry. I know I can work through it and change my life, giving myself what I didn't get as a child. I reparent myself using the tools of ACA recovery.

Solution – Love

"We learn to reparent ourselves with gentleness, humor, love and respect." BRB p. 590

We may have grown up thinking that some people just knew how to love better than others. Perhaps we marveled at someone famous who seemed to have a deep, meaningful relationship with his or her romantic partner.

In meetings when we hear our truths being sung in another's voice, it affirms that we are not freaks; we are human beings no better or worse than the person sitting next to us. And as human beings, we can reparent the part of us that was cast aside. We aren't "finished products." We can give and take this confusing thing called love.

When we hear in others' voices and see in their eyes is that we have value. The "music" we are making together has meaning. It reaffirms our worth to recognize that we are not alone when we "sing" to each other. Our song, while it is ours and has parts to it that are ours alone, is not foreign to other ACAs.

The singing of truth at meetings is actually an expression of love for each other. What we can learn to feel, we can also share with our Inner Child.

On this day I will teach my Inner Child to sing to me the truth without fear, and to trust that real love takes commitment.

Addictions

"Many adult children find ACA and find recovery. A few seem to do well only to act out in addictions such as drugs, alcohol, food, gambling or compulsive spending." BRB p. 69

When we started attending ACA meetings, we may have heard words that triggered pain and confusion and hope, a baffling mix of emotions. After living a numbed-out life for so long, this new chaos inside felt threatening to many of us.

It may have been hard for us to listen to others speak; the pain it provoked seemed too much to bear. Soon, perhaps we couldn't find time for meetings. Maybe we turned to an old "friend" like alcohol, food, drugs, TV or another numbing behavior to quiet the stirred-up thoughts and feelings. But something had changed: "using" didn't feel the same because we now knew there was a better way.

Confused and alone, we returned to a meeting. We admitted we were having trouble just sitting still and listening because we were feeling *so much*, and feeling was scary. Our friends told us we were not alone, and that sometimes it gets worse before it gets better. They promised that if we kept coming back, sharing, listening, and working the program, it *would* get better.

They were right! With our Higher Power to guide us, we find "inside" answers when we begin to trust ourselves and our inner loving parent. We finally learn to comfort our Inner Child.

On this day if things get difficult, I will sit down, breathe, and reach for the strength and wisdom of the program. I will remember I am not alone.

Celebrate Success

"Our group members celebrate our growth and recovery with us." **BRB p. 404**

Our critical inner parent can whisper to us all day long, repeating the messages we heard as children from our parents, teachers, and other authority figures from our formative years. Sometimes we may not even hear the messages as thoughts; instead we just feel bad about ourselves off and on all day.

But in recovery, as we become aware of the influence this critical voice has over us, and by acknowledging the harm it is causing, we start to replace the negative messages with positive ones. We affirm ourselves for our willingness to change.

Since the ACA program requires courage, stamina, and perseverance, it can be very rejuvenating to celebrate our successes and reward ourselves for the progress we make. Sometimes after a rough day, simply making it to a meeting deserves a hug of congratulations. Or after working through a Step Four exercise, our reward might be calling a fellow traveler to receive affirmation as we talk about what we learned about ourselves.

On this day I will acknowledge the recovery actions I take by celebrating my progress with my fellow travelers who support and value me.

Self-Doubt

"We believe that something is wrong with us even though we cannot voice what the thing is. With this belief, we can go through our adult lives silently condemning ourselves and doubting ourselves as a normal course of living." BRB p. 30

When most of us came to ACA we had tried different approaches to change that may have helped move us forward a bit, but the underlying suffering and self-sabotage persisted. We were aware of our patterns, but we didn't know how to stop them.

It was easy for us to think there was something wrong that we couldn't stop. We thought we were doomed to this fate, and the hopelessness of it led to and perpetuated addictive and dysfunctional behaviors. This helped us feel alone and isolated, afraid to come out of hiding to expose the roots we were so ashamed of.

If we're fortunate and courageous enough to practice ACA recovery, we start to emerge from the "curse-like" nature of these painful thoughts. We feel glimpses of hope and promise that there is a way to stop repeating these painful patterns. We can stop condemning and doubting ourselves by speaking our truth in a safe and empathetic environment with other ACAs. We discover we're not alone; others have felt the same self-condemnation and self-doubt. This helps liberate us. We begin to build bridges that open ourselves to a new freedom and self-love that is ultimately what we've longed for.

On this day I will continue to be honest about my self-doubts and have the courage to tell my story. I will remember that I am not alone in this journey.

Inner Child

"Family dysfunction drives the Inner Child into hiding, leaving states of fear that wander the adult's soul. While the Inner Child or True Self can be the spark of our creativity, we must also remember the child is a deeply hurt part of ourselves." BRB p. 303

Long ago, in order to protect ourselves from the pain of having a dysfunctional family, we shut away our most vibrant essence, our True Self. Instinctively, we knew this tender and vulnerable part of us was unsafe and must be hidden away. Today, we may have lost touch with our True Self or Inner Child, forgetting he or she is waiting to be healed.

We have many buried hurts and disappointments that get triggered when we are reminded of the circumstances surrounding our original pain. It is then that our Inner Child reacts and we may find ourselves engaged in self-destructive behaviors if we don't provide appropriate comfort and reassurance.

When we work the ACA program and take the time to uncover our pain while treating our Inner Child with unconditional love, we begin to heal. Having the courage to listen will expose the pain we denied for so long. It also will bring back to life our childlike joy and wonder. We give voice to the child within so we can finally resolve the lifetime of pain he or she has shouldered.

On this day I unconditionally support my Inner Child so we both have the freedom to heal and feel safe.

Family Diagram

"We cannot overstate the need for creating an extensive family diagram, which reveals with greater clarity the effects of family dysfunction in our lives today." BRB p. 127

Many of our families told us we were screw-ups, and we ate that label hook, line, and sinker. We may have thought we were the only ones who were messed up – until we drafted a family tree with a twist.

Our ACA family diagram lists our ancestors, just as any family tree would. But we add at least one label from page 128 of the BRB to each person. We determine the labels by finding out whatever family history we can from our relatives. We probably know that Mom was a martyr and Dad was a loner. But maybe we didn't know that Grandpa was a ladies' man and Grandma worried excessively, or that Great Grandpa was a workaholic and Great Grandma drank too much, although they called it something else.

Our diagram helps us see that the way we talk, dress, walk, and smile may also belong to people from our past. This helps us decide what we want to keep, and what coping mechanisms we may have been imitating that no longer work for us.

When we realize that we may have been imitating what we observed, the family secrets stop and our own lives begin. Armed with this knowledge, we are free to make our own choices as we learn to reparent ourselves.

On this day I will remember the past so that I don't repeat the patterns of my family's dysfunction. The secrets are out in the open.

Spiritual Experience

"Who would have thought that talking, trusting, and feeling would equal a spiritual experience, but it does for adult children. We felt this new spirituality in our breathing and in the sense that we could face life on life's terms." BRB p. 285

It seems rather simple: show up at a meeting, listen, share and go home. These basic acts of self-care bring significant changes to our lives. When we make time in our day to attend a meeting, we practice self-love. When we give each other attention, we show each other that we care. When we listen quietly, attentively and respectfully, we become witnesses of another person's growth and our own. When we feel comfortable enough to share our recovery story, we demonstrate trust in the group. When we make an effort to accept the space we are in, we display our own vulnerability and move forward.

These simple acts of self-care yield a spiritual experience that far outweighs our efforts. Our fellow ACAs listen with empathy without interrupting our process, and they witness our spiritual experience, too.

As we learn to trust and surrender to the process, memories or feelings surface from beneath the weight of the now crumbling false self. We become free to breathe, to take positive, simple steps as we heal and truly live our lives.

On this day I take simple steps to practice self-care so that I may experience the spiritual nature of my recovery.

Workplace 'Family'

"It occurred to me while we were discussing the personality conflict that I was reacting to my co-worker's physical demeanor, which subconsciously reminded me of my brutal alcoholic stepfather." BRB p. 425

Sometimes we don't even hear the words. A glare or body posture that's reminiscent of our childhood is enough to send us into fear and shame. We were taught to react this way by caregivers we felt we had to placate in order to get our basic needs met. Some of us were sexually abused in the process or physically beaten. In that world, we had no alternative. We were stuck.

But now we are grownups who can take care of ourselves. When we experience fear and shame brought on by someone else's actions, whether in the workplace or elsewhere, we no longer play the game. We start to let others be accountable for what they say and do and how they feel; we let go of the non-verbal cues. When it is safe, we ask questions. "It seems like you're upset. Is there something you would like to talk about?" We no longer pretend and try to manipulate people and things. If the situation is dangerous, we remove ourselves, going to where we are nourished and loved. We are no longer controlled by others. We claim our power as an act of self-love.

On this day I will own my power. If others seem grouchy or unapproachable, I let that live with them and don't make it mine or try to fix it.

Service

"Service work is a key aspect of the ACA recovery program. Service is our way of giving back to ACA what was freely given to us by the fellowship." BRB p. 348

We were pressed into service as children. So giving service in ACA may mistakenly feel the same. But there is a critical distinction: our families did not allow us to choose to do service. However, in ACA we are asked if we wish to be of service.

The choice is ours. No guilt trips or manipulation. If we don't want to do service, the members will still accept and love us. It may be that service is not something we are willing to do for a while because we are still working on ourselves. "First things first" we say, and others support that decision.

ACA gives us the room and time to grow into the wonderful human being we were meant to be. Somewhere along the way, though, we may begin to understand that service is a form of thank you – of giving back.

We can give back by doing service at the group level, the intergroup level and the world level. We all do service at the individual level every time we attend a meeting and share.

On this day, if I have grown to the point where I have authentic love to give to my fellow ACAs, I will give service from that space of love.

Mistakes

"Each time we judged ourselves without mercy for common mistakes, there was loss." BRB p. 199

Many of us raised in dysfunctional families got the message that there was no room for error. We may have been raised by controlling parents who expected perfection. We were scolded or even abused for making mistakes. We weren't allowed to be kids and learn from our mistakes or taught that making mistakes was part of being human.

We internalized this judgment. Even after we left our childhood homes, we treated ourselves harshly when we made mistakes. Recurring thoughts may have kept an underlying anxiety alive within us, such as "I'm afraid I'm going to get in trouble. I'm afraid I'm going to get caught." Some of us were so ashamed of mistakes that we lied or cheated to cover them up. We might even have tried to numb ourselves from the anxiety of it all by engaging in addictive or compulsive behavior.

When we embrace ACA recovery, we discover that we can reveal our imperfections in a supportive fellowship. We can openly share stories of what we used to hide, and receive loving acceptance. We know we're not alone when we hear someone else share. We feel exhilarated and free when we work the Steps.

On this day I will identify a mistake I made and judged myself harshly for. I will tell this to at least one person whom I trust and feel unconditional acceptance from.

Promise Nine

"*Healthy boundaries and limits will become easier for us to set.*"
BRB p. 591

As children, our integrity was badly mangled. Physical, psychological, social, and spiritual boundaries were rarely, if ever, respected in our homes. As a result of this conditioning, we didn't learn to honor our own boundaries or those of others. If we grew up in a house where our toes were continually stepped on and no one took responsibility, we may have become toe-steppers and believed it was normal.

We "come to" at ACA meetings. We learn about respecting boundaries at our first meeting when we observe the no cross talk rule. This healthy boundary allows each of us to express our reality without comment, judgment or placating behavior. As we continue to attend meetings and share our experiences, we may discover other levels of toe-stepping that we are still acting out.

Through the Steps, we discover how our childhood boundaries were violated. From there, we progress to acknowledging how those violations affect us today. Through reparenting ourselves, we reestablish healthy internal and external boundaries. We begin to restore our integrity by making others – even those in authority – aware of the healthy limits we are setting in our lives.

On this day I will honor healthy boundaries at my ACA meetings. I will use them as stepping stones to acknowledging my buried childhood memories and feelings. I am learning to set boundaries with integrity.

Finding Value in the Past

"Through recovery, we realize our childhood experiences have great spiritual value. We recognize that we can help ourselves and others." BRB p. 334

In ACA, our journey back to the trauma of our childhoods does not come without pain. For some of us, the intensity of the feelings may be greater now than they were then because we were not allowed to feel or show our feelings as children. As adults, until we started this journey, most of us did not let ourselves feel the powerlessness and vulnerability that is necessary to heal our woundedness.

At the start of recovery, if someone had said that one day we would look at our childhood experiences as having value, many of us might have had great doubt that would occur. Some of us avoided this journey because we thought that if we ever started to cry, we wouldn't be able to stop. But with faith in our Higher Power and the strength of our fellow travelers, we became willing.

The guidance of the Steps and the support of other ACAs helped us release the pain of our past. The sharing of our experiences helped us see spiritual value in what we were finding, not only for ourselves, but because of the hope we offered to other recovering adult children.

On this day I know that being willing to share my journey helps me first and foremost, but it also helps others understand that this journey is spiritual. I am now able to reconcile my past and live in serenity.

Geographic Cure

"Even though we were whipped emotionally, we held out hope that a new relationship, a new job, or a move would be the cure, but it never was." BRB p. 334

We gave our all to other people. We were trained to do that. Who we were as people, our hopes and dreams, were not important.

We found ourselves in old situations again and again, with different faces. We moved to a new city to get out of messes, we changed jobs and we ended relationships. But our parents continued to appear in different forms, or there was the destructive relationship we had with our uncle or sister, but with a different face.

Some ACA meetings use this version of the Serenity Prayer.

> *Higher Power, grant me the serenity*
> *to accept the people I cannot change*
> *the courage to change the one I can*
> *and the wisdom to know that one is me.*

It hurts when we start to come out of denial, but it doesn't hurt forever. We hold on to our program and to our Higher Power. We learn to nurture those parts of us that need attention in order to grow. We bring light where there is no light by shining the love in the universe onto those wounded parts that still hide inside us. They want to come out to tell their stories and heal.

On this day, with my Higher Power's help, I will focus on myself to find the solution that will keep me from repeating my past patterns.

Healing

"Being in an ACA Twelve Step meeting was being in a place where without speaking I sat with others who genuinely knew me." BRB p. xviii

All we knew was that our lives weren't working. In the midst of the dysfunction we found the strength to reach out for help. It was suggested that our childhoods were still affecting us and that ACA might be a good idea. So we took a leap of faith and attended our first ACA meeting.

Almost immediately we felt a sense of comfort without really knowing what this group was all about. We began to hear what others were saying; it was as if they knew us without actually knowing us. We came to realize that we all had similar characteristics as a result of being brought up in dysfunctional madness. We knew we had arrived at a potential solution for so often feeling alone and different.

We found that this process of healing showed us how to grow from the inside out, and we knew we were on the right path. We found great comfort in the knowledge that the 12 Steps were leading us to spiritual recovery and growth. ACA was helping us find a way out of isolation, fear, and terminal uniqueness.

On this day I will remember the feeling of safety I find in my meetings. I know that I am no longer alone.

Sexual Abuse

"If you were touched, fondled, forced to perform sex acts, asked to perform sex acts, or watch sex acts as a child, it was not your fault no matter what the circumstance or no matter what was said by the adult or teen abusing you." BRB p. 174

Many of us came from sexually charged homes. We became part of our parents' sex life if they had sex in front of us. We may have been forced to listen to them talk about sex at the dinner table like it was no big deal. We might have been made a part of their extra-marital affairs when they fought about it in front of us and talked about it behind each other's backs.

We may have felt responsible for all of this. Our youth and sexuality were stolen from us because we couldn't protect ourselves. Their words became ingrained in us before we knew we were hurt. We may have acted out with other children to try and make sense of what we had heard, felt, and been exposed to. But then shame set in. Even so, it was hard to stop ourselves from sometimes being excited by the attention. We knew intuitively that this was a way we could get love, even though it felt bad.

Through ACA, we learn that no matter what happened to us, we know today that we are not alone, and that we aren't to blame.

On this day I will acknowledge my intense feelings that are tied up with any sexual abuse I experienced. I will stop myself from taking responsibility for what was done to me.

Prayer

"Keep it simple, but create a prayer that is specific to you and your relationship with the Divine, Higher Power, or God."
BRB p. 278

Due to the trauma of childhood, we have had many unanswered questions. "Who can I trust? How should I live my life? Will anyone or anything ever help me?" It has been almost impossible for many of us to rely on something outside of ourselves to help us find our truth, until we get to ACA.

Working the Steps helps us reconnect with a Higher Power of our own choosing. And prayers, or affirmations, can help us focus. There are many meaningful prayers in ACA; the Serenity Prayer that starts and ends most of our meetings and prayers at the end of many of the Steps in the BRB.

Creating a personal prayer can also be a way to confirm that we are part of the Power that helps guide us and gives us the strength we need. Our voices are finally heard when we speak our own truth. Our personal prayer can be as simple as "Higher Power, please guide me today. If I get scared, help me know I am not alone."

We can ask for the strength to work the 12 Steps, for understanding of what it means to be our own loving parent, and for help to learn how to heal our Inner Child. We remind ourselves we are not alone when we reach out to someone or something beyond ourselves.

On this day I know I am not alone, that my Higher Power is ready to help when I am ready to ask.

Unexpressed Grief

"Every adult child has unexpressed grief, which is usually represented by the symptoms of depression, lethargy, or forms of dissociation." BRB p. 199

We pretended for years that we were responsible for our own depression. We took drugs and acted out to combat the feelings that came up. We hung out with others who minimized and wallowed in pity and inaction. When the topic of sexual abuse or child abuse came up, we floated around the room, sometimes forgetting what other people were saying entirely. When we saw violence in a movie or on TV, we may have felt uncomfortable, but we ignored it.

Because we're the lucky ones who have found ACA, we are now seeing that there's a better way to live. When we go to meetings, we find people who speak their truth openly. We listen as those who came before us and after us spill the beans about their real thoughts. They talk about what they're doing to uncover the grief that underlies their depression and other symptoms that are a result of their childhoods. Through their examples, we learn to speak the language of the heart ourselves and we heal.

On this day I will go to a meeting to listen to the healing that's in evidence. If a meeting is not available, either in person or by phone, I will make contact with a fellow traveler so I can hear healing words.

Step One

"We run about attempting to control others and situations in an effort to avoid our own unmanageable lives." BRB p. 104

The need to try to control the people and things around us can be so strong. We may have this idea in our minds about how things "should" be. If only life were a certain way, we could feel good about ourselves. So we feel compelled to make the "should" a reality.

We push and prod and manipulate to try to get others to do what we want, completely missing the fact that we have to clean up our own house first. In the meantime, the harder we push, the crazier we feel because others never quite measure up to our ideals.

Step One tells us that control over others is a myth. Even though some things may change as a result of our efforts, we leave a lot of wreckage in our wake. Until we realize our powerlessness, until we realize the only ones we can truly change are ourselves, we will continue on a downward spiral, often driving the ones we care about from our lives, whether that happens emotionally, physically or both. It's a paradox of this program that only by admitting our powerlessness can we gain true manageability in our lives.

On this day I will remember to focus on myself and the changes I can make in my own life. I let others be so they can find their own path, even if it isn't the one I would choose for them.

Resentment

**"Before recovery, some of us spent countless hours in resentment."
BRB p. 380**

Many of us come into ACA with seething resentments. We can be recognized by the hundred-pound resentment rock around our necks. Convinced that the rock was placed there by others, we hang onto it as if to let it go would cause us harm. The rock is content to remain where it is. However, the pain of carrying it may be too much.

ACA teaches us that forgiving others has nothing to do with the other person. We do it for ourselves so we can let go of our own pain. We hear others say that praying daily to forgive the person we resent will eventually rid us of that resentment. We learn that we don't forgive the act, but do forgive the person.

Many of us who hear these things for the first time think it sounds foolish. But what else have we done that has been able to chip away at the poison our resentment has brought into our lives? So we try it, repeatedly, every day.

After a while, we notice a remarkable thing happening. The details that seemed so important and were feeding our ongoing resentment seem to be fading. Our rock is losing some of its weight.

On this day I do what has worked for so many others in recovery; I pray that the resentment I've been mired in for so long will be removed.

Staying Present

"We learn to be in the moment and to be present in our bodies. We learn that our thoughts can end." BRB p. 266

When we got to ACA we may have never felt what it was like to be in our bodies and experience our feelings. We may have had extreme emotion, but we didn't know how to feel our feelings. The sense of panic that often washed over us seemed so familiar we may not have noticed it for what it was.

As we became full participants in our meetings, learning to bare our souls, we began to crack. Sometimes this was painful, but we knew we didn't have to go through the pain alone. We made phone calls and did the work. We asked a fellow traveler to work the Steps with us. We believed other ACAs when they said we were not alone.

We gathered the courage to sit through the pain of withdrawal from what was keeping us tied up inside. Maybe for the first time we felt the shame and abandonment from our childhood – they were like ticking time bombs inside of us. As our bodies unwound, we learned not to panic.

We gained trust in ourselves and our Higher Power. We moved out of our pain and the mental and physical lethargy that may have held us down. We accepted that we weren't perfect and life got better. We became authentic in our words and actions.

On this day I will not travel this journey alone. When I need help, I know I have my fellow ACAs and my Higher Power.

Boundaries

"I had no modeling for having, stipulating, or enforcing boundaries. I would allow children, family members, and others to use me to their advantage. I would do many things for others and then receive nothing in return." BRB p. 413

When we're new to recovery, boundaries can be a mystery because most of us came from families that had none. Even if we know what they are, we still may not know when to have the courage to set them.

Boundaries can be very confusing and overwhelming. But by working the Steps and going to meetings, we learn from others. We talk to fellow ACAs about how they know when it's right to set a boundary, and about the language they use. We begin to have faith that we can do the same.

Then, sometimes without even thinking, we find ourselves setting limits with family members and others. Our anxiety begins to lessen because we know we are able to take care of ourselves with the help of others in the program and our Higher Power. We feel less resentful, too.

Letting others use us so we gain their approval may still be occasionally tempting. It can seem easier than standing up for ourselves. But when we experience the self-esteem we gain from saying no, we know that's what we really want.

On this day I will have the courage to set the boundaries that are important to me.

Humility

"With humility, we become more thoughtful in our decisions, and we are slower to anger. We begin to become actors rather than reactors to life's situations." BRB p. 224

As children, we may have been humiliated and told we didn't measure up. As we grew, we decided we needed to prove our worth. When we accomplished things, we expected validation. Most decisions we made were geared to gaining this outward affirmation. If anyone disagreed with us, it felt like an attack. We lashed out and tried to punish them. We may have even further reacted by increasing our efforts to prove our worth.

In ACA, we learn about humility, and that it has nothing to do with humiliation, a core wound. ACA teaches us that humility is the way to inner peace and finding our True Self. If we do something for others, the world doesn't have to know. We don't need accolades. And where it was second nature for us to react first and lash out, we now take a step back and examine reality.

This change is not easy. Our insecurities and triggers are often just below the surface, and we can fall into old patterns. But when we use our new tools, we have more self-awareness. We learn to look in the mirror and feel at peace with what we see.

On this day I will remember that humility keeps me grounded and on equal footing with those around me. I don't have to be 'greater than' to have value.

Identity Crisis

"'The adult child is an identity crisis having an identity crisis.' That means that we were born in crisis and cannot easily recognize another way to live other than crisis." BRB p. 70

Many of us came to ACA broken, bruised, and torn. The crazy thing is, we didn't notice our hearts were barely attached as a result of all the abuse. We may not have noticed that our faces were pale and withdrawn. We couldn't truly see ourselves for months or maybe years in the condition we were in. We were the walking dead, usually surrounded by other zombies.

Then we started to get better, one day at a time. The first time we asked to do the Steps with someone else, chose a home group, did service at a meeting, or told our stories in front of a group, we picked up little pieces of ourselves in the process and were restored to sanity. It was awesome. We didn't know that we could feel so good after feeling so bad. It was counter-intuitive, but going into our pain, with the help of those who had gone before us, made us feel better. It hurt, but it passed.

On this day I will look for yet another little way to improve my life. I embrace this recovery process that teaches me more about who I am each day.

Spiritual Experience

"Education alone is not enough to gain the greatest benefit from our spiritual experience. We also learn that spiritual experiences have greater meaning when matched with a dedication to work the ACA program." BRB p. 284

Most ACAs like to read. Our bookshelves, nightstands, or e-readers may be full of books, and certainly some of them provide guidance. But all the knowledge we may gain from reading will only be as good as the effort we make to use that information in our recovery process.

Recovery *work*, that four-letter word that many of us have avoided at great lengths, seems to be the catalyst for our spiritual growth. Our spiritual work may consist of reading, regularly supplemented with attending and sharing consistently and honestly at meetings, taking the Steps with fellow travelers, journaling, and giving service. Yes, it seems like a daunting list of tasks. It may even seem impossible. It's hard to get used to taking care of ourselves.

We know we can be gentle with ourselves, that some of the work will become a habit after a time, and that some of the work will have a different feel at different stages of our recovery. We practice patience and tolerance with ourselves, and softly allow the spiritual experience to flow naturally and easily.

On this day I will practice working the ACA program's many facets with ease and grace, realizing that the spiritual experience comes with work.

Tradition Nine

"With service grounded in love, ACA creates service boards and committees directly responsible to those they serve. The committees have bylaws and procedures but, as such, are not organized into a governing body." BRB p. 536

We come to an ACA meeting because we hear it's where we can talk about our childhood stuff. When we walk in, someone starts the meeting, someone else makes a secretary's report, someone else collects the donations, and others straighten thing up at the end. No one in the meeting is in charge; the group is in charge of all its affairs.

The upside-down pyramid represents our corporate structure, with the membership at the top and committees or service boards underneath. The newcomer has as much right to speak up as the most seasoned member. If an issue comes up and the group decides to form a committee, the committee still answers to the group. If a meeting or an intergroup makes inquiries to the World Services Organization, they must answer.

None of our trusted servants are given any power over an individual unless the individual presents a risk to other members. Then, the overall safety of the members must be cared for, with a measure of compassion and appropriate assertiveness.

Our love for each other and the realization of the enormous pain we have been in are what support the structure that keeps our fellowship functioning.

On this day I will be a responsible member of the ACA fellowship, responding to my fellow ACAs with the same gentleness, humor, love, and respect I have been given and have learned to show myself.

Trait Eleven

"We judge ourselves harshly and have a very low sense of self-esteem." BRB p. 15

Many of us habitually experienced critical thoughts in our heads all our lives. If anyone suggested that we "think positive thoughts," we tried. Sometimes it made us feel better, but it didn't last. We still found ourselves getting stuck and believing the critical voice inside. We thought that something must be wrong with us, but we certainly didn't want others to know how bad we felt and how hard we were on ourselves.

When we came to ACA, we identified with Trait 11 right away. "Yes, I definitely judge myself harshly," we thought. "But you mean I'm not alone in this curse? You mean I don't have to be ashamed of this because thousands, if not millions of others do this, too?"

In this program we find hope. We learn there is a Solution: to become our own loving parent. We learn what being a loving parent means and begin to practice reparenting ourselves. And just as with all parenting skills, we know that it takes practice to get it right. But it can eventually become as natural as our harsh self-judgment once was.

On this day I will practice reparenting myself with gentleness and self-love. This includes forgiving myself if I slip and find myself being self-critical.

October

"We learn how to play and enjoy life in ACA." BRB p. 572

Keep Coming Back

"We keep coming back because ACA is a way of life that fulfills us emotionally and spiritually." BRB p. 334

When we first walked into an ACA meeting, we may understandably have felt apprehension. We may have hit a bottom and went to the meeting hoping to find relief, but were equally afraid that we might not find any answers.

We may have found a meeting where there were some light-hearted people who didn't seem at all like our family members. Or maybe the meeting resonated with a pall of silence and sadness. In either case, what we found was a group of authentic people willing to be happy or sad and not deny their truths.

Someone asked us if we were new and if we had any questions. Perhaps we found it hard to even speak at that point. But we were invited to "Keep Coming Back," and told that when we had questions, someone would be glad to help us find the answers.

Now, as we keep coming back, we see the beauty of it all. Since our first meeting, members were receptive, open, and honest. They encouraged us to get comfortable. As we have heard the format repeated each time, our sense of safety and trust has grown. The people in the meeting have allowed us to be ourselves. All of this occurred through actions that radiated love, acceptance, and understanding.

On this day I renew my commitment to be part of a group whose actions come from an attitude of love and understanding of my needs as an adult child.

Walking Wounded

"Adult children have been described as the 'walking wounded,' strutting about in a state of emotional and spiritual bankruptcy while claiming to be 'fine.'" BRB p. 71

We carried around deep wounds from childhood. When we were asked how we were, we said "fine" because we felt they wouldn't really want to know. But our actions and attitude spoke our truth.

None of us would be in ACA if life had not been difficult for us. We didn't learn good coping skills when we were kids because our role models either masked their pain with something, often alcohol or drugs, or they took their anger out on the most defenseless people in their midst: us.

We learn in recovery that we have the ability to change our attitudes and our lives. We don't need to carry our wounds with us forever. We can consciously change our attitudes, and thus change not only ourselves but our part in the interactions we have with others. If we hang onto past hurts as if they are badges of courage, we rob ourselves of the promise of today.

We now choose to use the tools of ACA that will take us from the depths of our victim role into the warm sun. We shed our victim clothing for a new spring wardrobe.

On this day I will work my program as if my life depends on it, because it does.

Step Ten

"Continued to take personal inventory and when we were wrong promptly admitted it." *BRB p. 250*

As we read Step Ten, we see a way of staying current in our daily lives. When we take our daily inventory, we notice where we have succeeded as well as where we have fallen short or need to change. And when we are wrong, we have the courage to deal with it real time. We no longer shrink from our reality. We embrace the recovery process.

We listen in meetings and talk with our sponsors about difficult things. We are getting opening up channels of communication with our Inner Child by educating our inner loving parent.

The changes we see are magnificent, and we pause to deeply breathe in the love we have surrounded ourselves with. We no longer choke ourselves with fear. We are not perfect and recognize that we are a work in progress. This admission creates a personal circle of compassion and gentleness that we need for our recovery.

We reach toward the sky like the beautiful seedlings that we are, stretching out towards the sun as we fulfill our destiny. We do not know exactly where we are going, but we know we need never be alone again. We look at our lives as symphonies that are always playing to us if we are willing to listen.

On this day I will hold the ship steady as I cruise along, regardless of what the sea looks like. When I make mistakes, I will remember that practicing the Tenth Step helps me feel free.

Spiritual Experience

"ACA holds out hope and acceptance to the hurting adult children of the world, who can 'hit a bottom' and reach out for help. Allowing the True Self to emerge in the nurturing atmosphere of ACA is a spiritual experience that awaits any adult child stepping onto the broad highway of ACA recovery." BRB p. xv

Coming to ACA was a long and complicated journey for many of us. We might have known that our families were not right. Some of us may have even thought that maybe we were the problem and sought any number of ways of adjusting ourselves to the family's dysfunction.

At some point, we finally hit a bottom, surrendering to the fact that we needed something different, but not knowing what it was.

Somehow our Higher Power opened the path, our eyes, and our minds so that we could find our first ACA meeting. Perhaps it was the suggestion of a friend or trusted counselor, or an internet search. Our Higher Power found us searching.

As we attend ACA meetings, we get the sense of belonging we had unknowingly sought. Here, the spiritual experience unties the entanglements of our childhoods. Our True Self comes out of the dark hidden places and sits among our fellow ACAs.

On this day I remind myself that my search has led me to my Higher Power, my True Self, and support from my fellow ACAs.

Enjoy Life

"We learn how to play and enjoy life in ACA." BRB p. 572

Many of us who grew up in alcoholic or dysfunctional homes had little time or opportunity for play. Faced with adult chaos, much of our early life was spent in survival mode.

In ACA, we learn that living life in our rearview mirror is not really living. Letting go of the past allows us to experience the present without the blinders that keep us from joy.

But where is the joy? It's not something that we can just sit around and wait for. Joy is to be sought. It's everywhere, but it must be found; it will not find us. We must open our eyes, our minds, and our hearts to search it out.

Joy is giving to others with no expectation of return. It's hugging someone who needs it or stopping at a shelter to walk a homeless dog. When we bring joy to others we bring it into our own lives.

On this day I will find the joy that is all around me that's just waiting for me to experience it.

Inner Critic

"We stop in mid-sentence if we are putting ourselves down or criticizing our thoughts or behaviors. We identify the source of the negativity which is the inner critic inside all adult children." BRB p. 299

Who tells us each day whether we live up to a standard?

Who lies awake each night running over the "could haves" or "should haves" for the day or for days gone by?

We weren't born with shame; it was instilled in us. We had no experience to measure or reject that shame when we were children, so we had to accept it. But who is keeping that shame alive in us today?

It's our inner critic that reflects the negative voices from our past. But we now have the choice to change that voice – to live life on our own terms and bury the "could haves" and "should haves." We are no longer required to listen to the messages that keep shame alive in our everyday thoughts.

Who puts a value on us if we do not value ourselves?

In ACA, we are accepted for who we are. We join together, not to bemoan our imperfections, but to find "the courage to change the one I can, and the wisdom to know that one is me.*" Our strength in numbers gives us that courage and assures us that we are now and always have been valued human beings.

On this day I look at myself through the eyes of my fellow ACAs and my Higher Power. Instead of listening to my inner critic, I believe what they say – that I am valued.

---

*Page 424 of BRB

Moderation

"Today, when I am acting compulsively, I take a breather from that activity to moderate my behavior. Sometimes I have to say aloud, 'I'm turning this over to God.'" BRB p. 138

We have homes with automatic temperature controls. The heat doesn't engage until the thermostat senses there's not enough warm air, and the air conditioning does the reverse.

This process of modulation (regulating according to measure or proportion) was not present in our families of origin. Nearly every life situation either received a maximal response or was virtually ignored (denial). A parent could rage over a traffic jam, but never discuss a tragic family death.

This lack of modulation or moderation in response to life's events sent most of us into our adult lives without effective role models or acceptable ways to handle our emotions. We had two settings, MAX ON and MAX OFF, and we didn't understand why. We blew up with anger and had no clue why we were unable to grieve serious life events. We now know we were programmed to be that way.

In ACA, with the Steps and the help of a fellow traveler, we see that we're not alone. We gain serenity and can thoughtfully assess a life event, and then decide on a reasonable course of action, if action is required. We learn to do our part and then "Let Go and Let God." As we go through this process, we gain serenity.

On this day I can choose a modulated response to a situation. I choose NOT to use the reactionary or denial behaviors I learned as a child.

Uncovering the Truth

"We are looking for the truth so that we can live our own lives with choice and self-confidence. We want to break the cycle of family dysfunction." BRB p. 27

Most of us grew up telling lies so the outside world would think that things were okay at home. We hid the truth because of the shame we felt, and because we understood the family rules, whether they were unwritten or not.

As we became adults, we often found it easy to continue lying about ourselves. Maybe we embellished to make ourselves look better because we weren't even sure what the truth was anymore. Or maybe we did so because we "knew" that people wouldn't accept us for who we really were. But the more lies we told, the harder it became to keep track, which made us terrified of slipping up.

In recovery, we begin to uncover the truth of who we are and where we come from, seeing the necessity of breaking our dysfunctional cycle. We learn to be honest about ourselves in our meetings where we learn we're not alone. We begin to see that others respect our honesty in a way that is constructive and hopeful. By choosing to be genuine, we find that this is actually the easier, softer way many of us have always looked for.

On this day I will honor myself by recognizing when I am tempted by an old habit. I will do what's right for my True Self.

Perfectionism

"Perfectionism is a response to a shame-based and controlling home. The child mistakenly believes that she can avoid being shamed if she is perfect in her thinking and acting." BRB p. 36

As children, many of us were either subtly or overtly shamed on a regular basis. We lacked true acceptance from our parents and learned to internalize the shame. We got the message that we were not okay as we were. Some of us tried to act in ways that garnered the approval and love we so longed for.

Further, we secretly blamed ourselves for our parent's alcoholism or dysfunction, thinking that if only we could be perfect, things would get better and our pain would end. But that was a losing battle. So we learned to associate being imperfect with being unlovable.

With our Higher Power as our true parent, in ACA we learn the right message: that we are worthy of love in all of our imperfection. We could not have changed our parents' sickness by being perfect, even if perfection was possible.

This is generational; our parents passed down the dysfunction in which they were also raised. But we are choosing to hear a different message and putting an end to the cycle of shame.

On this day I let go of my drive to be perfect by embracing the knowledge that I am enough and am lovable just as I am.

Hypervigilance

"In adult children PTSD tends to manifest itself in hypervigilance, compulsive behavior, and hard-to-detect body sensations. It is as if our bodies have 'rewired' themselves to protect us from severe harm or severe harm that almost occurred." BRB p. 178

Soldiers learn immediately what hypervigilance means: Watch out! The enemy is close!

In our family of origin, we experienced hypervigilance on a regular basis. If we didn't watch out, we or someone close might get hurt. In the middle of these experiences, we vowed we'd never do that to our own families.

But alas! The lessons were too well taught. Something seems to snap, and it's as if we go into a trance, screaming, belittling, or calling our loved ones names. We scold, threaten, slam doors, and drive away in a cloud of dust. We push away those we love most. We've become the multi-generational living triggers that cause hypervigilance in our loved ones.

When we realize we've become the perpetrators, we look for help in the rooms of ACA. It's in the Steps that we identify the root of our hypervigilance. We look at our triggers to try to determine how and where they originated. Triggers derived from our hypervigilance are what make us inexplicably react, freeze, hold our breath, or shake in our shoes. As we learn more, we usually find fear and guilt at our core, and those feelings are often frozen. We bring them to life so we can heal.

On this day I will slow down and breathe deeply if I find myself feeling triggered by my hypervigilant reactions. I can nurture myself through this.

Addiction to Excitement

"Gossip, dramatic scenes, pending financial failure, or failing health are often the turmoil that adult children create in their lives to feel connected to reality. While such behavior is rarely stated as such, these behaviors are an 'addiction' to excitement or fear." BRB p. 16

Many of us came into ACA perhaps unaware of the depth of chaos we had created around us. We felt we were in a fog we couldn't see our way out of. We didn't consciously cause this chaos. Our behavior resulted from the emotional and perhaps physical chaos we experienced in our childhood dysfunctional, abusive homes.

As we learned more about our addiction to excitement that drove us, we began to see how our fear was feeding us. And we realized that we needed this inner drug store to be closed for business. The adrenaline rush that we were not even aware of was blocking any progress. We knew the chaos had to stop.

As we find the answers in our meetings and by talking to others, we begin to nourish ourselves with a healthy program that brings us peace and serenity. We become committed to change because we've had the pain and anguish and we want to be done with it. We now have the inner radar to see what is coming, and when something feels wrong, we pause as long as we need to. Then we move away. We realize the health of our Inner Child is at stake!

On this day I will give my Inner Child and my adult the gift of freedom from fear and unhealthy excitement that we both need and deserve.

Asking for Help

"ACA recovery begins when the adult child gives up, asks for help, and then accepts the help offered." BRB p. 123

Many of us grew up in families where it wasn't okay to give up, much less ask for help. We were just supposed to know how to do it, and if we didn't figure it out, then we were punished in some way.

As adults, we knew we had to do it all ourselves because we didn't know how to rely on others. To ask for help would make us seem inadequate, or maybe it would give people a reason to think we weren't smart enough.

So we kept at it and at it until one day we just couldn't do *it* anymore. Something gave way, and we hit a bottom. We couldn't manage life anymore; we were never given the right tools.

We are the lucky ones in our families because we found help in an ACA meeting. We learned that it's okay to ask for that help—we were never meant to do it alone. We were given the wrong messages.

On this day I will remember that my support system in ACA is always available to me. I just have to be willing to ask.

Breaking the Ties

"As children we are tied to our families by our physical needs."
BRB p. 88

Many of us lived our childhood thinking what happened to us was our fault. But we existed at the whim of others. We were able to eat, but the price was being shamed by an angry parent or ignored by one who was self-involved. Some of us felt we were only given a place to sleep if we didn't talk about the sexual abuse going on in our house. We blamed ourselves because we had no other way of understanding the situation.

Today, as we see our childhood for what it was, we learn to replace the abuse by cultivating an inner loving parent. This parent protects our Inner Child and allows us to sit with things until they sort themselves out. We don't jump to conclusions or overreach for an outcome that we can't see. If we don't know what to do, we call someone and get help to turn it over. We allow our feelings to flow freely. It is cathartic.

No longer are we tied to our families in an unhealthy way. We focus on ourselves and begin to accept a Higher Power of our understanding. We don't rush to judgment when there is no clarity. We are a part of an awesome universe and we know we can't see all sides of it at once. We accept that we are where we need to be for today.

On this day my inner loving parent creates boundaries that make my Inner Child feel safe and whole, regardless of what's going on around me.

Service

"Red flags that warn that a bottom or relapse is coming involve: dropping out of meetings and isolating; being argumentative or unreasonable; gossiping; losing focus and returning to one of the family roles of hero, lost child, or mascot; general noncommitment to recovery; avoiding the Steps and intellectualizing; failing to give service to ACA; binging on sex, drugs, food, or other compulsive behaviors; and acting with perfectionism and failing to talk about feelings and critical inner messages." BRB p. 70

ACA deals with deep attitudes and behaviors that sometimes are difficult to stay conscious of. Sure, the blaring ones are easy to recognize and to admit into our consciousness. But others lie beneath multiple layers of self-deception or socially-celebrated attributes.

When we miss meetings on a consistent basis, it may seem like a way of avoiding unwanted pain and disappointment. But it also provides the opportunity for our critical parent to distract us from our healing journey. This false self is masterful at finding ways to avoid doing the work that gives us a lifeline of hope.

In ACA, one way that keeps us coming back is to give service from a space of love. This is a sure-fire way of keeping ourselves tuned into our True Selves and our inner loving parent, which leads to taking care of our Inner Child. By having consistent check-ins with ourselves, we can stay focused on what is right with our program and how to best help fellow ACAs begin their recovery process.

On this day I will give service to my ACA group as a way of staying conscious and focused on my recovery process.

Promise Ten

"Fears of failure and success will leave us, as we intuitively make healthier choices." BRB p. 591

While most folks believe they want to be successful, we know that many ACAs fear success. This is a fear born from years of regular servings of failure with side orders of abandonment, shame and humiliation. To be successful means that the spotlight can be turned on us, which recalls painful memories of never being good enough.

As we learn to connect with our inner loving parent, our Inner Child, and our Higher Power, our intuitive sense is sharpened. No longer dependent on old tapes or the critical voice inside of our heads, we are free to use this intuitive sense to make healthy decisions. At the same time, we are clear that we are on a spiritual path and that every situation is a spiritual lesson. There is no way to fail on this path.

Failure is the domain of our inner critic's all-or-nothing thinking. As we learn to see this for what it is, we filter everything around us through our inner loving parent. We become attuned to our Inner Child's quiet and steady voice as it tells us the better course for our spiritual, physical, and emotional development. We release our fears.

On this day I will listen for guidance from my purest Inner Child's perspective and trust that my fears will lose their grip on me. I am open to being guided to higher levels of spiritual, emotional, and physical consciousness.

Self-Love

"I lived my life in an endless cycle of harmful relationships, lost jobs, and lost friends. I could never be a friend, actually. I stopped getting into relationships to stop the pain. I had no choice. I was compulsive and getting more out of control with each passing year." BRB p. 141

It's amazing how we can be unaware that we're harming ourselves. We choose the wrong people, places and things to make us happy for the wrong reasons. Sometimes we know we're allowing people to use us so we can use them. We use people as Band-Aids to cover our unhealed wounds until we notice we still hurt and the Band-Aids can't help us. Our sponsors suggest that we work on loving ourselves. But how?

We read ACA literature, give ourselves affirmations and journal. We look at our past, deal with our hurts, forgive ourselves and others. We do the work. And one day we notice that it's happening. We've started to love ourselves and even like ourselves. We stop using Band-Aids and now have authentic friends who love us as we are, while we continue the journey of recovery. The greatest gift is that we learn to be a friend to ourselves.

On this day I will do the work. The journey to self-love is not an easy one, but the payoff is priceless.

Changing Inside

"As we greet co-workers or friends, we feel that we are changing inside. We begin to recognize a power inside we had not known before." BRB p. 273

Regularly taking a quiet time helps us to grow up emotionally and spiritually. How we take it depends on our choices. At first, we spend time by ourselves when we need to, letting others do what they will to take care of themselves. If they spend it getting drunk and high, we let them, but we no longer seek that outlet for our pain and suffering, if that was how we previously coped.

Later, we see that we actually enjoy spending time alone. We don't fill ourselves up with others just to pass the time and keep us numb. We no longer pretend to be excited when we're not. We seek those we can truly connect with and enjoy. We talk not just about superficial things, but about who we are and what's important to us.

People respect us more at work and elsewhere because we don't seek constant approval as we did in our families. We no longer do things we're uncomfortable with just for the sake of fitting in. As we become more genuine, we allow others to find their own paths; instead of labeling them, we now make room for our differences. If some don't like the new us, we have to let them go. We adjust our list of whom we can trust.

On this day I will own my power to be genuine and feel how comfortable it is to focus on being myself.

Reparenting

"With the Steps and by reparenting ourselves, we can further remove the 'buttons' that have been pushed by others to manipulate us or to get a reaction out of us." BRB p. 326

As children, others manipulated us at will. Sometimes it seemed we were born to be used by others. We showed up for horrible people who sucked us dry of our courage and strength, because that is what we learned from our families. That's what they told us we were meant for by the way they treated us every day.

As adults, we now know we can set boundaries with those who abuse us. When we find that we have recreated an unmanageable situation at work, we get new jobs. We change our living arrangements when we find that we are once again living with addicts who keep us awake at night and need us to look after them.

In recovery, we make space to feel the anger and shame that were handed to us in our childhoods, and we heal. We may even detach from abusive family members permanently if that's what it takes to maintain serenity.

On this day I will write down what I want my life to be like as a way of turning things over to my Higher Power.

Effort

"Recovery takes effort." BRB p. 50

A Higher Power provides food for all the birds on earth but doesn't put it in their mouths.

It would be nice to just sit in the rooms of recovery and let the program sink in by osmosis without having to work at it. Some of us have tried this, a few for many years, and wondered why we were not experiencing much change. We may be substance-free but we continue to have emotional chaos and dysfunction in our lives and in our heads.

Eventually, if we're lucky, it will dawn on us that, try as we might, change will not happen without significant effort on our part. And we need the program, our fellow travelers, and most of all our Higher Power. If we're stalled, we open our minds and hearts to see what works for others. Maybe the same thing will work for us.

We've been continuously told that recovery takes effort. And as we do the work, we realize that recovery does not bring the absence of storms, but it gives us a much needed umbrella we never had before.

On this day I will leave "the nest" and do the work necessary for the recovery that will change my life.

Relationships

"Adult children intuitively link up with other adult children in relationships and social settings." BRB p. 13

No matter how much we told ourselves that we wouldn't repeat the patterns of our parents, most of us reached adulthood and found ourselves inevitably attracted to others who came from similar backgrounds. It was like we could see each other in the dark, like we had some type of special radar. This didn't just happen by accident. It was a well-established pattern that we saw all around us in childhood.

Through it all, we found ourselves clinging to the fairy tale that one day we would find Mister or Miss Right and we would magically live happily ever after. But we kept meeting the "wrong" ones. Our dysfunctional coping behaviors only allowed us to relate well to certain people.

When we finally saw the writing on the wall, that things were not going to change unless we found the courage to change ourselves, we were lucky enough to get to an ACA meeting. There we found others like ourselves, but these others were doing the work to dig out from under their messy lives. As we listened to what they had learned, we became willing to make the journey that would require us to be truly honest with ourselves, perhaps for the first time. This journey will take us to where we are entitled to be – happy, joyous and free.

On this day I will have the courage to make the changes in my life that will make me whole. I will reach out and I know someone will be there.

Patience

"Rebuilding, or building, our lives takes time. It takes patience and steady focus." BRB p. 431

Many of us never knew what focus or patience really looked like until we came to ACA. We had spent our lives moving frantically from one thing to another.

As we began practicing new behaviors, we started by first being consistent in our attendance at meetings. We then began reaching out by making phone calls and asking for help to stay focused. When we became willing to take on service roles in meetings, it was to both feed our own recovery and to give back. We were searching for balance, realizing it took patience to recover from the years of dysfunction we'd experienced.

We learned to take care of our physical needs, resting when we were tired and eating healthy food to nurture our bodies and minds. We began retiring our compulsive behaviors as we became more aware of them.

Now we see our efforts paying off as we experience serenity. We have learned to ask for what we need in our jobs, friendships and romantic relationships because we know we're worth it. If others don't hear us, we move on. We have walked courageously into the light of recovery, feeling safe, perhaps for the first time.

On this day I pray for patience, and value the opportunities that present themselves. I ask for the guidance I need to stay focused on my needs.

Grief

"ACA meetings can unlock the grief that has not been addressed for years." BRB p. 68

The thought of doing grief or loss work doesn't sound inviting. It sounds as if we are going to a funeral. There's a deep sense of sadness just thinking about it. But when we review our childhoods, we realize that our sadness is actually waiting for an opportunity to be expressed.

In meetings we witness strong survivors of family alcoholism and other dysfunction as they visit their childhood funerals. We hear them share the current effects of their harrowing childhood experiences. This helps many of us to start recalling the events that led to the feelings we have had of a continuous sense of loss.

As we keep coming back, our memories and feelings keep coming back also – sometimes gradually, sometimes haltingly. But they do come if we are consistent in our meeting attendance. This is where we find the space to express the grief of our childhood losses. It's where we learn to heal after years of denying our feelings.

On this day I will remember that it's important for me to share my memories in order to heal. It also allows me to connect with others who have had similar experiences.

Safety

"Our meetings offer a safe environment for adult children to share their common experiences." BRB p. 333

Because of the many kinds of abuse and/or neglect we've experienced, both as children and adults, it is a huge issue for us to be able to connect with ourselves, other adult children, and a Higher Power.

We can begin by just showing up at ACA meetings. We are not forced to share; the choice is ours. We work at our own pace, perhaps just observing and getting a feel for things. And when we are ready, we can begin to absorb and actually work the ACA program.

As we break out of isolation, we realize we are not alone. We start working the Steps and understanding the Traditions. We may use the tool of journaling as a way to uncover what's going on for us. But however we do things, we let the ACA program, other people, and our Higher Power into our lives.

There is no special order to how things have to work. We are unique, and we do recovery in the way that works best for us. It's only important that we do it, because we deserve the safe, healthy connections that are now available to us.

On this day I know that my meetings provide the safety that helps me continue my personal growth.

Step Two

"Came to believe that a power greater than ourselves could restore us to sanity." BRB p. 130

Many of us have never known what sanity is, and the very word can set us on edge. We know everything that sanity is not, because that's how we grew up. We think, "How can I be restored to a state I've never experienced? If this Step is about restoration, maybe ACA isn't for me." This thinking might have moved us to walk away before we invested any hope in the process.

But we were fortunate enough to hear from others who take a more gentle perspective. They say, "Calm down. Try not to jump to conclusions too soon. Some of us had the same thoughts and feelings as you." They suggest that coming to believe in a Higher Power of our own choosing and working the Steps can give us the promise of a new life, one free of the character defects that have kept us from living purposefully. They assure us that the program and their Higher Power have worked miracles in their lives.

This feels comforting and helps us see that we are where we belong. We change our perspective and come to believe, act, and feel…sane. For many of us, sanity simply means peace of mind, which we gratefully welcome.

On this day I recognize that the insanity in my life was rooted in the dysfunction of my childhood. It no longer has the same hold over me because peace and serenity are what I focus on as I experience recovery.

Control

"Our attempts at control bring spiritual death to a relationship with ourselves and others." BRB p. 41

How many forms of control are there? On entering the rooms of recovery, we find there are almost as many as there are people.

But don't all people attempt to control others? Yes, but not with the feverish pitch present in adult children.

As young children, we had no control in our family of origin. When chaos surrounded us and threatened our physical, emotional, and spiritual well-being, we could only cower to the powers that caused the abuse.

The almost fierce need many of us have to control others stems from being these abused children. We fear that if at any moment we let go of the reins and allow others to take control, history will repeat itself, and we will again be that five-year-old hiding behind the sofa.

This helps explain why we use all the methods we can to keep control of our environment, or the illusion of control. And we attempt to hide what we're doing by saying things like, "I'm just looking out for everyone's welfare."

In ACA, we learn that control is fear-driven, and we learn to face our fears. We bring our 5-year-old out from behind the sofa and reparent ourselves with love and kindness.

On this day I will face my fears with the help of my fellow travelers and release my need to control others.

Self-Forgiveness

"Many adult children struggle with self-forgiveness because we are oriented to doubt ourselves or to be hypercritical of ourselves as children." BRB p. 234

We carry messages in our heads that if we do something and anyone has a negative reaction, we must have made a mistake. And if anyone tells us we did something wrong, our first thought is, "Of course they're right!" It doesn't matter whether we actually did something wrong or not.

We tell ourselves things like "I should have known better!" "What's the matter with me?" "Look at his expression; of course he's mad at me." These are like the messages we heard as children that became so ingrained that we learned at a very early age to say them to ourselves.

Now as adults in ACA, we stop "beating ourselves up" and see the full story. Our healthy support system can help us understand the reality of our situation, to determine what's really ours and what actually belongs to someone else.

On this day I will remember that I deserve to treat myself better! I will use the tools of the program to separate myself emotionally from an uncomfortable situation and take on only what belongs to me.

Trait Twelve

"We are dependent personalities who are terrified of abandonment and will do anything to hold on to a relationship in order not to experience painful abandonment feelings, which we received from living with sick people who were never there emotionally for us." BRB p. 17

We held on to relationships that died years ago. We were ashamed that we couldn't stand up for ourselves, but we told ourselves that at least we had somebody. It was a roller coaster – things got worse, then better, then even worse than before. We were going deeper and deeper down a never-ending hole with no light, and we were running out of time.

Today we breathe the crisp cool air of discovery in the sunlight of ACA. We choose to be honest with ourselves and others because it's become a habit for us, one that was born out of our Step work and calm commitment to the program that guides us through the once-dark regions of our lives. We hide from no one.

We are alive, whole, and sane, and we like it. If someone wants to leave our life, we let them go. In ACA, we've learned we cannot do for others what they will not do for themselves. When we let things die, there's room for more love and new growth. We celebrate the old and the new, seeing their connection to our spiritual health.

On this day I will do the work to heal my past and learn to focus on the healthy things I've begun to experience. I will let go and let my Higher Power in.

Passive-Aggressive

"By addressing our fear, we release some of our glaring behaviors of manipulation, passive-aggressiveness, and false kindness."
BRB p. 40

We grew up in homes where love was conditional. How we were treated depended on how we acted. Many of us were so fearful of being punished or ostracized that we learned to manipulate those around us. Some of us became very good at passive-aggressive behavior; we learned to get what we thought we wanted or needed without directly asking for it by putting on a false mask.

Because these were survival mechanisms based in fear, as adults we realized that we weren't really getting what we needed. For some of us, the frustration of feeling like we had to operate in this manner often built to a point where we would explode, sending ourselves spiraling into some form of addiction to cope. Eventually, we landed in a place where we didn't know who we really were.

For those of us who are "lucky," when all of our tactics failed us, we found our way to an ACA meeting. This is where we begin to face our underlying fears and learn how to be honest with ourselves. We start to relate to others in a healthy manner. Yes, it's challenging to change such ingrained habits, but we know it's possible. We see others in the program doing it all around us.

On this day, if I am tempted to manipulate others with old behaviors, I will affirm for myself that I am capable of new, healthy, life affirming behavior.

Parental Blame

"It is not the purpose of the Twelve Steps of ACA to place blame on the parent or caregivers; however, the adult child also must not shield the parents during the inventory process." BRB p. 109

Condemning or raging at ourselves for not doing something "right" is a carryover from our dysfunctional childhood. This behavior was programmed into us. In ACA, we learn to change that by re-programming ourselves to be kind to both our Inner Child and our adult self.

When we're tempted to get stuck in blaming our parents for everything that's wrong in our lives, we are reminded that ACA is not about blame. We revisit the past to learn why we think and act as we do and find out how to change our thought patterns. And we accept responsibility for our own actions as adults.

While we strive to forgive our parents so we can let go of our resentment, this doesn't mean we forgive their deeds. We learn to forgive the person separate from the action. Dysfunction is a family disease passed down through the generations. Even though we forgive, it may still be necessary to separate from people who continue to be unsafe.

We recognize where our self-harming behaviors originated and know that we don't have to hang onto them. We accept that we are human beings, and as such, we know that we will inevitably make mistakes. But we are not now, nor have we ever been a mistake.

On this day I honor myself as my own best friend. I will stop the cycle of self-inflicted emotional abuse learned through the generations of dysfunction.

Tradition Ten

"As a fellowship, we have no opinion on outside issues. We exist for one purpose: To carry the message to those still suffering from the effects of growing up in a dysfunctional family." BRB p. 539

The issues relating to the disease concept of alcoholic/dysfunctional family systems are endless. We could sit in meetings and talk about them continuously without ever focusing on ourselves. Many of us might even be moved to involve ourselves in an outside cause as a way of "trying to save the world." But this would be a re-creation of the dysfunction learned in childhood where we dealt with the needs of others instead of ourselves.

When ACA stays away from public controversy, our doors are open to all who desire to recover from the dysfunctional effects of their childhoods. Were we to take a position on any controversy, we might initially attract some people interested in that cause, but we could dilute our message and potentially make it unsafe for ACAs in general.

If we, as individuals, decide after careful thought, that we want to be involved with an issue outside of the bounds of ACA, we are mindful that we don't represent ACA. In this way, the meetings keep a singleness of purpose, remain free from emotional intoxication, and provide the adult child the greatest chance to recover.

On this day I will help my meeting keep its focus on ACA recovery. If outside issues arise, I will respectfully remind others of Tradition Ten, affirming for myself that ACA is my opportunity to champion myself as the most important cause in my life.

False Belief

"The effects of verbal and emotional abuse are hard to comprehend because we never thought to challenge what was said to us or about us until we found ACA. If we were told we were worthless or ignorant as children, we believed it without question." BRB p. 30

For many of us, our caretakers taught us in action and deed that we were worthless. When there was no food, we thought it was because we deserved none. We were bad. We cried alone in our rooms, but eventually learned not to cry when we saw that it made us more vulnerable. We retreated from our bodies and emotions until nothing was left but confusion. The trauma was complete. We had become numbed-out zombies compulsively seeking the next shock to remind us we were still alive.

We now allow ourselves to get angry at those who harmed us and others who knew and did nothing. We journal, we talk to friends. We rage and hit pillows with wiffle bats and scream if we have to, but we don't hold it all in. We let go of blaming ourselves. We know we weren't the cause of what happened.

We now choose to be around those who validate us when we talk about what happened and let go of those who stare blankly as we recount our childhood. We don't spell it out – we just let go.

On this day I choose to talk to those who can truly hear me and let go of those who can't. I know I am worthwhile and deserve to have caring people in my life.

November

"We are changing. We are beginning to see that we have choices." BRB p. 578

Giving and Receiving

"With our common experiences, we find that we can help one another in ways that others cannot because we carry with us empathy and understanding of the disease of family dysfunction."
BRB p. 515

An endless cycle of giving and receiving is at the very heart of the success and continuation of ACA. Adult children understand each other, because we have experienced similar effects from being raised with similar dysfunction. Being in the company of those who know of our pain brings comfort and reassurance that we are not alone.

When we hear others who have done the work and are reaping the benefits of recovery, we are filled with hope for our own future. As we work the Steps and see progress in ourselves, we willingly reach out to others in need. By honestly and openly sharing our experience, we help them open up to the possibility of their own growth.

We see that our pain is subsiding little by little, and we are finding a new happiness in the way others have. By giving of ourselves to fellow adult children, we are filled with gratitude for a new way of life, and share willingly to encourage others on their journey.

On this day I accept the love and support so freely given by my ACA brothers and sisters, and as I experience my own recovery, I open my heart to those seeking a new way.

Patience

"Another stumbling block involves taking on too much program work at once. Some members who smoke, overeat, and act out sexually might attempt to address all of the conditions at once. For these ACA members, we suggest two program slogans: 'Easy Does It' and 'First Things First.'" BRB p. 51

When we first decided to attend an ACA meeting, we entered these rooms alone, scared, angry, or exhausted. We knew we needed to do something, but we didn't know what – that's why we came here. Many of us were looking for ways to change the people in our lives, and we wanted to change them now.

We learned that our family of origin issues and failed relationships didn't happen overnight. We don't need to read every self-help book this week or hand the Laundry List to everybody we know. If we really want to trust that the program is going to work for us, we learn to follow in the footsteps of those who came before us – to slow down and "Take It Easy."

We learn how to take care of ourselves by attending meetings. We pray for the courage to ask someone to be our sponsor or fellow traveler who will help us work the Steps. We stop complicating, analyzing, and debating. We learn to keep the focus on ourselves and "Keep It Simple."

On this day I will remember to be kind to myself and use our slogans, especially "First Things First," "Easy Does It," and "Keep It Simple." They will help me stay grounded.

Step Eleven

"Sought through prayer and meditation to improve our conscious contact with God, as we understand God, praying only for knowledge of God's will for us and the power to carry that out." BRB p. 263

In ACA, we begin to get in touch with a loving Higher Power that some of us choose to call God. We realize we have an inner compass that is steering us, and we are not alone.

As we continue to pray and meditate, we often find that the image of our Higher Power changes. This is okay; it is a normal part of growth. We are changing, sometimes quickly, sometimes slowly. But we are always striving to move forward, seeking what is right for us.

We no longer struggle or fight when we get confused. When we are looking for answers, we stop and smell the roses until they come naturally. We don't let others throw us off. We no longer allow our dysfunctional families to control what we think and say about ourselves and our lives.

Our spiritual path does not need to match anyone else's. We pray for our own knowledge, not the answers for anyone else. If we truly listen, we see that our Inner Children are steering us closer to our Higher Power as they ask to be nurtured and loved. With guidance, we are choosing the next right thing to do for ourselves.

On this day I reach out to the source that is always there when I am open to listening, even if I don't have a specific definition of my beliefs.

Freedom from Fear

"I believe it is through the Twelve Step program of ACA that we no longer live life from a basis of fear. We live with self-care and love." BRB p. xxiv

We just sat and waited, or we tried to keep ourselves busy while we waited, even though it was difficult to concentrate. We waited in fear for the fireworks to start. We thought about what we could do to keep it from happening. But even if we had known then what we know now, we were children and we couldn't have stopped it. It was like a runaway train.

As adults, we found relationships where we could continue to do what we did best: wait. We waited in fear for the addict, for the abuse, for anything to go wrong. But as our emotional illness progressed, along with it often came physical illness. Gratefully, we eventually realized that this was no way to live.

In ACA, we can look back at the trauma we endured and know that our True Self was buried underneath the rubble, and we can resurrect it. We can now learn to sit peacefully, no longer worrying about what others are doing. We practice self-care and feel gratitude for the new insights that we continue to have.

On this day I will nurture my True Self by no longer living in fear and by not worrying about things that are none of my business.

HALTS

"Remember HALTS. Do not get too hungry, angry, lonely, tired, or serious. When you get overly tired, it is easy to over-react to a situation. Exercise, get enough sleep, write in a journal, and aim for a balanced lifestyle." BRB p. 427

HALT is an acronym that is well known in many Twelve Step programs. It stands for Hungry, Angry, Lonely, and Tired. When we feel out of balance, it's often that one or more of these things are in play. When we become aware of what's going on, we can take the necessary steps to mend ourselves.

There's often an "S" added at the end of HALT that stands for "Serious". It might also stand for "scared" or "sad" or "sick" – feelings or conditions we have had most of our lives, but haven't always identified the effect they've had. When the "S" is happening, it's time to be even gentler with ourselves.

We've learned that ignoring our reality doesn't make it go away. Even long-term ACAs can see their program seemingly fly out the window whenever HALTS isn't addressed. At these especially vulnerable times, the remedies might include connecting with our Higher Power, going to meetings, and talking to other ACAs. We are learning that these things help us have balance in our lives.

On this day I remind myself that when I feel down and don't see what's happening, remembering HALTS and doing the next right thing help me gently take care of myself in the way I deserve.

Adult Child Defined

"An adult child is someone who responds to adult situations with self-doubt, self-blame, or a sense of being wrong or inferior–all learned from stages of childhood." BRB p. vii, footnote

We may have grown up with parents who used anger and conditional love to control us. Maybe they were perfectionists and we could never measure up to their ideals. We were left with a feeling of certainty that our feelings, opinions, and perceptions were inadequate – that it was wrong to be an imperfect human being.

As adults, our sense of wrongness from childhood may have kept us from expressing our true opinions; we feared others would abandon us if we disagreed with them. This may have led us to make unhealthy choices about partners or careers because our self-doubt was more powerful than our ability to trust ourselves.

ACA meetings finally provide us with an opportunity to break the "Don't talk, don't trust, don't feel" rule. As we face our shame and feelings of abandonment, we begin to realize that our self-image is not actually based on objective reality. We start to see more of the middle ground in situations and to approach life as balanced adults. As we learn to experience our Higher Power's unconditional love, we see that our opinions matter, and that even when we don't think and feel as others do, we are still lovable.

On this day I validate and honor my own feelings and views. With the help of ACA, I see myself in a balanced way and know I am capable of handling situations as a mature adult.

Step Six

"By now, we have stopped punishing ourselves. We are asking God, as we understand God, to help us become entirely ready to have these defects of character removed." BRB p. 215

We used to beat ourselves up over things that we couldn't control. To help cope, many of us practiced compulsive behaviors. Some were more destructive than others, like using drugs, binging and purging, or getting high on controlling others. "Healthier" hang-ups, like excessive exercise, TV or sports, or being social butterflies may have been more acceptable, but ultimately made us almost as miserable.

Some of us felt a rush when we did something compulsive. Then we minimized the consequences in order to survive. Eventually we realized these things made us miserable and compromised our quality of life.

When we begin to uncover the roots of our self-punishing behavior, we see our defects for what they are, and we become entirely ready to have them removed. We realize that instead of numbing the pain, the only way to become whole is to work through it. We ask our Higher Power to lead us to a better place. As we do the work, we can make a list of our defenses and dialog with our Inner Child about how to give them up. We can reassure those parts of us that are still acting out that they are now safe and no longer need to find ways to escape.

On this day I will do all I can to help my Inner Child feel safe and loved. I now work through my problems instead of going around them.

Emotional Sobriety

"The pathway to emotional sobriety that endures time is through the Twelve Steps of ACA." BRB p. 91

The ACA program, if worked consistently and honestly, gives us a new route to emotional sobriety. We were unable to find this growing up with the dysfunctional people in our household.

As adults, most of us continued to seek advice from dysfunctional people. Whether it was someone we had a close personal relationship with or worked with, we were inevitably disappointed that the messages we heard, or thought we heard, were untrue. They seemed only to serve the best interests of others. This left us with a profound sense of betrayal and an increasing sense of mistrust, guessing at what normal was.

Stepping away from this mess, we encountered a program that asks us to recognize the truth within us. With the help of our sponsor, we can tap into a new way of thinking. We can establish reasonable boundaries with dysfunctional family members. We get to say no to situations that are not good for us.

When our internal alarms go off, we do not *react*; we call a fellow traveler instead to get centered and *act* in a healthy manner. Life moves from a state of DIS-ease to a state of ease as our program works in us. We are now able to easily solve situations that used to baffle us.

On this day, if I start to get off track, I will pick up the phone instead of giving in to the dysfunction. I choose emotional sobriety.

Mistakes

"Most of us agonize over mistakes because we internalize the error." BRB p. 38

When we were kids, making a mistake meant being verbally and often physically abused. Our mistakes provoked over-the-top reactions from the adults around us who did not have the tools to understand that we were just doing what kids and people in general do – make mistakes!

But instead, we heard shaming comments like, "What's the matter with you? Are you stupid? Are you an idiot?" or "You should have known better. Look what you did!" And on top of that, many of us were spanked, slapped, or beaten as well. It seemed like the end of the world when this happened. The mistake could never be undone.

Part of the result was that the more it happened, the better we got at shaming ourselves. We no longer needed to hear it from someone else –because those messages had become internalized. We carried this self-shaming behavior into our adult lives and many of us became merciless in the way we treated ourselves.

In ACA we learn to gradually reprogram those inner critical parent messages and understand that making mistakes is part of being human. We all do it. When we make a mistake, we talk about it, examine the nature of what we did, forgive ourselves, make amends when appropriate, and move on. We begin to think and act like true adults!

On this day I understand that when I make a mistake, I don't have to perpetuate my childhood abuse by beating myself up. I will call someone and process what happened, then move on.

Choices

"We are changing. We are beginning to see that we have choices."
BRB p. 578

Many of us used to think that making important choices was reserved for those who knew what they were doing, but that wasn't us. We almost fainted at the prospect of trusting our own intuition about what direction we should take in life. We felt we needed the help of others who were obviously more qualified. We had no faith in our ability to be independent.

As we become true partners in recovery with our Higher Power, we see that we actually are capable of judging what is best for ourselves. We learn to pray and meditate, and allow the answers to come naturally as we create space to hear in a new way. We walk forward fearlessly, knowing also that we may make mistakes, but that mistakes can become important lessons that lead to greater freedom and self-esteem.

Our problems, when faced, can guide us to a better place where we no longer doubt ourselves. We find that the creativity that comes from exploration nurtures our souls and helps us to live more fully. We are finally happy being ourselves and would not trade our lives with anyone else.

On this day I will trust in my ability to make the right choices for myself and I no longer depend on others to give me all the answers. If I need a sounding board, I have my Higher Power and fellow travelers, who are there when I ask for them.

Serenity

"Without help, we cannot recognize serenity or true safety."
BRB p. 16

What is this strange entity called serenity? How will we know if we have it? What will it feel like? Will we be different somehow? Is it something to strive for or is it an illusion?

Maybe it's easier to say what serenity isn't. It isn't waking up with the knowledge that this is going to be a bad day. It isn't focusing on what we don't have and what others do have. It isn't looking to others to affirm who we are. It isn't trying to make people like us by saying yes when we really want to say no.

In ACA, we learn that serenity isn't an entity; it's a feeling, an experience. It's the wisdom to know when we are powerless and to accept that truth without feeling *less than*. It's the inner strength that tells us we're okay regardless of how the world may view us. It's the ability to forgive others and ourselves for not being perfect or not living up to certain expectations. It's knowing that our best friend and strongest cheerleader is inside of us.

Serenity is a state of being where we feel accepted for who we are. It is unconditional peace with no strings attached. And yes it does exist, it's not an illusion. We invite it in.

On this day I will seek and hold onto the embrace of serenity. I will feel the peace of knowing I accept myself as an imperfect human being.

Old Tapes

"If our parents have said we are bad, dumb, or inferior, they were actually projecting what they believed about themselves. As children we were defenseless to throw off these projections. This is loss and grief carried into our adult years." BRB p. 200

The messages received during childhood can seem like an endless tape, the soundtrack of our often dramatic lifestyles.

Underneath the 'scapegoat' role one can hear the echoes of a caregiver who might have said, "You are a loser." Beneath the 'hero' role, the equally disabling charge of being a "perfect child" rings in the ears. As children, we may have accepted such words as true; what we actually felt was likely denied.

Whether we were belittled for being kids or praised for being perfect, we may have unwittingly carried these charges into our complex adult lives as a secret code of conduct. As we recover, we begin to realize that such messages stole from us our authentic internal sense of worth.

In ACA, we listen carefully for those messages, recognizing their debilitating effects and how we recreate or reinforce them. Then we gradually work to reduce their hold on us.

On this day I will notice the messages replaying from my childhood. I will begin to lower their volume in my life until I can hear the voice of my authentic, True Self instead.

Trust

"Do I trust the person I am with?" BRB p. 42

As children, most of us didn't learn trust in our families of origin, so we approached adulthood not trusting anyone. Paradoxically, we were actually often drawn to people who could not be trusted.

When we think of the people around us, we now ask ourselves "Can I tell them my deepest fears and insecurities and feel safe that they won't be used against me?" "Can I be sure they accept me and all of my flaws, or do I have to undergo a transformation in order to fit their ideal?" "If life brings financial difficulties, health problems, or other changes, will they stick around?"

As we grow stronger in our ACA program, we learn that we are healthy enough to ask the right questions, but also trust that we will be okay, even if our trust is violated. We affirm that we, too, can be trusted by others. Equally, or perhaps more important, we can trust ourselves to continue to work on our recovery.

On this day I choose to associate with those I can trust. If that trust is broken, I am able to determine how to handle it in an adult manner with the help of my fellow travelers.

Uniqueness

"By working the Steps and attending meetings, we see that we are not unique and that our family is not unique as well. There are millions of people like us." BRB p. 96

Many of us grew up thinking our families were different, that we were unique. We witnessed drama that was way beyond our understanding. Often the very people who should have comforted us were responsible for the trauma. The resulting shame and embarrassment left us feeling that we could never be like our peers. We felt "apart" from them, so we donned our masks and acted as if we were "normal."

In ACA we share our darkest history and find that others identify with it. Uncovering our memories helps take the sting out of our hurt. We cherish the freedom we feel because we realize we won't be judged for the actions of our family members. We are not alone.

We learn about patterns of behavior we developed to cope with our feelings of shame, hurt and anger. Once they are identified, we give ourselves a choice: we can continue to act as we did when we were in darkness or we can try new behaviors that work better. When we keep coming back, we are choosing new behaviors.

On this day I celebrate the freedom of knowing I am not unique – I'm not alone. I can now use the tools of recovery instead of the dysfunctional survival tools I learned as a child.

Promise Eleven

"With help from our ACA support group, we will slowly release our dysfunctional behaviors." *BRB p. 591*

Getting support to undergo the very challenging task of doing ACA work happens slowly. We might first hear of an ACA meeting and consider attending it, only to find that the day and time don't quite work for us. Then our schedule changes and we are able to venture into our first meeting, usually filled with apprehension. We might start out looking at the slogans hanging on the walls and just listening to hear if, in fact, we have finally found a place to work through our issues.

As we continue to attend meetings, we might start looking around at the members and begin chatting with them afterwards to see if we can begin to gather more support. When we are well-received, we might then become ready to make some inroads in our Step work with a fellow traveler.

As we begin to have experience our feelings and our memories return, the empathetic listeners we have gathered around us will encourage us to go forward. They have our backs. We then slowly let go of our dysfunctional behaviors and are released into the functional world.

On this day I will seek out ACA members who will support me as I learn how to practice more purposeful behavior.

Service

"Between the time we have decided to disconnect from our alcoholic beliefs but have not yet reached the security of a spiritual awakening lies a 'dark night of the soul' where we perceive there is no guiding force whatsoever. Our passage through this terrifying and often chaotic period of uncertainty and doubt is where we experience the power of our program and realize the importance of the service we give and receive." BRB p. 359

Between the familiar dysfunctional attitudes and thinking and emotional sobriety there can be a period of waiting in the spiritual hallway. Even here, there is an opportunity to grow in patience, tolerance, and self-acceptance.

As we wait for clarity, other ACAs encourage us to "keep coming back." We make forward movement, discovering a Higher Power that supports our healing. Thankfully, the pain lessens with time, and the relief comes more quickly than we imagined.

While parts of our work may remain undone, the satisfaction of having achieved some level of emotional sobriety, and of having grieved parts of ourselves and survived the process gives us strength to carry on with unfinished work. We know we can face other areas with the firm knowledge that the spiritual awakening we seek awaits us. With hope and love in our hearts, we encourage others in their passage. This is the highest form of service: speaking from experience about the strength and hope we have achieved.

On this day I will share my experience of being in the spiritual hallway between dysfunctional thinking and emotional sobriety, and how I was able to find the open door on the other side.

Generational Family Dysfunction

"We avoid blame because we are aware of the generational nature of family dysfunction." BRB p. 157

So many of us come into ACA blaming our parents for what has gone wrong in our lives. We tell ourselves, "If only I'd had a 'normal' family I wouldn't have so many problems; why couldn't things have been different?"

There's no doubt we deserved better; as innocent children we had few choices. But as adults, if we continue to focus solely on blaming our families, we *will* perpetuate the dysfunction. It's generational, and it's the same system in which our parents were raised.

Often we didn't want to see our role in the continued dysfunction before we started our recovery. Maybe we even told ourselves "I won't treat my children like that." But it's likely we either did some of the same things or maybe we moved 180 degrees the other way, trying to be more of a friend than a parent.

But all children need reasonable parents, just as we did. Until we uncover and deal with our own issues, we'll continue to repeat dysfunctional patterns. The ACA program gives us the middle ground where recovery lives. And we *deserve* to live in that space.

On this day I will remember that family dysfunction is a generational disease. I affirm my choice to break the cycle by working my program.

Personal Higher Power

"...each ACA member is free to choose a Higher Power, who is available and personal to the individual. No one will make this decision for us." BRB p. 79

During our childhoods, some of us were severely abused, tortured if you will. Maybe we were drugged or forced into sexual roles that seem unthinkable to a civilized society. Perhaps we were even forced to hurt other children.

As adults, we tried to come to grips with how there could have been a loving Higher Power that let that happen to us as sweet, vulnerable children. As we remembered the intense feelings caused by such devastating treatment, we asked ourselves, "Where was God on that day?"

When we are truly seeking an answer, something that will allow us to make sense of our lives, we are ready for the ACA Solution. This is where we learn that we have the freedom to choose a loving Higher Power of our new understanding. This loving presence helps us discover how we can heal all of our wounds. As we seek our truth, these wounds, no matter how deep, are being transformed into strengths.

On this day I will continue to seek an awareness of a loving Higher Power that is larger than all of the dysfunction I have endured.

Accepting Ourselves

"As we sit and think about our shortcomings, we do not judge ourselves." BRB p. 215

As children, we often had to endure verbal attacks that, as adults, made us vulnerable to even the slightest criticism. Even in ACA, it was difficult for some of us to hear that we had "defects of character" because we interpreted that as being defective, which felt shaming. Because we knew these were our core issues and that the program could help us, we might have found other words that made us feel more comfortable, such as "character defenses," "Step One issues," "spirit blockers" or simply "shortcomings."

No matter what we call them, it is essential that we look at them in the proper light and accept them as a part of who we learned to be. We also become aware that they are the very things that come between us and our Higher Power. They affect how we feel about ourselves and how we relate to other people.

In becoming willing to work the Steps, we gradually come out of the isolation we've used to protect ourselves. And we begin to acknowledge our strengths, one of which is our ability to intuitively know that the tools of ACA are giving us a new and better life. We're learning balance.

On this day I choose to face my shortcomings without judging myself harshly. I accept all the parts of me.

Dangerous Parents

".... some parents are so dangerous or perverted that the adult child must avoid them to stay safe and sane." BRB p. 232

Those of us who were sexually abused, either covertly or overtly, realize we were "soul raped." For a long time, we continually tried to do our part, to sweep off our side of the street, to seek change, but to no avail. The destruction was so severe that we were unable to maintain our integrity around our perpetrators afterwards for years. We felt there was no one who would understand, so we went on pretending, showing up, laughing when we didn't feel like laughing, smiling when we felt empty inside. And we always ended up feeling bad, holiday after holiday, and birthday after birthday.

With the help of ACA, we finally accept that the family we thought we had was really a fantasy we needed to believe in to keep ourselves alive as children. When we finally surrender and acknowledge the extent of the abuse, we detach from our perpetrators. We also detach from those who were supposed to protect us, but who instead protected the perpetrators by denying our stories; the ones who just wanted us to "get over it" so they wouldn't have to face reality.

On this day I will live in a new freedom that is based on truth and relationships with my new family and a loving Higher Power.

Grief is a Lifetime Journey

"We introduce grief work in Step Five, realizing that such work is a lifetime journey." BRB p. 200

Perhaps we thought that we could get through the ACA program without having to spend much time grieving the dysfunction we were required to endure, as well as the loss of what might have been. Perhaps we thought the Steps were a once-and-done process.

But gradually that notion faded. When we were ready for our Fifth Step, we were given perhaps our first opportunity to consciously grieve the losses we hadn't been able to share with others before now. But we got through it with the help of a trusted Sponsor, fellow traveler, or therapist.

As we continue to work the Steps, we begin to integrate the concept that recovery is a lifelong journey. We learn that each time we do a Fourth and Fifth Step we uncover more denial, sharing what we find as a continuing part of the process of becoming whole.

This journey is a quest to peel through the layers of the onion that go deep. As we work through our issues, we gain a stronger sense of integration, conscious contact, and spiritual awakening.

On this day I remain willing to remove more layers of denial as I grieve my losses. I am on a lifelong journey of discovery and recovery that I take one day at a time.

Trait Thirteen

"Alcoholism is a family disease, and we became para-alcoholics (codependent)* and took on the characteristics of that disease even though we did not pick up the drink." BRB p. 588

We felt like we were stark raving mad. We couldn't see what was happening to ourselves because we were so focused on controlling others and feeling their feelings for them. Or maybe we tried to shut others down because we didn't want to see or hear anything about feelings that would make us uncomfortable. It was a never-ending cycle of abandonment of ourselves and our Inner Child. But we were used to it; we didn't know any better.

Then one day we found ACA. Slowly, we learned to let ourselves be present in the moment. It wasn't easy. We watched as our sponsors and others with more emotional sobriety modeled what change looked like. We soaked it up. It was the best education we ever had – better than anything we learned or could have learned in school. We found something that could truly transform the world.

As we let go of our grandiosity, we saw that we could change ourselves if we were willing. We finally began to understand and believe that we were powerless over others and the choices they made. It was a great relief.

On this day I will keep my side of the street clean and let others take care of themselves. I will shun attempts to pull me back into that never-ending cycle of dysfunction I came from.

---

*Added by BRB Handbook Committee. Not part of original list.

Self-Sabotage

"By keeping the focus on ourselves, we will find freedom from our critical self as well as our addictive and destructive behaviors."
BRB p. 304

Many of us learned to victimize ourselves with self-destructive behaviors. We were taught to devalue ourselves early on, and had to join in our own victimization as a way to survive.

Unfortunately, the survival mechanisms we learned in order to cope hurt us just as deeply now as they did in the past, maybe even more so. Why? Because as adults we feel we should be able to change things at will. But without the necessary skills and insight, this is almost impossible.

In ACA we learn that no matter when or how our destructive behaviors and thoughts started, we *are* capable of experiencing new ways of being. But we don't do it alone. We invite our Higher Power and other ACAs to join us on our healing journey. When we have enough faith in ourselves to move in this direction, we become ready to release our self-destructive behavior.

As part of this process, we begin to grieve and heal the losses we've experienced, both because of our own actions and the actions of those who raised us. We learn to give ourselves unconditional love and draw upon the energy of other ACAs and our Higher Power. We embrace this positive support system that can get us through our darkest days.

On this day I will release any negative energy so that I am able to make the changes I want and deserve in my life.

Abuse

"Before finding ACA, many of us believed we deserved what we got or caused the abuse to happen." BRB p. 28

An ACA 'bottom' may take various forms. We say to ourselves "I can't stand being alone with myself," or "I hate myself." But if we analyze just these two statements, we can see they seem to speak of 'I' and 'self' as if they are two separate entities – and perhaps they are.

The 'I' is our essence, the soul that was placed in our human body. The 'self' in these negative feelings is only the person we think we are: the one who carries the past, is anxious about the present, and dreads the future. This false self is the creation of other people's words and deeds that caused us to hide our True Self. This hiding takes many forms, from physically isolating to being emotionally unavailable to ourselves and others. And when it becomes too toxic, we begin to seek help in order to find a new way of living.

In ACA we begin to question why we allow our false self to have so much control. We learn that the Steps are the pathway that helps us merge our 'I' with our True Self, while shedding the old self we created in our childhood. ACA brings us the knowledge that we are all gifted human beings who did not deserve what we got as children. We gradually begin to realize that we are more than good enough.

On this day I will recognize when my abusive false self is in control. This will then awaken my True Self so I can celebrate the wonderful creation that I am.

Internalized Messages

"Some parents routinely found fault with our thoughts or accomplishments without any apparent malice. If asked, the parent or caregiver would tell you that they meant well."
BRB p. 36

We felt as if we couldn't do anything right because we couldn't. No matter what our caretakers intended, their emotional daggers flew at us fast and furiously and stung deeply. Even long after leaving home, we carried that critical voice with us; only now it was internalized.

We told ourselves we were being babies, that we were over-reacting, that no one meant us harm: all our concerns were only in our heads. We just needed to toughen up and stop taking everything so seriously.

Internalizing these messages for so long left us unable to claim our birthright of serenity, which would allow us to face life's challenges in an adult way.

In ACA we eventually turn around to face ourselves and our past. When we finish Step Five, a burden is lifted. We can see where we came from, who we truly are and who we can be. We are grateful that we have begun to question the voices inside as we dialogue with and challenge them. We no longer push these voices away. We invite them in and sit with them. We see our story unfold before us as we write and talk. We see the courageous little person who was faced with a childhood full of doubt and shame – and we have compassion for ourselves. We find our serenity.

On this day I honor and cherish the child within who was blameless then and now.

Safety

"In ACA, there is a way to discuss and heal from the events of the past without minimizing these events and without remaining stuck with such memories." BRB p. 26

Arriving at the bridge between denial and acceptance was painful. What were we to do now that the brutality of the past was revealed? What were we to do with the internal mess that we had been left with from childhood? What were we to do with the tattered remains of a heart cast in stone, the plethora of emotions under lock and key, the inability to reach out?

When we find ACA, we realize we are about to cross over a bridge. We come to know that there will be no going back. This is an irreversible process of progress from pain, sorrow and suffering to health, joy and peace. All we need to do is avail ourselves of others and begin our journey with the first step forward. It isn't easy, but it is a lot less painful that staying stuck in our own absolute uncertainty. Once on the other side, we see how deeply self-protective we had become. No longer is it necessary to hide from others by looking down at the ground. We move our gaze into the eyes of those who understand how we feel, and we find safety in their unconditional concern for our well being.

On this day I will keep my head high and know that with the help of others in ACA, I am safe from the memories of the past.

Hitting Bottom

"Some ACA bottoms can be a chronic sense of aloneness in which the adult child never feels joy and never really connects with others in a meaningful manner." BRB p. 124

Loneliness is well known by adult children. Whether we were actually alone or in a group of people, we were lonely. Many of us were, or still are, in relationships where we are lonely. This is our experience because we missed a key piece of socialization growing up in a dysfunctional family: how to have a healthy relationship with another human being.

So we have become controlling, stand-offish, closed-minded, over-bearing, painfully shy or awkward, fearful of others, perpetual victims, people pleasers – the list goes on. Name the dysfunction and odds are we can relate to it.

We distrust people, expecting them to hurt us. But our actions cause the very hurt we try to avoid. We are hyper-sensitive and perceive any difference of opinion as a personal attack. We are less than forgiving and tend to hold grudges long into the future.

This is why we come into the rooms of recovery. The demons in our head need to be dealt with. We can't do that alone. We come in to gather knowledge and strength from the program, our fellow travelers, and our Higher Power. We come to face our past and put to rest the childhood survival traits that no longer work for us.

On this day I remind myself that living the ACA program will bring me the peace within myself that I have longed for. That peace will spill over into my relationships.

Incest

"Some incest victims have struggled with forgiving an offending parent or caregiver." *BRB p. 114*

Those of us who were sexually abused struggled for years trying to accept what happened to us. Mostly, people told us to shut up about it, or if they were a little more *polite*, they let us know that we should somehow just "get over it," put it out of our minds, stop dragging the family down, or some other such sentiment. We lived with this burden for years.

When we're working Steps Eight and Nine, the most important amends we make is to ourselves. We stop trying to push those wounded parts of ourselves down with food, anxiety, stinginess, and pornography – things that make us feel as if the abuse was either deserved or acceptable in some way.

We learn to set boundaries with our perpetrators and those who protected them, including our sisters and brothers who told us they couldn't talk about it. We put ourselves first for the first time in our lives. We detach with a hatchet if we have too, but we detach.

Forgiving our perpetrators, who we can finally view for what they are, may take time. But we will eventually find a way to move forward. Then forgiveness will be easier because we no longer have to pretend that the abuse didn't happen.

On this day I will make amends to myself by putting myself first for the first time. I will also learn to forgive my perpetrators so that I can focus on myself instead of them.

Tradition Eleven

"Ours is a program of attraction, not promotion." BRB p. 613

How exciting it is when we get the first dose of recovery. Issues that have plagued us for most of our lives can now be brought to an ACA meeting or discussed with a fellow traveler who knows how we feel and doesn't judge us.

Recovery is so powerful that we want to rush out and persuade many of our friends and relatives to join in this wonderful new adventure, probably because we believe some of them could benefit from the program more than we can. So some of us buy several ACA books to distribute to these people. This is called two-stepping: jumping right from Step One to Step Twelve, trying to give away what we don't even have yet.

But recovery requires patience. We find that as we work the Steps, practice the principles, and live the program, others will notice a positive change in us. They will be attracted by that change.

If their curiosity is piqued, they may ask about ACA. Then it's up to them to decide if they want to go to meetings and learn more.

On this day I will focus on my own recovery and respect that others have their own journey. If at some point our journeys merge, it will be a wonderful thing.

Seeking Affirmation

"Most adult children constantly seek affirmation but do not truly believe compliments and praise when they come." BRB p. 187

Some of us cringed at our own birthday parties because we were uncomfortable with the attention we had originally sought. When our partners found us attractive, we felt nervous and distracted. When others complimented us, the only way we felt worthy of the praise was by returning it.

We achieved all our goals only to find that we were not satisfied. Our dream life with our dream job and dream relationship still didn't fix us. The more successful we were, the more anxious we became.

As we heal in ACA, we learn to accept compliments without needing to return them. We can let the words hang in the air like sweet perfume. We can enjoy when we do something well, not because someone is watching, not because we expect affirmation from someone else, but because we know we did a good job.

More importantly, we can even allow ourselves to fail and still love those wounded parts inside of us – even when others do not. At least we made the effort. Maybe our mistakes will eventually lead to success, but even if they don't, we will be all right. Our relationships with our Higher Power and Inner Children become enough for us. We are enough, just as we are for today, and every day.

On this day, if I do something imperfectly, I will remember that I also do a lot of things right. I have many reasons to be proud of myself.

December

"Abandonment means more than being left alone or left at a doorstep." BRB p. 10

Perfectionism

"In other homes, the children are like objects of perfection to be displayed alongside dinners centered on tables with fine fixtures, perfect posture, and orderly spoons and forks. Holidays and celebrations bring guests who compliment the parents for sparkling floors and perfect children." BRB p. 37

A more subtle and powerful undercurrent in our alcoholic or otherwise dysfunctional families was ever-present control, although the type of control may not have always seemed clear. Whether our houses resembled museums or they were well-cluttered, expressions of love may have been flowery and superficial and had strings attached. The essence of these dysfunctional expressions was not authentic, and we knew it.

The actual object of all the cleanliness or sloppiness, the pseudo expression of love, was inauthentic. Deep inside, our True Self saw that the real motive was the suppression of the possibility of admitting that things were out of control.

So we bought in and "acted out" this subconscious conflict to both avoid being ostracized and to keep our own feelings of being out of control from surfacing.

Gradually, when the sense of chaos crept into our consciousness as adults, and we hit an emotional, spiritual and physical bottom, we found ACA. In this humbled state, we are given the gift of recovery as we recollect the memories of our upbringing, admit our terror and grieve our losses.

On this day I will examine the control in my family and the effect it's had in my adult life. I will practice the ACA program to help process the unexpressed traumatic fear and buried memories so that I may be free of control.

Spontaneous Feelings

"No longer willing or able to suppress my feelings, they came up effusively and erratically." BRB p. 409

When we entered our first meetings, we may have felt numb. Then, as we kept coming back, suddenly it felt like a roller coaster, with feelings flying blindly around a corner without warning.

As we progress in recovery, we learn to acknowledge all of our feelings and be unafraid. We don't put limits on how much we allow ourselves to feel. Whatever comes up for us at the moment is okay. We do not pretend we are fine when we are not. Claiming our truth becomes a basic need for us. We no longer allow others to try to shut us down when they're uncomfortable.

We maintain conscious contact with a Higher Power through our personal spiritual awakening, whatever form that takes. We cultivate affirming and soothing self-talk in the form of our inner loving parent – the parent we always deserved.

Recovery unfolds for us gently over time as we see each new direction we need to take, and then we seize it and run. We trust ourselves and our intuition. Our feelings are not overwhelming – they are what they are.

On this day I will allow my feelings to safely wash over me. This will give me the strength to be genuine with myself and others.

Step Twelve

"Having had a spiritual awakening as the result of these Steps, we tried to carry this message to others who still suffer, and to practice these principles in all our affairs." BRB p. 279

When we first entered recovery, we may have wanted to tell everyone we knew about this amazing program. But we soon found that most people were not interested in what we had to say. We probably sounded like we were preaching about what they should do.

We soon learned that carrying the message of recovery was not about chasing people down and forcing them to listen, but standing still and honoring our true space. We live the message through our words and actions, generating an environment that people want to be part of. They become more comfortable with us, but may not even know why.

In meetings, we help carry the message to each other when we tell our stories, agree to be a sponsor or fellow traveler, and take on service roles.

Our True Selves trust there will always be more to learn when we practice these principles in all our affairs.

On this day I will share who I have become with those who are willing to listen. I will remember that my actions speak louder than my words.

Escape

"I came to the program because I felt unhappy, abandoned, and generally miserable." BRB p. 413

Before ACA, many of us were scared. We knew that if something didn't change in our lives, we were likely to be emotionally or physically abused again, and we knew we couldn't take any more. To escape and to try to feel good, we had tried anything – burying ourselves in books all day, playing hours of video games, or compulsively shopping. We may have also used pornography as a way to numb ourselves. Our relationships were not with safe people. Our bodies were racked with tension that never seemed to go away.

Attending our first ACA meeting signaled the start of gradual change for us. As we come out of denial, we realize that we are capable of being healthy and sane. We find that sometimes this involves making hard choices, but ultimately those choices are worth it.

An important choice we make is to do the Steps with a Sponsor or fellow traveler who can be a witness to our positive change. We find that when we make bold, positive moves, the universe steps up to heal us. We are able to live a new story and feel free.

On this day I trust that I am going in the right direction and that I have all the support I need when I am willing to ask.

Cross Talk

"The word 'cross talk' means interrupting, referring to, or commenting on someone else's remarks made during the meeting....each person may share his or her feelings and perceptions without judgment from others." BRB p. 341

Some of us have a hard time with the no cross talk rule in ACA. We may believe others really need to hear our valuable opinions and insight! This can cause us to violate another's boundaries. And it may get in the way of others discovering their truth in their own time.

It has been found that when a nervous racehorse is left alone, it simply gets more nervous. But when a goat is in the stable, the race horse calms down. The goat, naturally, doesn't tell the racehorse, "Calm down; you're being silly!" It is the goat's *presence* that makes the difference to the horse. Presence can say what words cannot.

When we're tempted to give unsolicited advice or opinions, remembering this analogy of the horse and the goat may be helpful. We can do the most good for ourselves and others by just speaking our own truth and talking about our own feelings. By doing so, we can serve as living proof that this program can be trusted, that we can all get well in our own time. It is not our job to fix or parent each other. We learn to do that on our own when we are allowed to do so.

On this day I recognize that I don't have all the answers. Focusing on myself and being there for others instead of trying to 'fix' them is the best path for all involved.

Abandonment

"Abandonment means more than being left alone or left at a doorstep." BRB p. 10

We felt abandoned emotionally as children when we were criticized and felt we didn't measure up to expectations. These abandonment feelings were made worse when we felt compelled to keep family secrets, which brought a continual sense of shame that someone could find out how really dysfunctional our homes were.

As adults, this often resulted in feeling triggered to build up highly emotional responses toward the pain of loss.

Before ACA, living with all of this pain and shame caused us to look outside of ourselves for love and safety. But with the help and guidance of our program and each other, we learn that self-worth, self-nurturing, and a feeling of safety can be developed within ourselves. Thus, our confidence grows and recovery becomes real, especially as we strengthen our belief in a Higher Power.

Recovery works if we don't stare at the past, but decide to make new memories each day. We find that developing into a "new adult" is rewarding. At the same time, our Inner Child continues to grow in a healthy way.

ACA teaches us to be confident in the knowledge that we are in charge of ourselves. We can learn to live in the present and concentrate on each day's blessings.

On this day I know I am not alone. I have the support of my ACA family that is helping me heal my past and build a strong future.

Wholeness

"In ACA, we believe we were born whole and became fragmented in body, mind, and spirit through abandonment and shame. We need help finding a way to return to our miracle state."
BRB p. 143

When we find our way to ACA, we may feel like our outsides don't match our insides. We are used to acting as though everything is fine in our lives, knowing in our hearts this is not the case. We are adept at controlling how we appear to others, careful to conceal the pain behind a smile.

As children, we had to hide our true feelings, our True Self, in order to survive. We were sometimes shamed or abandoned when we expressed emotions our parents could not cope with. We learned to keep our thoughts and yearnings to ourselves out of fear.

With the help of our Higher Power and others in ACA who know of our pain, we begin to speak the truth of our experience and gradually align our thoughts, feelings, and actions. We know that wholeness is again available to us when we experience love and acceptance from others in recovery and from our Higher Power. With the help of ACA, we can learn to tap into all of our emotions, including joy.

On this day I welcome my True Self by acknowledging and accepting my feelings. I feel whole in my Higher Power's loving embrace.

Self-Love

"Self-love enables the adult child to back-fill the love or nurturing we did not get as children." BRB p. 436

Long ago we were yelled at, pushed aside, and neglected. In our quiet times, we wondered in our little child minds, "Why? What did I do wrong?"

We looked out at the world and saw a dad playing in the yard with his kids. Those kids looked so happy. We stood in our yard alone, feeling like the only kid in the world nobody loved.

This lack of love set the stage for years of searching. We found relief now and then when a teacher smiled or a friend bragged about us. But nothing made us feel loved enough to take away the pain. Some of us used drugs, alcohol, food, and other compulsive activities to fill the empty spot where love should have been.

When we got to ACA, we felt a connection when we heard others talk about their loveless lives because now we knew we weren't alone. We learned that the reason we didn't feel loved was because of something out of our control: true love can't co-exist along with alcoholic and dysfunctional thinking.

It wasn't our fault! We were always lovable. We made a commitment to start over and love ourselves.

On this day I will take positive action to love and nurture myself in a way only I can.

Fun

"We were not taught how to have fun." BRB p 39

Someone in a meeting once asked what adult children do for fun. In our families of origin, many of us were too hypervigilant to have fun or experience joy. When we look back, we often struggle to remember brief moments of fun. Some of us do catch glimpses of playing with dolls or trucks, blowing dandelions, or hollering "Let's play hide and seek – you're it!"

As we begin recovery, the idea of having fun may feel foreign, but we start to learn how important it is as a way to nurture our Inner Child and our adult self. As we get healthier, we see wondrous joy and freedom in having fun. We start doing things like drawing in a sketchbook, putting together a picture puzzle, coloring, working on a craft, going for a walk, riding a horse, fishing, hiking a mountain trail, skiing, swimming, calling a friend, going to the movies, painting a picture, singing, going to the library, learning to play a musical instrument, listening to music, hugging a friend, going to a museum, sitting by the river watching a sunset, laughing with friends, taking pictures, taking a class on meditation, playing a game… the list fun activities can go on forever.

On this day I will experience life to its fullest by being in the present and doing something fun.

Solution – Respect

"We learn to reparent ourselves with gentleness, humor, love and respect." BRB p. 590

As we learn to reparent ourselves with respect in ACA, we oftentimes find ourselves at odds with our Inner Child. Maybe our child is clamoring for an expensive cup of tea at a nearby coffee shop, or just wishing for a better car. We might have once quashed that inner voice in a shaming manner, and said things that we heard as children, like "Stop wishing for what you can never have." We can now be a responsible parent and respectfully say, "No, we can't afford that right now."

With the help of our program, we also learn to put things in perspective. Maybe we can decide that even though a chai tea latte is never going to be a daily habit, we can afford it this once if our Inner Child is having a bad day and wants a treat. And yes, the Lamborghini is out of our price range, but we can allow ourselves to visit the mental Lamborghini showroom, sit in the car with our Inner Child and say, "It's okay to wish for things we may never have." It's a tiny gift not to squash our hopes and dreams, but it is a lasting tiny gift.

On this day I will show respect for myself, my Inner Child, and others. I will remember that wonderful things I never thought possible have happened to me because I dared to dream.

Placing Ourselves Last

"Having an overdeveloped sense of responsibility, we preferred to be concerned with others rather than ourselves." BRB p. 589

When we arrived at ACA, many of us realized we had a pattern of putting all others before ourselves. It seemed their lives were more important than ours, and we just got the crumbs or whatever was left over. We had developed a "What about me?" victim persona.

Some of us noticed this when we finally became so tired of not being listened to by friends and family. We thought, "Hey, I want to talk about my life, my interests, my challenges, too!" This deprivation had led us to feeling lethargic, hopeless, and depressed. We were wallowing in self-pity, compulsions, or addictions to numb our pain.

In recovery, we find ourselves transforming this pattern. Our unconscious compulsive reactions are lessening. We find freedom from our survival traits when we talk in meetings and with our fellow travelers. We work the Steps. We meditate and pray. We read and write about our thoughts and feelings. We begin opening up, ready and willing to turn our dysfunctional patterns over to our Higher Power. We see how our wounded Inner Child is responding to our inner loving parent's compassion.

On this day I know there is an alternative to being overly concerned with others rather than myself. Gradually, more of my needs are met and I feel I am finally listened to.

Tradition Five

"I give it away to keep it – recovery." BRB p. 513

When we come to ACA, we are hurting. We find others like ourselves. Because we learn to trust these people, we gradually allow ourselves to open up and share our deepest secrets.

But in some cases, people we've grown close to leave, and we feel abandoned, just as in our childhoods. We wonder if we should go, too. Maybe we've done all we can and should move on; maybe this ACA program isn't the answer to everything; maybe we aren't having the big "aha" moments anymore.

So why *should* we stay when others might not? Because this abandonment we feel is different; we are using new tools that help us work through these feelings. Everyone doesn't have the same path, and we can feel sad when people leave and hope they find what works for them. But for us, ACA is the healthy choice. We decide to stay, first for ourselves and then for others. We give back what we've gotten to the next person who comes through the door. These are our peers. We may not all look and act alike, but it's amazing the help we can give one another. By being there for others in recovery, we learn more about ourselves.

On this day I will rededicate myself to my recovery in ACA. I know this is where I belong.

Responsibility

"Freedom from alcoholic insanity is a question of responsibility. We cannot be responsible for something we did not create." **BRB p. 88**

We thought of ourselves as something worthless at the center of the universe. We had tried to commit suicide in many ways, both emotionally and physically, thinking to ourselves "Maybe this time they will see what is going on." But nothing changed and neither did our perpetrators. We spent all of this energy for what?

In ACA, we learn that *we* are the ones who have to change. To do so, we first need to let go of the responsibility for the alcoholic insanity. It has always been unmanageable, with or without us.

We start to see that we deserve to have a chance at a sane life, even though we aren't quite sure what that would be like. We look out before us and see there is light ahead. We can't see what it is, but we also can't stop moving towards it. It feels good and warm. That scares us at first, but it also feels new and exciting.

We put down our shame and our addictions that no longer serve us. We release our character defenses. It is time to see what this thing called life is about. We allow ourselves to walk forward.

On this day I will remember that I am responsible for myself, but not for the insanity of my childhood. I will use the memories to heal myself, but then leave them in the past so I can be free.

Victim

"Our experience shows that we often lived as victims." BRB p. 14

Many of us may have gotten very good at playing the victim. But we tell ourselves that we didn't create that role for ourselves. Wasn't it those other people and circumstances that made us a victim?

Holding on to regrets and resentments is like wrapping ourselves in a blanket of thorns. Each minute of each day we are aware of the fact that the thorns are causing us pain, and the only comfort some of us get is thinking that at least others see how hurt we are. But nobody wants to live with a victim, not even the victim.

How different our lives and our world would be if we could go back and undo the past. But life doesn't offer us that option. What we do get is a choice, to either accept our past and work through it, or to remain a victim, letting it continue to influence who we are and what we do.

When we recite the Serenity Prayer in meetings, we need to believe the words "Accept the things I cannot change." Our past happened. As uncomfortable as it was, it can become the catalyst that helps make us stronger.

On this day I will continue to shed the blanket of thorns I've worn as a victim and wrap myself in the soft blanket of recovery.

Promise Twelve

"Gradually, with our Higher Power's help, we will learn to expect the best and get it." BRB p. 591

Our Higher Power is always ready to assist us in realizing our spiritual wholeness. If we take the time and effort to do the work, we will be repaid a thousandfold.

So what are we to expect after all our work? To be the singularly awesome human beings our Higher Power meant us to be with all our wonderful and our not-so-wonderful gifts. Our Higher Power unconditionally loves us from our gray hair to our mohawks, from our double chins to our crooked toes. We are loved for our humanness – creations as magnificent as the galaxies. We are spiritual beings who are having a human experience filled with hurdles and hoops, minor fender benders and colossal blunders.

We have many splendid gifts that we have only just begun to discover. We are learning to ask for the best and we stop placing limits on what we think that is. As we continue to work hard and have faith in our Higher Power, we are amazed to uncover even greater gifts that were just waiting for us to discover.

On this day I will not limit my expectations to small ideas. With my Higher Power's help on my recovery journey, I may get more than I can imagine: Me.

Hearing a Fifth Step

"In Step Five, the ACA member trusts another to hear his or her life story without judgment. For many, this is the first time the adult child has told the most intimate details of his or her life to another. Trust of another person is one of the spiritual principles of Step Five." BRB p. 632

The first time we did our Fifth Step with someone else, we may have been really nervous. Then we felt affirmed as the other person didn't run away or shame us for what we shared. We had broken the silence, and it was a huge relief as we unpacked years of baggage. In a haze, we stumbled in the dark with the loving presence of a fellow traveler by our side. We released our past. We walked away better, lighter, and with a sense of completeness we may have never experienced before.

Hearing someone else's Fifth Step can be such a privilege. When we are asked to do so, we remember our own vulnerability when we shared our lives in this manner. Recalling our own experience helps us honor the other person and treat them with the respect we were given. To help each other on such an important journey truly benefits both individuals.

On this day I will look forward to the time when I am ready to do my Fifth Step so that I can experience the freedom on the other side. When I am then asked to hear another's Fifth Step, I will honor that request as the wonderful gift that it is.

Expressing Feelings

"As we move out of emotional isolation, we regain the ability to recognize and express all of our feelings." BRB p. 361

As children, many of us were not allowed to show our feelings. So we stuffed them and pretended not to have them for fear of being ridiculed or punished.

Is it any wonder that we carried this over to adulthood, where we continued to stuff our feelings and convince ourselves that they didn't matter? Or perhaps we chose the route of medicating our feelings with addictions or obsessions until we didn't have to experience them.

We come into ACA as adult children with an armful of triggers. These triggers can turn what should be a mild reaction into rage, not because of the situation, but because what is said or done awakens our stuffed feelings.

These denied feelings interfere with relationships, as we leave in our wake people who can't figure out why we respond the way we do.

ACA reaches into these hidden areas and brings our childhood feelings into the light of day where they eventually lose their power over us.

On this day I will continue to trust and appreciate that ACA is a safe place for me to recognize and express my feelings.

Service

"The purpose of service in ACA is to support one another in becoming responsible for our own well-being." BRB p. 354

It can be difficult to start doing service when service seems to carry such a heavy responsibility. The idea that we can help another person recover feels similar to our having tried to save our families.

Yet service in ACA is what provides others the opportunity to assume responsibility for themselves. Opening the meeting, being the secretary, keeping the books, and picking up chairs after the meeting are all things that keep a meeting open and provide the means for ourselves and others to recover.

As members turn to us for guidance, we realize that we can share our experience, strength and hope, but that also, the directions are right in front of them. The "Newcomer's Pamphlet," the BRB, the Yellow Workbook, and other pieces of literature will answer any question the member may have.

Our goal is to support adult children as they become comfortable with the idea that they can be responsible for their own well-being. It may be very frustrating to the newer member to understand that by allowing them to find the strength to love themselves, we are expressing a deep level of love. However, if done with a spirit of love and a short explanation, they will feel the strength of the program filling in the vacuum they had long sought to deny.

On this day I will give service, realizing that every part of setting up a meeting creates an opportunity for ACAs to become empowered to love themselves.

Trait Fourteen

"Para-alcoholics (co-dependents) are reactors rather than actors."
BRB p. 17

Before ACA, many of us ran from one person to another, one idea to another, found "better" jobs, sought solutions for our medical ailments, read all the self-help books: we tried anything to change the way we felt. We were so mixed up inside, wondering why everyone else seemed calm and reassured, while we had fireworks going off in our brains and bodies. Each time we jumped into frantic action, the results were usually hurtful to ourselves or others.

How did we learn to react so intensely? As children, each step we took or *didn't* take caused "bombs" to go off. We were told things like "Can't you do anything right?" or "If you'd just stop acting like that, everything would be better." We were scapegoats. We became reactors in an attempt to try to fix things. And we carried this behavior into our adult lives.

In ACA we find relief, one day at a time. We learn to use the slogans, like "Easy Does It" when we feel an "emergency" inside. They help us act in healthier ways by doing nothing, even if we have to sit on our hands or zip our lips until the compulsion passes.

Self-reflection is imperative during these times. Stopping ourselves before we react inappropriately, and even in mid-sentence, helps us gain self-confidence and positively affirm ourselves.

On this day, when I feel a compulsion to react "Right Now," I will remember two slogans: "Don't just do something, sit there" and "Be Still and Know." I am learning to be calm in the face of internal chaos.

Dissociation

"Using a substance to alter the feelings is the second way to dissociate from feeling pain. The most easily available substances are alcohol, sugar, nicotine, and caffeine." BRB p. 87

Many of us came to ACA with addictions to drugs or alcohol. Others came with addictions to money, food, sex, or gambling. With the help of other 12 Step programs, we successfully worked on these presenting problems. But there were other seemingly more acceptable addictions that we picked as a way to mask our pain. In our quest for emotional sobriety in ACA, our feelings have to be available to us in order to locate the underlying trauma in our lives. Even if we're participating in these more acceptable addictions, like watching hours of TV each day, a nicotine habit that interrupts everything we do, or excessive caffeine, our feelings are being masked.

If we continue to alter our feelings in these or similar ways, it may be because the underlying trauma seems too scary to face. But to find true freedom for our Inner Child requires that our feelings to be accessible. We need to be "present" to work our program if we are to become our own loving parent, which means rejecting the role models of our childhood. We make a commitment that the abuse stops here! We allow ourselves to be imperfect and move towards our ultimate goal of being fully awake without reservation.

On this day I will be honest about what I may be using to numb my feelings. I will reach out for help so that I may find the peace I deserve.

Stuck Grief

"Grief is loss that is stuck beneath denial, willful forgetting, and the fear of being perceived as dramatizing the past. Grief is the built-up defeats, slights, and neglect from childhood." BRB p. 199

Before we came into ACA, we might have thought of grief as something we experience only from overt losses such as death of a loved one, divorce, or a devastating illness. With recovery in ACA, we also experience grief as something that comes from the loss of our identity in childhood. We're exposed to many suggestions of what those childhood losses might be, such as being regularly and unfairly criticized by a parent, being compared to a sibling who was more well-behaved, being told we were bad, dumb or inferior, being told to keep secrets – the list goes on.

Just as it's valuable to handle more overt losses by grieving in a healthy manner rather than avoiding, numbing, and dissociating, we learn in ACA to practice loving ways to grieve our childhood losses. By working the Steps and learning to have a dialog with our Inner Child, we discover that our bodies and minds remember the neglectful and shaming acts of the past. Unearthing these memories and facing the feelings buried within them isn't easy, but we discover an amazing payoff on the other side of this grief – being fully self-expressed and feeling alive, perhaps for the first time.

On this day I will be aware of and focus on one of the losses I experienced in childhood and practice a loving and compassionate way to grieve that loss.

Good Enough

"Yet, we come from homes in which doing our best was never good enough. Or it seemed never good enough." BRB p. 37

As children, many of us were expected to perform. But no matter how well we did, we didn't receive praise – just higher expectations. It was normal to want to hear we were valued and we yearned for affirmation that we were okay. But in its absence, we were left to believe we simply weren't good enough.

As adults, we heard those tapes in our head and kept setting higher expectations of ourselves. No matter what we achieved, we never felt good enough. Many of us were lucky that we inevitably hit a wall we couldn't climb and found ACA and the help we needed.

We began to also see that not getting praise had kept us from knowing how to give praise. For those of us who have children, we wanted to do it better but couldn't find the language, often believing that praise would give them permission to stop trying. We had repeated the pattern, not realizing that the disappointment in their eyes mirrored our own childhood feelings.

As we learn to erase the tapes in our heads, we begin to give ourselves the affirmation we didn't get – that we are good enough. We can now pass this sense of worthiness on to those who mattered in our lives.

On this day I remind myself that I am good enough, and I fill myself with praise and good feelings.

Forgiveness

"We cannot forgive another until we forgive ourselves."
BRB p. 233

As children, we learned to be critical of ourselves and to see ourselves as never being good enough. This was told to us so many times and in so many ways by the adults in our lives that it programmed itself into our self image. The thought of forgiving ourselves for doing or saying something wrong never entered our minds.

In ACA, we learn that self-forgiveness is essential for honoring and loving our True Self. It is how we learn to affirm our worth and build a foundation for being able to forgive others.

Learning to love ourselves unconditionally opens up a new world. It may not be easy for many of us because of the critical inner voice that seems to keep beating us down, but it's possible – we know that because we see it happening in others.

Once we begin to give ourselves this gift, we are then better able to give this same gift to those around us. But doing so does not mean we excuse unacceptable behavior; we simply learn to forgive and accept others for who they are. Only then can we make a decision about whether we want them in our lives. But we will make that decision from a healthy place, not one of anger and resentment.

On this day I will strengthen my spirit, showing myself unconditional love by accepting myself for being human.

The Problem

"This is a description, not an indictment." BRB p. 589

Even though it says in The Problem that it's not an indictment, it may still feel that way at first. Many of us felt locked forever in continually repeated patterns of family dysfunction. But in spite of that, we see the wisdom of what's written down. We come to realize that this description, based on The Laundry List, can actually feel comforting. We're no longer alone when we enter an ACA meeting and find we can share these Traits openly without criticism, because others have the same "habits."

We cannot change where we came from or what happened to us, but we can choose to work the ACA program of recovery and find a way out. Each day, we can use any of the tools of the program, such as the Steps, the phone, the meetings, a sponsor, and so much more.

We are no longer trapped in a horrible past. We may sometimes feel bad, but we are *not* bad in our inner core. Whatever traits or shortcomings we have, we look around us and see that we are not alone. We now have the support of others in the program and our Higher Power.

On this day I rededicate myself to living this new life. I will pick up the phone, go to a meeting or spend time reading the Big Red Book to nourish myself.

Serenity

"We can find serenity in ACA." BRB p. 442

We may not have experienced what we think of as serenity – we see it as something other people have, not us. We may not even know what serenity is, let alone where to look for it. What does it feel like?

It may be best to start by examining what we think serenity might be. Maybe it's a magical, peaceful feeling that totally engulfs someone 24 hours a day, seven days a week. With this feeling, people never feel stress, fear or anxiety. Well, that's a nice idea to contemplate, but we know in our heart of hearts it's not reality.

A more realistic view of serenity is to think of it as a core of acceptance that already resides deep inside us; something that we haven't yet tapped into or perhaps acknowledged. It may be small, even tiny now. But it will grow. We learn to recognize and feel little moments of it in our lives.

With the help of our ACA group, we find serenity when we accept our life – past and present, and learn to trust the future. As part of this shift in our mindset, we learn that serenity is achievable. We understand that we won't feel it 24/7, but it will be present enough to change our lives.

On this day I will remind myself that I already have serenity inside me. It is up to me to help it grow by building acceptance and trust through the ACA program.

Self-Forgiveness

"We realize that we are practicing the concept of self-forgiveness when we hear ourselves talking about being gentle with ourselves." BRB p. 113

Being gentle with ourselves is not second nature to us. Few of us had good role models in that respect. As a result, we learned to lock our thoughts inside our heads where we often fell prey to negative messages.

As we learn to care for the needs of our Inner Child, we begin to release the harsh self-criticism we honed through the years. We allow ourselves to be human, and we acknowledge that to be human is to make mistakes.

We may find ourselves incessantly reliving our actions because we *think* we made a mistake. ACA offers us many new resources that can help quell our critical inner voice. We can call a fellow traveler, read from the Red Text, attend an in-person or phone meeting, pray, meditate or practice any number of new behaviors. The list is long and purposeful.

We learn to take an inventory of our actions when we think we've done something wrong, and acknowledge our feelings. Maybe we made a mistake; maybe we took a small misstep. Maybe we are hearing false messages from childhood. By being open to a daily review, we can turn things around and practice healthy behavior. We can affirm our humanness and our desire to grow.

On this day I show my Inner Child love and acceptance by practicing gentleness and self-forgiveness.

Grief and Tools

"While grief can be perceptible through writing and talking about our memories, some grief is not always visible." BRB p. 200

ACA encourages us to journal and share our story to help with our grieving process. While some of us use *only* these tools, there are thankfully many other tools available.

That's important to know because for some of us, our grief doesn't always surface while we are writing or talking. The hidden Inner Child may be too terrorized to respond to these methods. If this is the case, we learn to experiment with other methods to gain our Inner Child's trust. One tool is the non-dominant handwriting exercise. Another is seeing a qualified therapist.

Whatever method works for us to uncover the grief, eventually sharing what we find will empower us to continue the journey toward wholeness with the support of our meetings and our fellow travelers. There's plenty of room in our toolbox for whatever tools we may find along the way that help us get to the heart of what we're dealing with.

But we are careful about advising others how to do this work, since what may work for us, may not work for someone else.

Our goals are what we focus on: to awaken spiritually, integrate our Traits, and reparent ourselves to wholeness with gentleness, humor, love, and respect.

On this day I will use the tools of recovery as well as any other tools that can help me to get in touch with my Inner Child.

Value of Therapy

"While therapy is not a replacement for the ACA program, many of our members have benefited from counselors who are familiar with ACA or Twelve Step work." BRB p. 447

After some time in ACA, many of us wondered about therapy and counseling. We heard our friends share about recovering with such help. We wondered if we should look into it. Some of us had never been to a counselor before, and we were nervous to start something new, thinking it might get us off track. We knew of others who had been in therapy before and it didn't seem to go well.

So we read Chapter 16 in the BRB, "ACA and Therapy," with an open mind. We learned what a therapist should and shouldn't do, because the BRB gave us the step-by-step process we needed. We said the "Therapy Affirmations" several days in a row. Then, while leaning on our Higher Power, we decided to use the "Questions to ask a Therapist" while calling a few of them. And we found someone who seemed like a good fit.

We bounced the results off our ACA friends. Then, with our support network in place, we took a leap of faith and tried something new. We opened the door to another tool of recovery. We knew that if we didn't like the results, we had the resources to talk about it. And if our gut says it's not working, we can change directions.

On this day I will remember that ACA has many suggestions for recovery, and I can try something new.

Fellowship

"In addition to the meetings, we chat after the meeting with others. We go for coffee at a nearby coffee shop, and we introduce ourselves. This is carrying the message as well, outside the walls of the meeting." BRB p. 514

We go to a meeting and afterwards people stand around and talk and maybe some go out for coffee. That's part of the fellowship of this program. But why is it important? Why should we participate?

When we begin our positive life changes, we often feel less comfortable with the non-program people in our lives. It can become a challenge to have more functional relationships.

For most of us, our meetings become another family - one built on trust and shared recovery experiences. But even so, it's often uncomfortable for a lot of us to have conversations with wonderful people we may not know well. Going out for coffee is a great way to practice new behavior and establish relationships, even if it doesn't come easy. We use this as a way of further introducing ourselves to our fellow ACA members.

On this day I will practice new behaviors by spending more social time with my new family.

Tradition Twelve

"Anonymity is the spiritual foundation of all our Traditions, ever reminding us to place principles before personalities." BRB p. 549

The Traditions are guidelines that help our meetings run smoothly and remain safe. If something goes off course, it's usually because one or more of the Traditions are not being followed.

Reminding ourselves to place principles before personalities is a healthy choice that keeps us individually and collectively grounded. When we forget this concept, some of us can slip into practicing old behaviors, such as allowing ourselves to become offended by or irritated with what another ACA says or does. Whatever the trigger is, we can build resentments and even become paranoid or blind to the reality of the situation. This can subtly or overtly infect our meetings. Strong, Tradition-focused meetings can help us uncover the truth and remain open to the differences among us.

The Serenity Prayer can also keep us in tune with Tradition Twelve. When we ask to accept what we cannot change and the courage to change what we can, we are above all asking our Higher Power for the wisdom to know the difference. This helps us stay centered on ourselves instead of others.

On this day I will ask myself what I am doing to contribute to the safety of my meeting. In doing so, I remind myself that I am choosing a healthier way to live my life.

The Slogans

"Keep coming back. It works!" BRB p. 565

This is a wonderful, simple old slogan we hear in recovery, but what does it mean? For newcomers, it may just seem like a nice platitude. But those of us with some experience in ACA know that little by little, small miracles happen as we continue to show up.

Perhaps we find ourselves picking up the phone more easily, or we talk to our fellow travelers with a greater feeling of safety. We start to feel less alone or unique in the world. We feel less shame in telling our stories. We start to disbelieve and detach from the messages the family disease trained us to integrate. We come to know we are innocent children and that we each have a Higher Power of our own choosing. We start to sincerely forgive ourselves for mistakes we've made. In doing so, we realize that even though we have made mistakes, *we* are not mistakes.

These are some of the miracles we start to experience simply by showing up. We do our part; our Higher Power does its part. Our efforts are accumulating. Invisible scales of compassion, not judgment, are beginning to tip in our favor. "Keep coming back. It works!" means what it says. Miracles can and do happen in this program.

On this day I will trust that my actions in recovery are cumulative, and nothing I do goes to waste. Little by little, my efforts pay off.

Index

$\mathcal{A}$

Abandonment, 51, 353
Abuse, 7, 340
Acceptance, 162, 335
Acting Out, 246
Acting Purposefully, 6
Actor vs. Reactor, 25
Addiction to Excitement, 295
Addictions, 259
Adult Child Defined, 45, 322
Affection, 44
Amends, 122
Apologies, 82
Applying the Program, 190
Asking for Help, 191, 296
Attraction vs. Promotion, 128
Authority Figures, 27, 42, 79, 143, 210
Autonomy, 74
Awakening Spirit, 155

$\mathcal{B}$

Balance, 162, 208
Beyond Survival, 164
Blame, 30, 59, 313

Body Shame, 106
Boundaries, 182, 249, 278
Buried Feelings, 29

C

Celebrate Success, 260
Change, 53, 76, 137, 301
Character Defects, 181
Choice, 238, 326
Codependence, 71, 199, 216
Conflicting Feelings, 184
Connection, 91, 119
Control, 309
Critical Inner Voice, 111
Critical Parent, 99, 115
Cross Talk, 77, 268, 352

$\mathcal{D}$

Dangerous Parents, 336
Disease of Alcoholism, 88, 125, 235
Dissociation, 142, 163, 223, 277, 367
Dreams, 43

The Laundry List

These are characteristics we seem to have in common due to being brought up in an alcoholic household.

1) We became isolated and afraid of people and authority figures.

2) We became approval seekers and lost our identity in the process.

3) We are frightened by angry people and any personal criticism.

4) We either become alcoholics, marry them or both, or find another compulsive personality such as a workaholic to fulfill our sick abandonment needs.

5) We live life from the viewpoint of victims and are attracted by that weakness in our love and friendship relationships.

6) We have an overdeveloped sense of responsibility, and it is easier for us to be concerned with others rather than ourselves; this enables us not to look too closely at our own faults, etc.

7) We get guilt feelings when we stand up for ourselves instead of giving in to others.

8) We became addicted to excitement.

9) We confuse love and pity and tend to "love" people we can "pity" and "rescue."

10) We have "stuffed" our feelings from our traumatic childhoods and have lost the ability to feel or express our feelings because it hurts so much (Denial).

11) We judge ourselves harshly and have a very low sense of self-esteem.

12) We are dependent personalities who are terrified of abandonment and will do anything to hold on to a relationship in order not to experience painful abandonment feelings, which we received from living with sick people who were never there emotionally for us.

13) Alcoholism is a family disease; we became para-alcoholics and took on the characteristics of that disease even though we did not pick up the drink.

14) Para-alcoholics are reactors rather than actors.

Tony A. 1978

The Problem
Adapted from The Laundry List

Many of us found that we had several characteristics in common as a result of being brought up in an alcoholic or dysfunctional household. We had come to feel isolated and uneasy with other people, especially authority figures. To protect ourselves, we became people-pleasers, even though we lost our own identities in the process. All the same we would mistake any personal criticism as a threat. We either became alcoholics (or practiced other addictive behavior) ourselves, or married them, or both. Failing that, we found other compulsive personalities, such as a workaholic, to fulfill our sick need for abandonment.

We lived life from the standpoint of victims. Having an overdeveloped sense of responsibility, we preferred to be concerned with others rather than ourselves. We got guilt feelings when we stood up for ourselves rather than giving in to others. Thus, we became reactors, rather than actors, letting others take the initiative. We were dependent personalities, terrified of abandonment, willing to do almost anything to hold on to a relationship in order not to be abandoned emotionally. Yet we kept choosing insecure relationships because they matched our childhood relationship with alcoholic or dysfunctional parents.

These symptoms of the family disease of alcoholism or other dysfunction made us "co-victims," those who take on the characteristics of the disease without necessarily ever taking a drink. We learned to keep our feelings down as children and kept them buried as adults. As a result of this conditioning, we confused love with pity, tending to love those we could rescue. Even more self-defeating, we became addicted to excitement in all our affairs, preferring constant upset to workable relationships. This is a description, not an indictment.

The ACA Twelve Steps

1) We admitted we were powerless over the effects of alcoholism or other family dysfunction, that our lives had become unmanageable.

2) Came to believe that a Power greater than ourselves could restore us to sanity.

3) Made a decision to turn our will and our lives over to the care of God as we understand God.

4) Made a searching and fearless moral inventory of ourselves.

5) Admitted to God, to ourselves, and to another human being the exact nature of our wrongs.

6) Were entirely ready to have God remove all these defects of character.

7) Humbly asked God to remove our shortcomings.

8) Made a list of all persons we had harmed and became willing to make amends to them all.

9) Made direct amends to such people wherever possible, except when to do so would injure them or others.

10) Continued to take personal inventory and, when we were wrong, promptly admitted it.

11) Sought through prayer and meditation to improve our conscious contact with God, as we understand God, praying only for knowledge of God's will for us and the power to carry that out.

12) Having had a spiritual awakening as the result of these steps, we tried to carry this message to others who still suffer, and to practice these principles in all our affairs.

The Twelve Traditions and Twelve Steps are reprinted and adapted with permission of Alcoholics Anonymous World Services, Inc.

The Solution

The Solution is to become your own loving parent. As ACA becomes a safe place for you, you will find freedom to express all the hurts and fears you have kept inside and to free yourself from the shame and blame that are carryovers from the past. You will become an adult who is imprisoned no longer by childhood reactions. You will recover the child within you, learning to accept and love yourself.

The healing begins when we risk moving out of isolation. Feelings and buried memories will return. By gradually releasing the burden of unexpressed grief, we slowly move out of the past. We learn to reparent ourselves with gentleness, humor, love, and respect. This process allows us to see our biological parents as the instruments of our existence. Our actual parent is a Higher Power whom some of us choose to call God. Although we had alcoholic or dysfunctional parents, our Higher Power gave us the Twelve Steps of Recovery.

This is the action and work that heals us: we use the Steps; we use the meetings; we use the telephone. We share our experience, strength, and hope with each other. We learn to restructure our sick thinking one day at a time. When we release our parents from responsibility for our actions today, we become free to make healthful decisions as actors, not reactors. We progress from hurting, to healing, to helping. We awaken to a sense of wholeness we never knew was possible. By attending these meetings on a regular basis, you will come to see parental alcoholism or family dysfunction for what it is: a disease that infected you as a child and continues to affect you as an adult.

You will learn to keep the focus on yourself in the here and now. You will take responsibility for your own life and supply your own parenting. You will not do this alone. Look around you and you will see others who know how you feel. We will love and encourage you no matter what. We ask you to accept us just as we accept you. This is a spiritual program based on action coming from love. We are sure that as the love grows inside you, you will see beautiful changes in all your relationships, especially with God, yourself, and your parents.

The ACA Twelve Traditions

1) Our common welfare should come first; personal recovery depends on ACA unity.

2) For our group purpose there is but one ultimate authority—a loving God as expressed in our group conscience. Our leaders are but trusted servants, they do not govern.

3) The only requirement for membership in ACA is a desire to recover from the effects of growing up in an alcoholic or otherwise dysfunctional family.

4) Each group is autonomous except in matters affecting other groups or ACA as a whole. We cooperate with all other Twelve-Step programs.

5) Each group has but one primary purpose—to carry its message to the adult child who still suffers.

6) An ACA group ought never endorse, finance, or lend the ACA name to any related facility or outside enterprise, lest problems of money, property, and prestige divert us from our primary purpose.

7) Every ACA group ought to be fully self-supporting, declining outside contributions.

8) Adult Children of Alcoholics should remain forever non-professional, but our service centers may employ special workers.

9) ACA, as such, ought never be organized, but we may create service boards or committees directly responsible to those they serve.

10) Adult Children of Alcoholics has no opinion on outside issues; hence the ACA name ought never be drawn into public controversy.

11) Our public relations policy is based on attraction rather than promotion; we maintain personal anonymity at the level of press, radio, TV, and films.

12) Anonymity is the spiritual foundation of all our Traditions, ever reminding us to place principles before personalities.